TO PROTECT AND DEFEND

Homeland Security Series

Series Editors:
Tom Payne, University of Southern Mississippi, USA
Tom Lansford, University of Southern Mississippi, USA

This series seeks to provide a body of case studies to explore the growing importance and prominence of homeland security to national defence policy and to examine the development of homeland security within the broader context of national defence policy in the United States and other major developed states. This series will identify and analyze the major threats that are particular to homeland security, as well as those that affect broader national security interests. Comparative studies will be used to elucidate the major similarities and differences in how states approach homeland security and works which advocate new or non-traditional approaches to homeland security. The series aims to integrate information from scholars and practitioners to provide works which will influence the policy debate and examine the ramifications of policy.

To Protect and Defend
US Homeland Security Policy

TOM LANSFORD
University of Southern Mississippi in Long Beach, USA

ROBERT J. PAULY, JR.
University of Southern Mississippi - Gulf Coast, USA

JACK COVARRUBIAS
Old Dominion University, USA

ASHGATE

Published by
Ashgate Publishing Limited
Gower House
Croft Road
Aldershot
Hampshire GU11 3HR
England

Ashgate Publishing Company
Suite 420
101 Cherry Street
Burlington, VT 05401-4405
USA

Ashgate website: http://www.ashgate.com

British Library Cataloguing in Publication Data
Lansford, Tom
    To protect and defend : US homeland security policy. -
    (Homeland security)
    1. United States. Dept. of Homeland Security 2. National
    security - United States 3. Civil defense - United States
    4. Terrorism - United States - Prevention
    I. Title II. Pauly, Robert J., 1967- III. Covarrubias, Jack
    363.3'25'0973

Library of Congress Cataloging-in-Publication Data
Lansford, Tom.
    To protect and defend : US homeland security policy / by Tom Lansford, Robert J.
Pauly, Jr., and Jack Covarrubias.
        p. cm. -- (Homeland security)
    Includes bibliographical references and index.
    ISBN 0-7546-4505-3
    1. Terrorism-Government policy--United States. 2. National security--United
  States. 3. National security--United States--History. 4. Terrorism--Prevention--
Cross-cultural studies. 5. United States--Foreign relations. I. Pauly, Robert J.,
1967- II. Covarrubias, Jack. III. Title. IV. Series.

    HV6432.L3675 2006
    363.325'15610973--dc22

        2006005438
ISBN-10: 0 7546 4505 3

Printed and bound in Great Britain by MPG Books Ltd. Bodmin, Cornwall.

Contents

Acknowledgments

This book would not have been possible without the assistance and support of a wide range of colleagues, family members and friends. In particular, the authors would like to thank our editor, Kirstin Howgate, for her encouragement and support throughout the editorial process.

Jack Covarrubias would like to thank Tracy, Sheron and Savannah for their love and patience; Anna for her friendship and kind heart; my mentors, role models and friends for putting up with me.

Tom Lansford would like to thank Denise von Herrmann and his colleagues in the Political Science department at the University of Southern Mississippi for support through this project. I would also like to thank my parents, Max and Ivy Lansford and siblings, David and Cynthia, and their respective families. Special consideration goes to both my family and to Mike Pappas and family, and Frank and Sue Reed, for their help following Hurricane Katrina. Without their assistance, this manuscript would not have been completed. As always, special thanks goes to Mr. James D. Buffett for assistance in manuscript preparation. I also owe a debt of gratitude to a range of friends and colleagues in the profession, but would like to particularly praise Dr. Robert P. Watson who has been a friend and collaborator for many years. Finally, my deepest thanks, appreciation and love go to Gina and Ella who have been both my inspiration and main comfort through these times.

Robert J. Pauly, Jr. would like to thank Peggy, Bob, Mark, Chris, Sami, John and Missy Pauly for their perpetual love and support in all of my personal and professional endeavors. He would also like to thank Maria Pasalidi for adding a warm smile, a bit of excitement and something to look forward to in the future in the continuing aftermath of Hurricane Katrina.

For the victims of Hurricane Katrina

9/11 and Homeland Security Policy in the United States

September 11 2001: A Shock to the American System

On September 11 2001, the perception of security threats to the territory of the United States underwent a change as fundamental as it was devastating. That morning, a transnational terrorist organization known as Al Qaeda prosecuted the costliest attack against US domestic targets in American history. At the behest of Al Qaeda leader Osama bin Laden, 19 Middle Eastern men hijacked four US commercial airliners, which they then used to strike targets in New York City and Washington, DC. Two of the planes flew into the north and south towers of the World Trade Center in New York, causing the eventual collapse of those structures, a third hit the Pentagon on the outskirts of Washington and a fourth crashed in a field in western Pennsylvania after a heroic group of crew members and passengers attempted to retake the aircraft from the hijackers. Collectively, the attacks resulted in the loss of nearly 3,000 lives, the vast majority of which were those of American civilians. The number of fatalities was the largest in a foreign strike on a US domestic target since the Japanese surprise attack on Pearl Harbor on 7 December 1941, an incident that delivered a similar shock to the American public at the time.[1] Yet, ultimately, the shock produced by the events of 9/11 was deeper, particularly given the number of civilian deaths and the fact that much of the tragedy unfolded live on national television. As scholar Arthur Hulnick, a former Central Intelligence Agency (CIA) officer, explains:

> For those of us who remember the Japanese sneak attack on Pearl Harbor in 1941, the terrorist attack was worse because we could watch it happen. The Pearl Harbor attack was a distant event for most of us, reported in the press, of course, and in scratchy radio broadcasts, but 9/11 was right there on TV or in smoky skies. The silence in the air that followed, broken only by the roar of fighter jets overhead, was an eerie reminder of what had happened.[2]

The implications of the attacks will continue to be felt for many years, if not decades, to come. American historian Victor Davis Hanson, for example, notes that:

> We will not grasp for years the full interplay of events set in motion by the sudden vaporization of thousands in the late summer of 2001. The orphans and children of orphans not yet born will not – cannot – forget September 11

because they are now part of it forever. The victims of the World Trade Center, the Pentagon, and the crashing airliners did not fall in pitched battle. They were not even armed. None were expecting their fate. Yet they were nonetheless combat casualties of self-described warriors – indeed, the first terrible fatalities of what may prove to be a long war. And because battle by its very nature radically changes history in ways that even other seminal events – elections, revolutions, inventions, assassinations, and plagues – cannot, it will require decades before historians can chart all the aftershocks that followed 9/11.[3]

At their core, the 9/11 attacks demonstrated to Americans from President George W. Bush and the members of his national security team to the general public that the United States was not as safe from foreign-based threats as they had previously believed. Based thousands of miles away in a remote corner of Afghanistan as guests of the puritanical Islamic Taliban regime, Bin Laden and his lieutenants planned and carried out an operation that was successful primarily because of Al Qaeda's ability to plant terrorist cells in the United States, whose members largely, albeit not wholly, avoided detection during the months and years preceding 9/11. The collective inability of America's domestic and foreign intelligence and security agencies to prevent Al Qaeda's catastrophic strikes understandably left US citizens with an immediate sense of insecurity, particularly relative to the perceptions of national invulnerability that had prevailed previously. That sense of insecurity coincided with a groundswell of anger over the attacks, which were the gravest within the continental United States since British forces overran Washington and burned the Capitol and the White House in August 1814 in the context of the War of 1812. According to Yale University's John Lewis Gaddis, a leading scholar of American national security strategy, there was at least "one eerie connection" between the latter events and those of 9/11, "for it's likely that the intended target of United Flight 93, which crashed in Pennsylvania after the passengers overwhelmed the hijackers, was one of those two buildings. History rarely repeats itself, but on this occasion it came damn close."[4] Indeed, as tragic as Al Qaeda's attacks were, matters could have been considerably worse. And with the clear revelation of US vulnerability to terrorism at home came a popular demand to respond to those attacks with significant government action both domestically and internationally, and in the short term as well as over the medium and long terms.

Above all, the events of 9/11 highlighted the need for American government officials at the national, state and local levels to consider much more seriously the emerging nexus between national security and homeland security, which is the principal topic of this book. Put simply, Al Qaeda's strikes demonstrated that transnational terrorist organizations now have a markedly greater capacity to plan and carry out operations with catastrophic consequences for US interests at home as well as abroad than most American policymakers had previously assumed. Consequently, preventing attacks on the scale of 9/11 has required a rethinking of the means through which to counter terrorist threats to the United States. While Bin Laden was by no means an unknown quantity to either the national security teams of Bush or his predecessor, William J. Clinton, neither administration took the necessary action to prevent Al Qaeda from carrying out its strikes on the World Trade Center or the Pentagon. Despite Bin Laden's orchestration of a series of operations against American targets during Clinton's tenure in office, including bombings of the US Embassies in Nairobi, Kenya, and Dar es Salaam, Tanzania, in August 1998 and the USS *Cole* in October 2000, 9/11 still came as a surprise to politicians and policymakers in Washington, let alone those at the state and municipal levels.[5] As is typically the case when governmental leaders are taken by surprise, the Bush administration was left to fashion a response, one that has required the use of a combination of traditional and revolutionary tools within, and outside of, the United States. As Stephen Flynn, a retired Commander in the US Coast Guard and current Jeanne J. Kirkpatrick Senior Fellow in National Security Studies at the Council on Foreign Relations, asserts, "While people know that their government can't prevent natural disasters, they do expect their officials to be vigilant in preventing out enemies from killing innocent civilians, toppling our landmarks, and destroying non-military property. Accordingly, there is a political price to be paid if politicians are perceived as being negligent or ineffectual in providing security."[6]

Confronting Terrorist Groups and their Sponsors Abroad

Understandably, the Bush administration wasted little time in fashioning its initial response to what it perceived as a clear act of war by Al Qaeda. And, predictably, it was one based primarily on America's military power generally and its logistical capacity to conduct effective operations against foreign adversaries abroad in an expeditious fashion in particular. As Walter Russell Mead, the Henry A. Kissinger Senior Fellow in US foreign policy at the Council on Foreign Relations, notes, "One must ... accept that others need to understand that Americans will respond to provocations like those of September 11 with massive and overwhelming force ... . Force remains an important element of international relations; America's enemies need to understand that the United States possesses more force than other powers and is, under the right circumstances, more than willing to use it."[7] Since 9/11, two such US adversaries – the regimes of the Taliban in Afghanistan and Saddam Hussein in Iraq – have learned the lesson to which Mead refers as a direct result of their past, or expected future, support for terrorist groups.

Within hours of the attacks in New York and Washington, Bush declared in an address to the nation: "We will make no distinction between the terrorists who committed these acts and those who harbor them."[8] Over the ensuing days, evidence implicating Al Qaeda mounted quickly. That evidence suggested that bin Laden had planned and orchestrated the attacks from Afghanistan, where he trained and then dispatched the hijackers responsible for carrying out the operation on 9/11.[9] The United States responded by building an international "coalition of the willing" to confront Al Qaeda and its Taliban hosts. Ultimately, following Taliban leader Mullah Muhammad Omar's refusal to surrender Bin Laden to the Bush administration to answer for the attacks, the United States launched Operation Enduring Freedom in

October 2001. With limited logistical and combat assistance from fellow North Atlantic Treaty Organization (NATO) allies, including France, Germany and the United Kingdom, along with somewhat more substantial support from the opposition Afghan Northern Alliance, American forces removed the Taliban from power and reduced markedly bin Laden's capacity to organize and direct future terrorist operations on the scale of the assaults on the World Trade Center and Pentagon. It did so over a period of less than two months that was followed by ongoing nation-building operations to develop a functioning democracy in Afghanistan.[10]

Operation Enduring Freedom demonstrated that the United States was willing to carry out the promise Bush made just hours after the events of 9/11: namely that it would seek to punish not only the terrorists responsible for the attacks but also those states or regimes willing to cooperate with or harbor bin Laden and his ilk. In reiterating that pledge in an address to Congress just over two weeks prior to the launch of operations against Taliban and Al Qaeda forces in Afghanistan, Bush had warned, "we will pursue nations that provide aid or safe haven to terrorism. Every nation, in every region, now has a decision to make. Either you are with us, or you are with the terrorists. From this day forward, any nation that continues to harbor or support terrorism will be regarded by the United States as a hostile regime."[11] Bush's stance reflected a changing perception among most Americans of the nature of the dangers to US interests posed by terrorism generally and Al Qaeda specifically and a corresponding willingness to support a more proactive approach to reducing and eventually eliminating those threats.

After the successful conduct of Operation Enduring Freedom, the Bush administration shifted its attention to other states it believed were guilty of sponsoring terrorism, including, most significantly, Iraq. In his January 2002 State of the Union Address, Bush characterized three states (Iraq, Iran and North Korea) as members of "an axis of evil, arming to threaten the peace of the world." Further, he referred explicitly to the threats posed by states determined to develop biological, chemical or nuclear weapons of mass destruction (WMD) and support terrorists, including, but not limited to, Bin Laden and his followers, concluding that Iraq, Iran and North Korea "pose a grave and growing danger. They could provide these arms to terrorists, giving them the means to match their hatred. They could attack our allies or attempt to blackmail the United States. In any of these cases, the price of indifference would be catastrophic."[12] Essentially, that address provided the rhetorical foundation for the planning and prosecution of the Second Iraq War.

As a result of Saddam's unwillingness to provide unequivocal evidence that he was adhering to a series of UN resolutions to which he acceded at the conclusion of the Persian Gulf War (including, most notably, prohibitions against the development of WMD and sponsorship of terrorist groups), the United States and United Kingdom launched Operation Iraqi Freedom in March 2003.[13] Within a month, US-led forces had eliminated Saddam's regime, laying the foundation for a liberal democratic transformation of Iraq that Bush still views as central to the global war against terrorism. Reiterating that point in his June 2004 commencement address to the graduating class of the US Air Force Academy, for example, he made three fundamental points. First, the US-led pursuit of the democratization of the Greater Middle East is – and will remain – critical to the effective prosecution of the war on terror. Second, the conduct of nation-building operations in Iraq since the removal of Saddam's regime represents the first step in the wider economic and political transformation of the broader Arab and Islamic worlds. Third, the maintenance of a sustained American commitment to the above objectives is indispensable to providing for the security of the United States at home and safeguarding its interests abroad.[14]

Most significantly, in linking the democratization of Iraq – and, eventually, the Greater Middle East as well – to the war on terror, Bush stressed that "[f]ighting terror is not just a matter of killing or capturing terrorists. To stop the flow of recruits into terrorist movements, young people in the region must see a real and hopeful alternative – a society that rewards their talent and turns their energies to a constructive purpose." Consequently, he continued, the "vision of freedom has great advantages. Terrorists incite young men and women to strap bombs on their bodies and dedicate their deaths to the deaths of others. Free societies inspire young men and women to work, and achieve, and dedicate their lives to the life of their country. And in the long run, I have great faith that the appeal of freedom and life is stronger than the lure of hatred and death."[15]

In casting Saddam's removal from power through the conduct of Operation Iraqi Freedom in March and April 2003 and ongoing efforts to develop representative political and free market economic institutions in the new Iraq as key parts of the war on terrorism, Bush drew parallels to past American conflicts with opponents of freedom across the globe. In particular, he emphasized, "it resembles the great clashes of the last century – between those who put their trust in tyrants and those who put their trust in liberty. Our goal, the goal of this generation is the same: we will secure our nation and defend the peace through the forward march of freedom."[16]

Enhancing American Security at Home

In addition to illustrating the dangers posed to the United States by the development of transnational terrorist organizations abroad, the events of 9/11 highlighted the glaring weaknesses of America's domestic security system. Put simply, Al Qaeda spent no more than $500,000 in planning and carrying out an operation that the US intelligence and law enforcement communities failed to uncover beforehand and proved incapable of preventing on the morning of 9/11.[17] As the plot unfolded, a lack of coordination among agents and analysts within the Federal Bureau of Investigation (FBI) and CIA and between the two agencies reduced the potential of either organization to uncover Al Qaeda's plans. And, on the day the attacks were executed, the hijackers had little trouble penetrating a porous airport security system in order to board their chosen flights, three of which then hit their selected targets in New York and Washington. Apportioning blame in the immediate aftermath of the attacks was neither difficult nor particularly productive as there were plenty of weaknesses in the system to be exploited. More significant was the subsequent acknowledgment of the need to transform that system in a manner that would reduce security risks to the American public in the future.

Since the 9/11 attacks, the Bush administration, US Congress and broader public and private academic and policymaking communities have attempted to create a more effective domestic security system to guard against terrorist threats to America. Those efforts have moved forward on three interconnected fronts: the creation and refinement of the US Department of Homeland Security (DHS); the establishment of and subsequent issuance of a detailed report by the National Commission on Terrorist Attacks Upon the United States (9/11 Commission); and the restructuring of the American intelligence community to include an integrated National Counterterrorism Center (NCC) under the leadership of a Director of National Intelligence.

Two weeks after 9/11, Bush announced that he planned to create the DHS, which was formally established through Congressional passage of the Homeland Security Act in November 2002. Specifically, the act folded 22 federal agencies, either wholly or in part, and 180,000 of their employees, into the DHS. Those agencies, which now fall under the administrative umbrella of the Secretary of Homeland Security, include the Coast Guard, Immigration and Naturalization Service (INS) and Transportation Security Administration (TSA). The same month that the DHS was created, Bush also authorized the establishment of the 9/11 Commission as a means to determine precisely what the United States did wrong in failing to prevent Al Qaeda's attacks. The commission spent the ensuing 18 months investigating the prologue to the attacks and the events that unfolded on 9/11, before issuing its report in July 2004. The report featured a detailed set of recommendations on how best to improve US intelligence and security institutions over the short and long terms. Collectively, these recommendations, which emphasized the need for much more effective cooperation and collaboration between the CIA and FBI, and enhanced safeguards along America's land and sea borders, set the stage for the development and Congressional passage of the Intelligence Reform and Terrorism Prevention Act in December 2004.[18] Ideally, that act will help to further integrate US intelligence assets and provide the necessary data to better defend the American homeland against terrorist groups, including but not limited to, Al Qaeda. As Bush stressed at the signing ceremony for the act:

> A key lesson of September 11, 2001 is that America's intelligence agencies must work together as a single, unified enterprise. The Intelligence Reform and Terrorism Prevention Act of 2004 creates the position of Director of National Intelligence, or DNI, to be appointed by the President with the consent of the Senate. The DNI will lead a unified intelligence community and will serve as the principle advisor to the President on intelligence matters. The DNI will have the authority to order the collection of new intelligence to ensure the sharing of information among agencies and to establish common standards for the intelligence community's personnel ... The many reforms in this act have a single goal: to ensure that the people in government responsible for defending America have the best possible information to make the best possible decisions.[19]

Homeland Security vs. National Security: The Emerging Debate

In addition to – and largely concurrent with – Bush administration, Congressional and other governmental and private efforts to enhance the available means to minimize future terrorist threats to America, an academic debate on that issue area has also progressed. The majority of scholarly works that have appeared in the context of that debate fall into two general categories. The first category features books that examine the intricacies of US homeland security policy. Such monographs typically discuss and evaluate the developing homeland security system at the federal, state and local levels or deal with specific threats to homeland security. The second category features books that offer critical analyses of current or emerging homeland security policy. Included in this category is a range of works that examine the broader, often philosophical, implications of evolving homeland security policy.

This monograph, on the other hand, provides one of the first scholarly overviews of homeland security policy that places the field in the larger context of national security policy studies and international security in general. It also introduces a debate over the role of homeland security policy in response to non-military threats to homeland security, including natural disasters. It does so through the presentation of seven chapters, which address the following issues in particular.

Chapter 1: Security Studies and US Policy

This chapter examines the main theories and paradigms that guide security studies in the context of the history of US national security policies as they have been applied to national defense and international security commitments and threats. Further, it discusses American policy approaches within the framework of accepted models of national security.

Chapter 2: Evolution of Homeland Security

This chapter analyzes the changes in the conceptualizations of homeland security in the United States and the ramifications of these changes for security policy. Specifically, it examines the professionalization of homeland security, in such areas as the transformation of militias to professional military/police forces and the establishment of new federal agencies, in the context of the revolution in military affairs.

Chapter 3: National Security and Homeland Security

This chapter explains the role of homeland security in the broader patterns of contemporary US national security policy. Specifically, it examines the evolution of threat perceptions and national responses in the contemporary period.   It also addresses the longstanding American preference for preemptive action as a core security option.

Chapter 4: Structure of Homeland Security

This chapter presents an overview of the current organization of homeland security at the national, state and local levels. It details the structures, capabilities and responsibilities of the agencies involved in homeland security and their relationship with the other organs of national security, including the National Security Council, the Defense Department and the US intelligence community.

Chapter 5: Homeland Security Policies and Processes

This chapter describes the impact of the American governmental system on efforts to develop effective homeland security policies through an analysis of the impact of such factors as: the system of checks and balances; state and local capabilities and priorities; and funding.

Chapter 6: Homeland Security in a Comparative Perspective

This chapter compares emerging US homeland security policy with similar policies in other developed, industrialized states as a means to identify strengths and weaknesses within the American approach. It includes comparative case studies focusing on the domestic security systems in France, the United Kingdom, Israel and Russia.

Conclusion: Present and Future Threats

The concluding chapter examines how well US homeland security policy will react to contemporary and emerging security threats, including: superterrorism; the proliferation of WMD; and natural disaster response and recovery.

Notes

1. For an in-depth account of the events of 11 September 2001, see Thomas H. Kean, Lee H. Hamilton, Richard Ben-Veniste, Fred F. Fielding, Jamie S. Gorelick, Slade Gorton, Bob Kerrey, John F. Lehman, Timothy J. Roemer and James R. Thompson, *The 9/11 Commission Report: Final Report of the National Commission on Terrorist Attacks on the United States* (New York: W.W. Norton & Company, 2004), 1-46, 278-323.
2. Arthur S. Hulnick, *Keeping Us Safe: Secret Intelligence and Homeland Security* (Westport, CT: Praeger, 2004), 1.
3. Victor Davis Hanson, *Ripples of Battle: How Wars of the Past Still Determine How We Fight, How We Live and How We Think* (New York: Doubleday, 2003), 11.
4. John Lewis Gaddis, *Surprise, Security and the American Experience* (Cambridge, MA: Harvard University Press, 2004), 10-11.
5. Kean *et al.*, *9/11 Commission Report*, 108-214.
6. Stephen Flynn, *America the Vulnerable: How Our Government is Failing to Protect Us from Terrorism* (New York: HarperCollins Publishers, 2004), 9-10.
7. Walter Russell Mead, *Power, Terror, Peace, and War: America's Grand Strategy in a*

World at Risk (New York: Alfred A. Knopf, 2004), 127-28.

8. George W. Bush, "Presidential Address to the Nation," 11 September 2001, excerpted in *We Will Prevail: President George W. Bush on War Terrorism and Freedom* (New York: Continuum, 2003), 2.
9. Bob Woodward, *Bush at War* (New York: Simon & Schuster, 2002), 42-57.
10. For a detailed examination of the organization and conduct of Operation Enduring Freedom, see Tom Lansford, *All for One: Terrorism, NATO and the United States* (Aldershot, UK: Ashgate Publishing Limited, 2002).
11. George W. Bush, "Presidential Address to a Joint Session of Congress," 23 September 2001, excerpted in *We Will Prevail*, 15.
12. George W. Bush, "President's State of the Union Address," 29 January 2002, excerpted in *Ibid.*, 108.
13. For an in-depth account of the diplomatic prologue to, and prosecution of, Operation Iraqi Freedom, see Tom Lansford and Robert J. Pauly, Jr., *Strategic Preemption: US Foreign Policy and the Second Iraq War* (Aldershot, UK: Ashgate Publishing Limited, 2004).
14. George W. Bush, "Remarks by the President at the United States Air Force Academy Graduation Ceremony," 2 June 2004, *White House Office of the Press Secretary* (www.whitehouse.gov).
15. *Ibid.*
16. *Ibid.*
17. Kean *et al.*, *9/11 Commission Report*, 169.
18. *Ibid.*, 361-428.
19. George W. Bush, "President Signs Intelligence Reform and Terrorism Prevention Act," *White House Office of the Press Secretary*, 17 December 2004 (www.whitehouse.gov).

Chapter One

Security Studies and US Policy

Introduction

Within the disciplines that study security, mainly history and political science, the tendency in the twentieth century has been to concentrate on the international factors which influence and often determine national policy. Indeed there is a rich body of literature on the role of the international system in global conflict and strife. In the study of international relations, security studies, with its implicit concentration on the nature of the global state system has tended to dominate the debate, even if only to serve as the counterpoint for the development of new approaches and divergent perspectives.[1] Security studies itself is dominated by the theoretical paradigm of realism, and its various sub-fields, including classic realism, neorealism, and offensive realism.[2] All of these various strands have in common an emphasis on the implicit importance of the nationstate as the primary actor in international relations and the explicit concentration on the role of power and force in the global system.

With the end of the Cold War, transnational problems have developed into one of the main security threats to the traditional nationstate. For instance, international terrorist groups have demonstrated an ability to attack on several fronts using a range of non-conventional tactics. While the attacks of September 11 2001 represent the most visible and costly modern terrorist strikes, there is a long legacy of non-state actors using force in an effort to gain political or economic objectives. This legacy is complicated by an equally long legacy through which non-state actors, in the form of revolutionaries or self-determination movements, transform themselves into state actors by establishing new nationstates or taking political control of others. While terrorism represents a hard security threat, in its ability to directly destroy infrastructure and kill citizens, soft security threats, including the transnational drug trade, human trafficking and financial crimes, also present new challenges for states as they develop and implement security policy.

In response, nationstates have endeavored to improve their security capabilities along two tracks. First, many states have increased international and regional cooperation and collaboration to counter the emerging threats. This approach has generated a range of successes by pooling information and capabilities without a significant loss of sovereignty or control of security and defense policy and priorities. Second, states have concurrently worked to increase internal or domestic capabilities by integrating the military, intelligence and law enforcement branches of government with a host of other agencies ranging from customs and border control to medical and emergency responders. It is within this latter category of internal security that the concept of homeland security emerged. This chapter examines and integrates contemporary scholarship and perspectives on the policy process at a broad level in an effort to identify and elucidate the main theories and paradigms that serve as a foundation for the study of national security. It seeks to trace the evolution of the field of security studies within the broader framework of international relations, as contemporary debates relate to the development of homeland security studies. New and emerging national security threats are analyzed in the context of doctrinal changes and the growing recognition of the likelihood that contemporary and future conflicts will be unconventional in nature, including terrorism and asymmetrical warfare. Finally, the chapter explores US policy within existing models of national security.

Security Studies

In the aftermath of World War II, there emerged a broad effort to develop a new field of academic inquiry. Military history had a long and distinguished record of contributions to the study of strategy and policy, but with the escalating Cold War, many scholars began to work to develop a framework that would integrate past studies of tactics and military policy with other areas of grand strategy, including diplomacy and politics. The result was the creation of a new field of inquiry, security studies. Security studies is the analysis of national defense and military policy within the context of the international system.

By its very nature, security studies concentrates on the role of force and coercion in the global system. Stephen Walt writes that security studies "... explores the conditions that make the use of force more likely, the ways that the use of force affects individuals, states, and societies, and the specific policies that states adopt in order to prepare for, prevent or engage in war."[3] Noted scholars Joseph Nye and Sean Lynn-Jones assert that in security studies "the central questions are concerned with international violence."[4] This theme is present throughout the development of the study of international relations and was expressed by a range of prominent thinkers and philosophers, including Thomas Hobbes who argued that anarchy was a natural and recurring component of human nature. In *Leviathan*, Hobbes writes that "... if there be no power erected, or not great enough for our own security; every man will, and may lawfully rely on his own strength and art, for caution against all other men."[5] The development of the theme of international anarchy significantly influenced later international relations scholars, especially in the latter half of the twentieth century. These scholars included the likes of E.H. Carr and Hans J. Morgenthau.

The father of neorealism, Kenneth Waltz, expands on the theme of violence and international politics (or international anarchy) in his seminal work, *Theory of International Politics*, explaining that:

> The state among states, it is often said, conducts its affairs in the brooding shadow of violence. Because some states may at any time use force, all states must be prepared to do so – or live at the mercy of their militarily more vigorous

neighbors. Among states the state of nature is a state of war. This is meant not in the sense that war constantly occurs but in the sense that with each state deciding for itself whether or not to use force, war may at any time break out.[6]

Central then to the traditional approach to security studies is the role and place of violence within the state system. And the use of violence for political goals remains, in principle, the prerogative of the nationstate in what realists contend is the continuing anarchical system of contemporary international politics.

Any peace or stability within the international system is the result, not of broad patterns of cooperation or collaboration, as neoliberalists[7] would assert, but is, instead, the result of the forced stability provided by a hegemonic power or through simple balance of power politics in which a rough equilibrium forestalls conflict. The hegemon is simply a state or actor with the economic and military power to set and enforce the rules of the international system. Usually states either bandwagon with the hegemon or balance against it through coalitions. The result can be a balance of power system or hegemonic war, after which either a new hegemon emerges or the primacy of the existing hegemon is reaffirmed.[8] Not that warfare or strife is ever-present. As Robert Jervis attests, "To conceive of international politics as a Hobbesian state of nature means not that warfare is constant, but only that it is always a possibility and that actors understand this."[9]

Realism as a Paradigm

At its core, security studies is an effort to integrate domestic level variables with those of the international system in order to create a synthesis to explain the defense and security activities of actors. The discipline is interdisciplinary and reaches across boundaries of method and theory. In the contemporary period, a number of institutes and programs have emerged which concentrate on security studies. In addition, new approaches and models of security analysis have emerged. Security studies has long been dominated by an emphasis on power and the dynamics of international politics. Feminist international relations scholar, J. Ann Tickner, grudgingly notes that "Power, autonomy, self-reliance, and rationality are all attributes that realism – the approach in IR [international relations] that has had the most influence on security studies – deems desirable for state behavior if states are going to survive and prosper in a dangerous 'anarchical' international system."[10]

Roberta N. Haar furthers this line of argument when she writes that "the most prevalent approach used to explain foreign policy emerges out of the realist tradition."[11] Haar goes on to assert that "the paradigm, in both its classical realist and neorealist forms, focuses on the external milieu, basing foreign policy decisions on a traditional, geopolitical analysis of identifying the strategic goals of a state and then considering the alternative means available to that state for achieving those goals."[12] Contemporary realist scholar John Mearsheimer summarizes the principle tenets of realism in the following manner: states are the main actors in an international system that lacks a global government; the international system is anarchical and states face constant threats from other states; states are unitary actors; they are also rational actors that engage in cost-benefit analysis and rational choice; states are driven by self-interests; and because of the anarchical nature of the system, states must be both offensive, in order to accrue power, and defensive, in order to protect their interests.[13] Often peace is achieved in the realist conception not through cooperation, but through a balance of power equilibrium that precludes conflict.[14]

Against the realist paradigm, a number of alternative approaches have emerged, although none has gained the prominence of realism or neorealism as either a methodological framework or a body of scholarship to oppose in the deconstructionist model. Central to continued dynamism of security studies has been the constant effort to develop theories that contain both an explanatory and predictive value. Tickner notes that the:

> Goal of theory building for conventional IR, which includes most realists, has been to generate propositions that are testable and that can help explain the security-seeking behavior of states in the international system. Neorealism, the devolution of realism committed to scientific methods, believes that theory should be explanatory and separated, to the largest extent possible, from norms and political practice.[15]

From the 1950s onward, rational choice models have significantly increased their impact on the field. Consistent with traditional and neo-realism, rational choice now dominates the discipline. This approach uses mathematical formulas and models to test hypotheses. The rational choice approach has been credited by many with providing a scientific basis to security studies as a field of political science. Stephen M. Walt notes that as much as 40 percent of contemporary scholarship is based on rational choice.[16] He defines rational choice "formal theory" as the "construction of specific mathematical models intended to represent particular real-world situations and the use of mathematics to identify the specific solutions ('equilibria') for the models."[17] Nonetheless, Walt also criticizes the increasingly quantitative trend in security studies. In a powerful and sweeping criticism of the trend, Walt argues that formal rational choice theory may be useful for improving existing theoretical frameworks and for proving contested conclusions. However, the approach has not led to the development of broad new theories. Worse, rational choice has, in Walt's words, "relatively little to say about important real-world security issues ..." and, instead, "... much of the recent formal work in security studies reflects the 'cult of irrelevance' that pervades much of contemporary social science."[18]

Rational choice theory's greatest strength is, as Lisa L. Martin explains in a counter essay to Walt's arguments its "ability to generate linked, coherent sets of propositions and insights."[19] Martin criticizes Walt for concentrating on a small number of "individual, isolated hypotheses, finding them lacking in originality, empirical support or policy relevance."[20] Nevertheless, Walt's denunciation of the practical utility of mathematical models for policymakers and the general public does underscore the danger of specialization and the narrowing of the security studies to focus on case studies with limited practicality, but clearly defined parameters and variables.

Explanations and Predictions

The end of the Cold War and the rise of ethnic and substate violence during the 1990s caught many security studies scholars napping. Eminent historian John Lewis Gaddis asserts that the inability of security studies and international relations scholars to predict the end of the Cold War raises "questions about the methods" employed to understand conflict and strife in the global system.[21] Gwyn Prins points out that "Security studies provided notably little help in understanding, let alone foretelling, the eruption of the largely bloodless velvet revolutions at the end of a bloody century, and the agenda of global issues is proving to be awkward."[22] Likewise, the field failed in large part to recognize the growing danger of transnational terrorism as a direct threat to the international order, let alone the economic and political stability of settled nationstates.

One response has been the rise of alternative approaches to international security. Although they offer insightful and meaningful criticisms of the dominant modes of inquiry, newer theoretical constructs such as world systems theory, critical theory and feminist analyses of international security, remain outside of the mainstream of the discipline and offer only limited utility for policy proscription. World Systems theory, like neorealism, is a structural theory, but instead of concentrating on the distribution of power within the system, it focuses on the impact of capitalism and the resultant inequities of the global system. Based on the work of Karl Marx, as modified by Immanuel Wallerstein, world systems theory is expressed through modern dependency theory and other critiques of globalization.[23] Critical theory deconstructs existing theoretical frameworks in an effort to understand the biases of scholars and to critique existing models in order to create a more equitable global system.[24] There are a range of feminist approaches to international security, but all are linked by their emphasis on the importance and role of gender. The emphasis on gender even carries over into the feminist critique of traditional international relations theory with realism roundly criticized as an overtly masculine framework that mainly rationalizes aggressive male behavior. Feminist theories collectively assert that international security would be dramatically different in a world dominated by women.[25]

Other new approaches have gained adherents within the debate over the primacy of realism and rationalism. In contrast to traditional rationalist lines of argument, constructivism, or social constructivism, has emerged as a popular means to explain change in the international system.[26] This approach emphasizes the role and importance of international norms. Theo Farrell defines norms as the "intersubjective beliefs about the social and natural world that define actors, their situations, and the possibilities for action."[27] Farrell goes on to contend that "norms regulate action by defining what is appropriate (given social rules) and what is effective (given the laws of science)."[28] Robert Herman reinforces Farrell's definition norms as he writes that they are "collective beliefs that regulate the behavior and identity of actors."[29] Hence, norms define the behavior of states and other actors in the international system by creating the standards and codes of acceptable conduct.[30]

The emphasis on norms within the international system provides a means to account for changes in state behavior over time as the constraints on and opportunities afforded to actors are modified allowing previously marginalized factors to play an increasingly important role in the international system. For instance, norms on security cooperation can change over time. The post World War II era demonstrated the potential for security cooperation as the western states of the transatlantic region developed a comprehensive security regime. Katja Weber describes security regimes as:

> mechanisms for aggregating the capabilities of states in situations in which individually the states have inadequate capability to deal with threats that confront them. In fact, the scale required to generate the capability to assure survival often exceeds that of any one state, so that cooperation becomes necessary.[31]

Jervis notes that linkages in security matters often lead to cooperation and collaboration in other area, thus propelling norms linked to cooperation to expand:

> Common goals give each state a stake in the well-being of the others: to the extent that they expect to cooperate in the future, they want all to be strong, especially if they think they may again have to contain the former enemy. Far from states' values being negatively interdependent (as is often the case in world politics), they are positively linked: each gains if the other is satisfied, and willing and able to carry out its international obligations.[32]

Hence, just as cooperation norms have evolved over time, threat norms have changed as well. At the end of World War II, military doctrine and planning, and indeed the emerging field of security studies, initially continued to perceive the main threat to transatlantic security to be a conventional, mass invasion. Over the course of the Cold War, the threat norms evolved so that nuclear exchanges rose to be the dominant challenge to world peace. At the end of the Cold War, both policymakers and scholars were slow to accept the changing nature of security threats as substate terrorism, accompanied by ethnic and religious strife, increasingly dominated defense and security planning.

State and Substate Actors

Efforts to combine the core arguments of traditional realism, especially as expressed in balance of power equations, and constructivism have led some scholars to argue in favor of a "minimalist" or "soft-realism."[33] This shift seeks to combine many of the elements of realism with constructivism, while lessening the importance given to the state. One manifestation of this trend has been the ongoing effort to assign a degree of importance to substate actors within the field of security studies. While traditional and neo-realism, as well as neoliberal institutionalism, all emphasize the importance of the state or supra-state actors, scholars are increasingly interested in analyses which examine the role of substate and domestic actors on the policy process. In addition, scholars increasingly question whether states really act as unitary actors. For instance, in his study of Southeast Asian, Amitav Acharya argues that regional security cooperation occurred both because of external threats, as realism or neoliberalism would predict, and in response to the perceived internal threat posed by communism and other insurgency movements.[34] With the end of the Cold War and the rise of international terrorism, the emphasis on substate actors has dramatically increased within security studies as some groups have increasingly posed a threat to both domestic governments and the peace and stability of the international system.

Two-Level Games

One framework through which domestic and foreign actors can be reconciled is two-level games. This game model contends that policymakers must negotiate on two levels: one with domestic actors; and the second with international actors. The results of these twin sets of negotiations can be one of four outcomes or win-sets: 1) domestic win – international win; 2) domestic win – international loss; 3) domestic loss – international win; or 4) domestic loss – international loss (or some degree of win/loss in each of the areas along a continuum from twin wins to twin losses).[35]

Different circumstances determine the acceptable win-sets for negotiators and the likelihood of success. Robert Putnam asserts that after leaders, or Level I players, achieve their objectives or goals at the international level, they then must win the domestic game by convincing the public to accept the agreement or goal.[36] Players can use international agreements to force domestic consensus or use domestic attitudes as a factor in their negotiations with foreign actors. Either the international and domestic wins can be formal, in the form of a treaty or agreement on the international level or some form of formal ratification at the domestic level, or they can be informal as tacit agreements or simple manifestations of public support.

The significance of two-level games, which have mainly been analyzed in terms of economic negotiations, to security studies is that the model provides a means to incorporate domestic level variables and actors into the policy framework.[37] While realism is based on the premise that states function as unitary actors within the international system, two-level games also provides a means to explain interaction between domestic groups within involved states, including substate coalition-building and the articulation of common goals and interests among like actors.[38] It also explains what may be perceived as irrational actions by leaders, in that actions which appear impolitic at the international level may be perfectly logical or acceptable in light of domestic constraints or variables.[39] Realism also accepts the potential for irrational policy or actions by actors within the international system as the result of poor quality of information.[40]

Security, Threats and Threat Quotients

Contemporary security studies has its genesis during the Cold War era. Currently the field includes a range of subfields, including strategic studies, which explores the use of force in the policy context, and military science, which specifically examines tactics and military doctrine. Among these areas of inquiry, Thomas G. Mahnken points out that the military aspects and strategy of the Cold War continue to have a significant impact on scholarship: "The topics of arms competition, arms control, force structure, strategy, and deterrence dominated the field."[41] However, the military actions of the 1990s led to recalculation of both threat assessment and doctrine. For instance, during the Cold War, one of the main military doctrines was that of deterrence. Even in the wake of the end of the superpower conflict, nuclear states have continued to rely upon nuclear deterrence as a main ingredient in overall security strategy. Meanwhile, other states have sought to acquire weapons of mass destruction (WMDs) for their bargaining or deterrent value. In light of the growing risk of terrorism, however, the value of deterrence is increasingly questioned. Mahnken has this to say about the contemporary debate over deterrence:

> A related question is the applicability of deterrence to terrorists. The orthodox view is that a person who is willing to give his life cannot be deterred. But of course a suicide bomber kills himself and his victims in the belief that their death will pave the way toward the attainment of some goal. At least in theory it might be possible to demonstrate that such actions are not only futile but also counter-productive, leading to a sort of deterrence.[42]

The twentieth century has witnessed a continuous recalculation of security threats. Through the first two wars of the century, the main security threat to states was the use of force to conquer territory or to capture or destroy interests, including economic interests or allies. The degree of threat was measured through a threat quotient. The higher the threat quotient, the more likely a state would use its array of resources and assets to deter or defeat the threat. With the onset of the Cold War, the main security focus of the United States shifted to the threat of nuclear war. Military planners still prepared for large-scale conventional warfare, but an increasing amount of resources and planning was devoted to the doctrine of deterrence and to the development of the American nuclear stockpile.

Technology has been the main determinant of new security threats. As Michael Mandlebaum points out, "... strategy followed technology."[43] As was the case with the development of the airplane, the revolution in military affairs (RMA) that accompanied the spread of nuclear weapons led to dramatic changes in the way nations prepared for conflict. In his classic work on modern warfare, Theodore Rapp notes that the RMA of World War II produced not only atomic weapons, but "... such improved means of delivery as the snorkel submarine, a true under-water rather than a submersible ship, jet planes, long-range rockets, and new guidance and navigation systems."[44] In response, states have endeavored to develop both offensive and defensive military systems to deter attack and counter threats.

One major result of the RMA and the changing military doctrine of the Cold War era for the United States was the creation of a security strategy based on nuclear deterrence. The "New Look" developed by the Eisenhower administration was a strategic plan that incorporated various existing elements of American security policy and capabilities in an effort to counter the emerging Soviet threat. Mandlebaum writes that the "New Look":

> marked, as well, a shift in emphasis in American defense policy, toward atomic weapons. For the first time the American government gave a formal answer to the first two questions that the atomic age had pressed upon it: What political purposes would atomic weapons serve? And how should they be deployed to serve these purposes?
>
> The answer to the first question turned out to be deterrence. The concept of deterrence is simple: prevention by threat.[45]

Deterrence, as a pure military or security doctrine, matched the broader American foreign policy goal of containment. Since policymakers in Washington believed that Soviet foreign policy was inexorably tied to expansion, deterrence and containment could serve to constrain the Soviets until the inherent flaws in the Soviet system led to the demise of America's superpower rival.[46] Deterrence was especially important in light of Soviet conventional strength; however, the eventual build-up of Soviet nuclear forces resulted in a nuclear stalemate with both superpowers relying on deterrence to counter the other. As military historian Jeremy Black writes:

> The threat of retaliation by American nuclear strength, both tactical ... and strategic, served to lessen their threat [Soviet conventional forces], but in the 1970s, the Soviet Union was able to make major advances in comparative nuclear potency, producing a situation in which war was seen as likely to lead to MAD (mutual assured destruction).[47]

As the threat to the United States changed, so too did American security policy, including the drive in the 1980s, to develop anti-missile systems through initiatives such as the Strategic Defense Initiative (SDI).[48]

Asymmetrical Warfare

The end of the Cold War marked the beginning of a period of decline in interstate conflict, accompanied by a rise in intra-state strife. For instance, in 1993, there were 22 wars being fought around the globe, and all but five were intra-state conflicts. The 1990s witnessed a dramatic increase in the number of ethnopolitical conflicts as substate actors challenged existing state structures.[49] During this decade, there was a marked increase in asymmetrical warfare, especially through the rise in international terrorism. Asymmetrical warfare is a conflict in which a weak actor battles a powerful one. Usually the term refers to wars in which the opponents are so unequal, that the weaker side has no choice but to utilize unorthodox or unconventional tactics and strategy.[50]

Asymmetrical warfare was common during the Cold War in the numerous struggles for independence and in the range of counterinsurgency conflicts fought around the globe by both superpowers. Indeed, in many regions, asymmetrical warfare became the norm after World War II and the subsequent demise of interstate conflict. Black notes that "in areas where international conflict was uncommon, such as Latin American after 1941, the prime activity of the military could be asymmetrical internal confrontations."[51] Indeed, asymmetrical warfare has been a historical constant and has ranged from conflicts such as the American Revolutionary War to the Vietnam War.

Terrorism

One manifestation of asymmetrical warfare is terrorism. Terrorism is defined by the US law (Title 50, Section 1801) as "violent acts or acts dangerous to human life that are a violation of the criminal laws of the United States or of any State, or that would be a criminal violation if committed within the jurisdiction of the United States or any State;" the US Code goes on to note that terrorist acts include those designed:

> to intimidate or coerce a civilian population; to influence the policy of a government by intimidation or coercion; or to affect the conduct of a government by assassination or kidnapping; and occur totally outside the United States, or transcend national boundaries in terms of the means by which they are accomplished, the persons they appear intended to coerce or intimidate, or the locale in which their perpetrators operate or seek asylum.[52]

Domestic terrorism refers to acts that are committed within the borders of the Untied States by domestic actors. The United Nations still does not have a consensus definition of terrorism, since memberstates are reluctant to try to distinguish between terrorism and self-determination movements or insurgencies. However, the United Nations Office on Drugs and Crime offers this very thorough 1988 definition developed by A.P. Schmid:

> Terrorism is an anxiety-inspiring method of repeated violent action, employed by (semi-) clandestine individual, group or state actors, for idiosyncratic, criminal or political reasons, whereby – in contrast to assassination – the direct targets of violence are not the main targets. The immediate human victims of violence are generally chosen randomly (targets of opportunity) or selectively (representative or symbolic targets) from a target population, and serve as message generators. Threat- and violence-based communication processes between terrorist (organization), (imperiled) victims, and main targets are used to manipulate the main target (audience(s)), turning it into a target of terror, a

target of demands, or a target of attention, depending on whether intimidation, coercion, or propaganda is primarily sought.[53]

Asymmetric warfare does not necessarily mean terrorism, although in asymmetrical conflicts, the weaker actor may utilize terrorist tactics. In addition, international terrorist groups, although often substate actors, employ the same strategies and resources often used by weaker states in asymmetric wars. Mahnken characterizes the current war on terror as "violent clash of wills" in which "while Al Qaeda looks and operates much differently than a conventional state adversary, it is nonetheless a strategic actor. Its leadership has political objectives and attempts to use force to achieve them."[54] Hence in the contemporary global struggle against various linked terrorist groups, the principles of conflict and the methods utilized by America's adversary parallel those utilized by weak actors in other asymmetric wars.

While asymmetric warfare is not new in the history of conflict, what is different is the ability of international terrorists to conduct direct attacks on the United States. In addition, terrorist groups have also demonstrated a willingness and desire to conduct attacks on a massive scale that threatens the infrastructure and economy of America. As early as 1998, the potential for devastating September 11 – style attacks was recognized in the National Security Strategy which warned that "potential enemies, whether nations, terrorist groups or criminal organizations, are increasingly likely to attack US territory and the American people in unconventional ways."[55] Indeed, in 1999, the US Commission on National Security for the Twenty-First Century forewarned of the potential for attacks on the American homeland. The Commission also correctly reported that the notable military capabilities of the country were not capable of deterring terrorism. The group noted that "America will become increasingly vulnerable to hostile attack on our homeland and our military superiority will not entirely protect us."[56] At the core of the Commission's inquiry was the call for a recalculation of security policy to better prepare the nation for homeland defense against terrorism. The Commission prophetically foresaw the need to integrate national security policy with domestic security programs through what has become homeland security policy. It reported that "traditional distinctions between national defense and domestic security will be challenged further as the new century unfolds, and both conventional policies and bureaucratic arrangements will be stretched to and beyond the breaking point unless those policies and arrangements are reformed."[57] It would take the devastating terrorist attacks of September 11 to prompt the type of reorganization and reform that the Commission had recommended almost exactly two years earlier.

Interests and Security Policy

Central to security studies is the articulation and identification of national interests. Interests drive policy and often represent both the domestic internalization, and the outward expression, of international norms. Just as norms revolve around state behavior, interests serve as a means to formulate and articulate policies to implement norms. National security policy refers to actions undertaken and choices made to protect or defend interests.[58] In the United States, national security strategy is codified through the annual publication of a formal National Security Strategy (a requirement since the 1986 passage of the Goldwater-Nichols Defense Department Reorganization Act).[59] The terrorist attacks of September 11 confirmed the need for a recalculation of American security interests to more fully develop policies that would utilize the nation's resources in a manner to better protect the homeland.

The identification and articulation of US national interests is the key to adapting to changes in the security environment. The internationalism of Woodrow Wilson or the commitment to European and Asian regional security advocated by the Truman administration or the transition to the "New Look" or the effort at SDI were instances of interest recalculation. However, the ability to define core interests is often complicated by both domestic and international factors. Leaders must also decide how the national interests should be manifested: should those interests be expressed in clearly defined, quantifiable terms, or should they be broad goals and objectives? Glenn Hastedt and Kay Knickrehm point out some of difficulties:

> The term *national interest* [italics in the original] has a compelling ring. It conveys a sense of urgency, importance, threat, concreteness ... Unfortunately, just as with the concept of power, the concept of the national interest is not easily defined. At the core of the debate over its definition is the question of whether the national interest should be treated as an objective, measurable asset of a normative political stance.[60]

For example, in the 1999 National Security Policy, the Clinton administration identified three broad goals: 1) "to enhance America's security"; 2) "to bolster America's economic prosperity"; and 3) "to promote democracy and human rights abroad."[61] General objectives such as these characterized US security policy throughout the 1990s, as first the administration of George H.W. Bush and then the Clinton administration endeavored to identify new or changing interests in light of the end of the Cold War and the demise of America's superpower rival.

Interests Defined

In a widely used reader on US national security, Sam C. Sarkesian, John Allen Williams and Stephen J. Cimbala contend that, for the United States, "national interests are expressions of US values projected into the international and domestic arenas."[62] The nation's values reflect the core political culture of the United States and include its moral, legal, political, economic, historic and cultural priorities.

These interests guide US foreign and security policy and serve to project American goals into the international system. Consequently, these interests are formulated to ensure "an international environment that is most favorable to the peaceful pursuit of values. It follows that interests nurture and expand democracy and open systems.

Similarly, the United States wishes to prevent the expansion of closed systems by the use of force or indirect aggression."[63] In the 2000 National Security Strategy, the Clinton administration, on the eve of its departure from office, characterized the national interests in the following manner: "Our national interests are wide-ranging. They cover those requirements essential to the survival and well being of our Nation as well as the desire to see us, and others, abide by principles such as the rule of law, upon which our republic was founded."[64]

The 2000 National Security Strategy also presented a utilitarian model of how to rank or assess national interests:

> We divide our national interests into three categories: vital, important, and humanitarian. Vital interests are those directly connected to the survival, safety, and vitality of our nation. Among these are the physical security of our territory and that of our allies, the safety of our citizens both at home and abroad, protection against WMD proliferation, the economic well-being of our society, and the protection of our critical infrastructures – including energy, banking and finance, telecommunications, transportation, water systems, vital human services, and government services – from disruption intended to cripple their operation. We will do what we must to defend these interests. This may involve the use of military force, including unilateral action, where deemed necessary or appropriate.
>
> The second category, important national interests, affects our national well being or that of the world in which we live. Principally, this may include developments in regions where America holds a significant economic or political stake, issues with significant global environmental impact, infrastructure disruptions that destabilize but do not cripple smooth economic activity, and crises that could cause destabilizing economic turmoil or humanitarian movement. Examples of when we have acted to protect important national interests include our successful efforts to end the brutal conflict and restore peace in Kosovo, or our assistance to our Asian and Pacific allies and friends in support of the restoration of order and transition to nationhood in East Timor.
>
> The third category is humanitarian and other longer-term interests. Examples include reacting to natural and manmade disasters; acting to halt gross violations of human rights; supporting emerging democracies; encouraging adherence to the rule of law and civilian control of the military; conducting Joint Recovery Operations worldwide to account for our country's war dead; promoting sustainable development and environmental protection; or facilitating humanitarian demining.[65]

In their analysis of the three-level ranking of national interests, Sarkesian, Williams and Cimbala note the importance of developing such a categorization as a means to define priorities and allocate resources. The authors explain that "categories of priorities such as these can be used not only as a framework for systemic assessment of national interests and national security but also as a way to distinguish immediate from long-range issues."[66] In the post-September 11 world, there has been another reformulation of interest. This recalculation was presented in the twin 2002 publications, the *National Security Strategy* and the *National Strategy for Homeland Security*.

Homeland Security Strategy

Unlike the security strategies issued over the previous decade, the Bush administration's 2002 *National Security Strategy* contained far more defined goals. Following the attacks of September 11, the Bush administration announced changes in threat assessments and national security policy. A major component of the new national strategy was a clearer and more robust identification and articulation of homeland security policies. However, even the development of a more defined homeland security strategy came within the framework of the elevation of international terrorism as the main imminent threat to the United States and the concurrent enunciation of a more assertive policy to counter global terrorism.

Central to the new US foreign and security strategy was a transition away from the deterrence-based policies of the late Cold War period to a more flexible response, including, most controversially, the promulgation of a doctrine of unilateral preemption. Specifically, the Bush *National Security Strategy* states that:

> The United States has long maintained the option of preemptive actions to counter a sufficient threat to our national security. The greater the threat, the greater is the risk of inaction – and the more compelling the case for taking anticipatory action to defend ourselves, even if uncertainty remains as to the time and place of the enemy's attack. To forestall or prevent such hostile acts by our adversaries, the United States will, if necessary, act preemptively.
>
> The United States will not use force in all cases to preempt emerging threats, nor should nations use preemption as a pretext for aggression. Yet in an age where the enemies of civilization openly and actively seek the world's most destructive technologies, the United States cannot remain idle while dangers gather. We will always proceed deliberately, weighing the consequences of our actions. To support preemptive options, we will:
> - build better, more integrated intelligence capabilities to provide timely, accurate information on threats, wherever they may emerge;
> - coordinate closely with allies to form a common assessment of the most dangerous threats; and
> - continue to transform our military forces to ensure our ability to conduct rapid and precise operations to achieve decisive results.
>
> The purpose of our actions will always be to eliminate a specific threat to the United States or our allies and friends. The reasons for our actions will be clear, the force measured, and the cause just.[67]

The strategic document also makes three broad pledges: that the United States "will defend the peace by fighting terrorists and tyrants"; that it will "preserve the peace by building good relations among the Great powers"; and, finally, it "will extend the peace by encouraging free and open societies on every continent."[68]   The core sentiments of the new broad strategy would be tested with the 2003 invasion of Iraq. The *National Security Strategy* reflected the attempt by the Bush administration to redefine national security interests and, subsequently, recalculate national security policies. One of the major changes in the operational definitions of interests and policies was the endeavor to formulate and implement a new policy of homeland defense within the broader framework of national security.

Homeland Security in the Post-9/11 Context

Homeland security, as a strategic imperative, has significantly evolved since the end of the Cold War. Homeland security used to mean the defense of national borders and the protection of the United States from large-scale enemy attacks, including ballistic missile strikes. Current homeland security doctrine is less about countering traditional military threats and more about counter-terrorism. As a result, US homeland security priorities more closely resemble the nation's counter-terrorism programs of the 1980s and 1990s rather than Cold War military doctrine.

The nation's main security organization, the Department of Defense currently defines homeland security as "the preparation for, prevention of, deterrence or preemption of, defense against, and response to threats and aggressions directed toward U.S. territory, sovereignty, domestic population and infrastructure; as well as crisis management, consequence management, and other domestic civil support."[69] In addition to the publication of the *National Security Strategy*, the Bush administration also codified its homeland security policy in order to incorporate changing interests and values. In the 2002 *National Strategy for Homeland Security*, the Bush administration presented an operational definition of homeland security, based on four main goals. The administration also acknowledged that the concept was an amorphous one, open to different interpretations:

> In the aftermath of September 11, "homeland security" has come to mean many things to many people. It is a new mission and a new term. The federal government defines homeland security as follows ... Homeland security is a concerted national effort to prevent terrorist attacks within the United States, reduce America's vulnerability to terrorism, and minimize the damage and recover from attacks that do occur.[70]

The administration's definition rests on two main interrelated pillars: homeland defense and civil support. Homeland defense can be defined as the "protection of US territory, sovereignty, domestic population, and critical infrastructure against external threats and aggression," while civil support is "support to US civil authorities for domestic emergencies, and for designated law enforcement and other activities."[71] Traditionally, the concept of homeland defense has revolved around the necessity to protect America's borders, including its maritime waters, from both conventional attacks and potential strikes from WMDs by national actors, rather than substate or terrorist groups. For instance, in 2000 there was a broadly accepted "consensus" that homeland security involved "national missile defense, counterterrorism, WMD preparedness, consequence management of WMD events and protection against cyber attacks."[72] Prior to the September 11 2001 attacks, the Office of Management and Budget under the Bush administration presented a strategic vision for homeland security that rested on three main points: counterterrorism, defense against WMDs and the protection of critical infrastructure.[73]

US Homeland Security Objectives

These different operational definitions provide an overview of the transition from Cold War to post-September 11 homeland security doctrine. In the changed security environment, several main points emerge over the purpose and scope of contemporary American homeland security policy. First, the main responsibility of homeland security policy is defense against terrorist acts. This marks a major transition away from traditional defense policy in which states were viewed as the main threats to US national interests. The *National Strategy for Homeland Security* specifically states that "homeland security is focused on terrorism in the United States."[74] Within the statement of strategy, the administration offers a specific and detailed definition of what it considers to be terrorism: "Any premeditated, unlawful act dangerous to human life or public welfare that is intended to intimidate or coerce civilian populations or governments."[75] The administration follows this definition with the following explanatory clause:

> This description captures the core concepts shared by the various definitions of terrorism contained in the US Code, each crafted to achieve a legal standard of specificity and clarity. This description covers kidnappings; hijackings; shootings, conventional bombings; attacks involving chemical, biological, radiological or nuclear weapons; cyber attacks; and any number of other forms of malicious violence. Terrorists can be US citizens or foreigners, acting in concert with others, on their own, or on behalf of a hostile state.[76]

Second, but related to the first responsibility, is the increasingly important role that crisis management plays in homeland security. Support for federal, state and local authorities in the event of a terrorist attack becomes one of the main priorities of homeland security policy. For instance, the Secretary of the new Department of Homeland Security was given a specific set of coordinating duties:

> In discharging his responsibilities relating to coordination (including the provision of training and equipment) with State and local government personnel, agencies, and authorities, with the private sector, and with other entities, the responsibilities of the Secretary shall include: 1) coordinating with State and local government personnel, agencies, and authorities, and with the private sector, to ensure adequate planning, equipment, training, and exercise activities; 2) coordinating and, as appropriate, consolidating, the Federal government's communications and systems of communications relating to homeland security with State and local government personnel, agencies, and authorities, the private sector, other entities, and the public; 3) directing and supervising grant programs

of the Federal government for State and local government emergency response providers; and 4) distributing or, as appropriate, coordinating the distribution of, warnings and information to State and local government personnel, agencies, and authorities and to the public.[77]

This reflects the language of the administration's definition of homeland security, which calls for a "concerted national effort" and acknowledges that while the "federal government has a critical role to play in homeland security ... The administration's approach to homeland security is based on the principles of shared responsibility and partnership with the Congress, state and local governments, the private sector and the American people."[78]

Third, homeland security is not defined as a purely military mission, although the US military plays a role. Instead, homeland security involves a variety of federal, state and local agencies and not just the Department of Defense or the intelligence agencies. In fact, the lead agency in homeland security has traditionally been the Federal Bureau of Investigation (FBI). Under the new concept of homeland security, the FBI retains a significant role and is assigned as the lead coordinating agency through the Joint Terrorism Task Forces, which integrate federal, state and local law enforcement agencies with the intelligence services and the military.

Fourth, and finally, the key to effective homeland security is prevention. A report by the Brookings Institute concludes that "a sound Homeland security strategy should focus first and foremost on prevention – by ensuring that would-be terrorists and their materials do not enter the United States, identifying would-be terrorists already here, and securing dangerous materials so that they cannot be used for attack."[79] Only in the aftermath of the September 11 attacks has the United States begun to develop a cohesive and multi-faceted homeland security strategy that focuses on prevention. Prior to the attacks, both the Clinton administration and the early Bush administration employed a homeland security strategy that was primarily reactive in nature. The Bush administration's commitment to prevent terrorism is manifested through the doctrine of preemption within the 2002 *National Security Strategy* and is reaffirmed with the *National Strategy for Homeland Security* where the administration pledges to "strive to detect terrorists before they strike, to prevent them and their instruments of terror from entering our country, and to take decisive action to eliminate the threat they pose."[80]

The main principles of American homeland security policy would shape the administration's vision for a Department of Homeland Security whose primary goals would be "reducing the vulnerability of the United States to terrorism at home, and minimizing the damage and assisting in the recovery from any attack that may occur."[81]

The Reordering of National Security Priorities

The subsequent chapters examine the historical evolution of US homeland security policy and frame the nation's priorities within the broader context of the international system. Central to understanding this analysis is an examination of the importance of the shifts in US security policy that resulted in the development of a new homeland security strategy and its resultant institutions, including the Department of Homeland Security.

Security considerations under traditional realism were based on the preservation and enhancement of state power. As Pinar Bilgin points out in an essay on alternative approaches to security which emphasis the individual, "The concept of security has traditionally been related more to states than to people."[82] Within this tradition, there was a significant emphasis on the acquisition of, and maintenance of control over, geographic territory, and economic resources. The changing nature of threats within the international community has led to a subsequent recalculation of interests.

Within the field of security studies, this has led to the emergence of what many scholars refer to as "human security." For instance, under the auspices of Harvard University's Program on Humanitarian Policy and Conflict Resolution, the Human Security Network has begun a long-range program to develop an annual Human Security Report. This publication is a response to what Andrew Mack identifies as a need "because the forms of global violence are changing – and quite dramatically. Not only has international terrorism captured headlines since September 11 . . but almost all wars now take place within, not between, states ..."[83]

Much of the vanguard scholarship in this area has been the result of the "Copenhagen School" which seeks to redefine security away from an interest-based concern. As Michael G. Williams writes, the Copenhagen School treats security "not as an objective condition but as the outcome of a specific social process: the social construction of security issues (who or what is being secured, and from what)."[84] One method by which the development of a new homeland security doctrine can be analyzed is through the securitization models developed by prominent thinkers within the Copenhagen School, including Barry Buzan and Ole Weaver.[85] Williams argues that the Copenhagen School, while not immune to a range of criticism, is particularly useful owing to the manner "... in which securitization theory combines themes common within social-constructivism and a particular reading of the classical Realist tradition, and especially the legacy of Carl Schmitt."[86]

Other approaches to the reordering of security come directly from the social constructivist schools. For instance, the recalculation of the nexus between threat and interest can be examined through the framework of risk evolution. Ulrich Beck defines risk as "a systemic way of dealing with hazards and insecurities induced and introduced by modernization itself."[87] The intricacies of modernization have, of course, played a significant role in facilitating the rise of supra-national terrorism and international terrorist networks such as Al Qaeda.

Homeland Security Studies

Ultimately, the rise of homeland security as a field of academic inquiry is in line with the continuing evolution of security studies. Just as strategic studies emerged as a major subfield in the 1950s and 1960s, in response to the RMA and changes in the global security system, homeland security represents the latest, but not last stage in the maturation of security studies. The multitude of approaches described within this chapter provide a range of lenses through which to examine the transitions in American national security policy as they relate to the rise of homeland security as a means to counter global terrorism.

The rise of the threat quotient posed by terrorist groups such as Al Qaeda has forced states to reorder their security and defense priorities in order to better counter and contain the threat. Central to these efforts has been the redefinition of security interests in the manner in which the Bush administration codified and clarified US homeland security doctrine through the 2002 *National Strategy for Homeland Security.* States also have had to recalculate policy to better distribute resources and to coordinate the assets of national governments in order to prevent, prepare for and respond to terrorist attacks.[88] The central role of the state in these processes reaffirms the utility of realism and neo-realism to the study of homeland security, especially in an examination of the manner in which the United States has projected homeland security, in the form of a national interest, into its relations with other states and, indeed, the rise of global terrorism as a reaction to American primacy in the international security system.

Meanwhile, scholars outside of the realist tradition will continue to challenge the prevailing tenets within security studies, especially as they apply to homeland security. Social constructivism and other alternative approaches provide reasonable means to assess the changes in the international system and the evolution of security paradigms. Such analyses propel the debate over actor action and reaction, and help delineate the most fruitful areas of inquiry. This book seeks to initiate a broad debate within security studies over the utility of developing a line of inquiry devoted to homeland security. As such, the following chapters offer a starting point in terms of concepts, definitions and history, and the broad evolution of homeland security within the framework of the US response to the September 11 attacks.

Notes

1. There is an immense body of literature on realism in international relations. Among the more notable or influential works are: E.H. Carr, *The Twenty Years Crisis, 1919-1939: An Introduction to the Study of International Relations* (London: Macmillan, 1939); Hans J. Morganthau, *Politics Among Nations* (New York: Knopf, 1948); Kenneth N. Waltz, *Man, the State and War: A Theoretical Analysis* (New York: Columbia University Press, 1959); or Kenneth N. Waltz, *The Theory of International Politics* (Reading, MA: Addison Wesley, 1979). Works which elucidate the key differences between realism and other approaches to international politics include: David Baldwin, ed., *Neorealism and Neoliberalism: The Contemporary Debate* (New York: Columbia University Press, 1993); Robert O. Keohane, ed., *Neorealism and its Critics* (New York: Columbia University Press, 1987); or Paul Viotti and Mark Kauppi, eds., *International Relations Theory: Realism, Pluralism, Globalism* (New York: Macmillan, 1993).
2. On offensive and defensive realism, see George Quester, *Offense and Defense in the*

International System (New York: John Wiley & Sons, 1977). Some scholars argue that offense – defense theory, which maintains that the nature of global politics is determined by the degree of difficulty of offensive military operations, "resolves many problems in the standard neorealist theory of Kenneth Waltz and enhances its explanatory range and power;" Sean M. Lynn-Jones, "Preface," in Michael E. Brown, Owen R. Coté, Jr., Sean M. Lynn-Jones, and Steven E. Miller, eds., *Offense, Defense and War, An International Security Reader* (Cambridge: MIT Press, 2004), xii. Some contend that by integrating offense-defense theory into realism, scholars are better able to predict the likelihood of war and conflict in the international system; ibid; xiii. Lynn-Jones further cites Stephen Van Evera who "calls offense-defense balance and other related variables the 'fine-grained structure of power' and argues that 'Realism becomes far stronger when it includes these fine-grained structures and perceptions of them';" Stephen Van Evera, *Causes of War: Power and the Roots of Conflict* (Ithaca: Cornell Univeristy Press, 1999), 256; cited in Lynn-Jones, xiii.

3. Stephen M. Walt, "The Renaissance of Security Studies," *International Studies Quarterly,* 35-1 (1991), 212.
4. Joseph S. Nye and Sean Lynn-Jones, "International Security Studies: A Report of a Conference on the State of the Discipline," *International Security*,12/4 (Winter 1988), 6.
5. Thomas Hobbes, *Leviathan*, Richard E. Flathman and David Johnson, eds., Norton Critical Edition, (New York: W.W. Norton, 1997), 93.
6. Kenneth Waltz, "Anarchic Orders and the Balance of Power," *Theory of International Politics* (Boston: McGraw-Hill, 1979); reprinted in G. John Ikenberry, ed., *American Foreign Policy: Theoretical Essays*, 5th ed. (New York: Pearson Longman, 2005), 60.
7. Neoliberalism, often referred to as neoliberal institutionalism, differs from realism in its willingness to accept non-state actors, including institutions such as the United Nations or the World Bank, as being just as important and powerful as states within the international system. Neoliberalism has a long history which includes the work and ideas of Immanuel Kant and Woodrow Wilson, and is often expressed through sub-theories such as the Democratic Peace Theory or Institutionalism, both of which emphasize cooperation over conflict and the impact of evolutionary trends in international relations. Neoliberalism is based on rational choice theory and accepts that states "learn" over time. See David Baldwin, ed., *Neorealism and Neoliberalism: The Contemporary Debate* (New York: Columbia University Press, 1993); or Charles W. Kegley, Jr., *Controversies in International Relations: Realism and the Neoliberal Challenge* (New York: St. Martin's, 1995).
8. See Robert O. Keohane, *After Hegemony: Cooperation and Discord in the World Political Economy* (Princeton: Princeton University Press, 1984); or David A. Lake, "Leadership, Hegemony, and the International Economy: Naked Emperor or Tattered Monarch with Potential," *International Studies Quarterly*, 37/4 (December 1993):459-89.
9. Robert Jervis, "Realism in the Study of World Politics," *International Organization*, 52/4 (Autumn 1998), 986.
10. J. Ann Tickner, "Feminist Responses to International Security Studies," *Peace Review*, 16/1 (March 2004), 44.
11. Roberta N. Haar, *Nation States as Schizophrenics: Germany and Japan as Post-Cold War Actors* (Westport: Praeger, 2001), 5.
12. *Ibid.*
13. John Mearsheimer, "The False Promise of International Institutions," in Michael Brown, *et al.*, eds., *Theories of War and Peace* (Cambridge: Massachusetts Institute of Technology, 1998), 337.
14. Balance of power can describe the resultant equilibrium which emerges when rival states or blocs form coalitions to counter each other, it can also refer to the policies pursued in order

to reach that equilibrium; see Robert Jervis, "From Balance to Concert: A Study of International Security Cooperation," *World Politics*, 38/1 (October 1985): 58-79.

15. Tickner, 44.

16. Stephen M. Walt, "Rigor or Rigor Mortis: Rational Choice and Security Studies," *International Security*, 23/4 (Spring 1999), 5.

17. *Ibid.*, Walt relies on the work of Barry O'Neil to distinguish between three broad categories of formal rational choice theory. These include "proto-game theory" which uses models to develop "analogies" or other means to enhance the explanatory value of case studies. An example of this would be the familiar prisoner's dilemma. The second category is that of "low game theory" in which broad theoretical outcomes are compared with real world scenarios. Finally, there is "high game theory" that endeavors to build broad or sweeping generalizations that cover entire categories of games or case studies; Barry O'Neill, "Game Theory and the Study of Deterrence in War," in Paul C. Stern, Robert Axelrod, Robert Jervis and Roy Radner, eds., *Perspectives on Deterrence* (London: Oxford Univeristy Press, 1989, 135; cited in *ibid.*, 9.

18. *Ibid.*, 46.

19. Lisa L. Martin, "The Contributions of Rational Choice: A Defense of Pluralism," *International Security*, 24/2 (Fall 1999), 74.

20. *Ibid.*

21. John Lewis Gaddis, "International Relations Theory and the End of the Cold War," *International Security*, 17/3 (Winter 1992/93), 6.

22. Gwyn Prins, "The Four-Stroke Cycle in Security Studies," *International Affairs,* 74/4 (October 1998), 781.

23. See Immanuel Wallerstein, *The Modern World System: Capitalist Agriculture and the Origins of the European World Economy in the Sixteenth Century* (New York: Academic Press, 1974); or Immanuel Wallerstein, *Geopolitics and Geoculture: Essays on the Changing World-System* (Cambridge: Cambridge University Press, 1991).

24. See Andrew Linklater, *Beyond Realism and Marxism: Critical Theory and International Relations* (New York: St. Martin's, 1989).

25. See J. Ann Tickner, *Gender in International Relations* (New York: Columbia University Press, 1992).

26. On the emergence of constructivism, see Emanuel Adler, "Seizing the Middle Ground: Constructivism in World Politics," *European Journal of International Affairs* 3 (September 1997): 319-363; Jeffrey T. Checkel, "The Constructivist Turn in International Relations Theory," *World Politics*, 50/2 (January 1998): 324-48; Ted Hopf, "The Promise of Constructivism in International Relations Theory," *International Security*, 23/1 (Summer 1998): 171-200; or John Ruggie, *Constructing the World Polity: Essays on International Institutionalization* (New York: Routledge, 1998).

27. Theo Farrell, "Constructivist Security Studies: Portrait of a Research Program," *International Studies Review*, 4/1 (Spring 2002), 49.

28. *Ibid.*, 50. Farrell points readers to Friedrich Kratochwil, *Rules, Norms and Decisions* (Cambridge: Cambridge University Press, 1989) and Jan Golinski, *Making Natural Knowledge* (Cambridge: Cambridge University Press, 1998) for a more thorough overview of this line of argument; *ibid.*

29. Robert Herman, "Identity, Norms, and National Security," in Peter J. Katzenstein, ed., *The Culture of National Security: Norms and Identity in World Politics* (New York: Columbia University Press, 1996), 274.

30. Ann Florini, "The Evolution of International Norms," *International Studies Quarterly*, 40/3 (September 1996), 364.

31. Katja Weber, "Hierarchy Amidst Anarchy: A Transaction Costs Approach to International

Security Cooperation," *International Studies Quarterly*, 41/2 (June 1997), 326.

32. Robert Jervis, "From Balance to Concert: A Study of International Security Cooperation," *World Politics*, 38/1 (October 1985), 67.

33. See Sorpong Peou, "Realism and Constructivism in Southeast Asian Security Studies Today: A Review Essay," *The Pacific Review*, 15/1 (2002),136.

34. Amitav Acharya, *Constructing a Security Community in Southeast Asia: ASEAN and the Problem of a Regional Order* (London: Routledge, 2001).

35. See Robert Putnam, Diplomacy and Domestic Politics: The Logic of Two-Level Games," *International Organization,* 42/3 (Summer 1988): 427-60; or Keisuke Iida, "Involuntary Defection in Two-Level Games," *Public Choice*, 89/2 (1996): 283-303; or Michael D. McGinnis and John T. Williams, "Policy Uncertainty in Two-Level Games: Examples of Correlated Equilibria," *International Studies Quarterly*, 37/1 (March 1993): 29-54.

36. *Ibid.*

37. For a further explanation, see Jongryn Mo, "The Logic of Two-Level Games with Endogenous Domestic Coalitions," *Journal of Conflict Resolution*, 38/3 (September 1994): 402-22.

38. Robert Pahre, "Endogenous Domestic Institutions in Two-Level Games: Parliamentary Oversight in Denmark and Elsewhere," *Journal of Conflict Resolution*, 41/1 (February 1997) 132-62; and Keisuke Iida, "When and How do Domestic Constraints Matter? Two-Level Games with Uncertainty," *Journal of Conflict Resolution*, 34/3 (September 1993): 403-26.

39. On this theme see Thomas H. Hammond and Brandon Prins, "Domestic Veto Institutions, International Negotiations, and the Status Quo: A Spatial Model of Two-Level Games with Complete Information," *Political Institutions and Public Choice Working Paper 98-05* (East Lansing: Michigan State University, Institute for Public Policy and Social Research, 1998); Helen V. Milner and B. Peter Rosendorff, "Democratic Politics and International Trade Negotiations: Elections and Divided Government as Constraints on Trade Liberalization," *Journal of Conflict Resolution*, 41/1 (February 1997): 117-46.

40. See Robert Jervis, *Perception and Misperception in International Politics* (Princeton: Princeton University Press, 1976).

41. Thomas G. Mahnken, "The Future of Strategic Studies," *The Journal of Strategic Studies*, 26/1 (March 2003), x.

42. *Ibid.*, xi.

43. Michael Mandlebaum, *The Nuclear Question: The United States & Nuclear Weapons, 1946-1976* (Cambridge: Cambridge University Press, 1979), 46.

44. Theodore Rapp, *War in the Modern World*, revised edition (New York: Macmillan Books, 1962), 393.

45. Mandlebaum, *The Nuclear Question*, 46-47.

46. *Ibid.*, 47; see also the seminal work by John Lewis Gaddis, *Strategies of Containment: A Critical Appraisal of Postwar American National Security Policy* (Oxford: Oxford University Press, 1982).

47. Jeremy Black, *War: Past, Present &Future* (New York: St. Martin's Press, 2000), 251.

48. On SDI, see Mira Duric, *The Strategic Defense Initiative: US Policy and the Soviet Union* (Aldershot: Ashgate, 2003).

49. Ted Robert Gurr and Barbara Harff, *Ethnic Conflict in World Politics* (Boulder: Westview Press, 1994), xiii, 1-5.

50. On asymmetrical warfare, see Ivan Arreguin-Toft, "How the Weak Win Wars: A Theory of Asymmetrical Conflict," *International Security*, 26/1 (Summer 2001): 93-128; T.V. Paul, *Asymmetric Conflicts: War Initiation by Weaker Powers* (Cambridge: Cambridge University Press, 1994); or Steven Metz and Douglas V. Johnson, II, *Asymmetry and US Military*

Strategy: Definition, Background, and Strategic Concepts (Carlisle Barracks: Army War College, 2001).

51. Black, 5.

52. United States, US Code, Title 50, Section 1801, Chapter 36, Subchapter 1, online at http://www.law.cornell.edu/uscode/.

53. United Nations, Office on Drugs and Crime, "Terrorism: Definitions," online at http://www.unodc.org/unodc/terrorism_definitions.html.

54. Mahnken, xii.

55. United States, White House, *A National Security Strategy for a New Century* (Washington, D.C.: White House, October 1998), 7.

56. United States, Commission on National Security for the Twenty-First Century, "New World Coming: American Security in the Twenty-First Century," the Phase I Report on the Emerging Global Security Environment for the First Quarter of the Twenty-First Century" (15 September 1999), 138.

57. *Ibid.*, 1.

58. For more on the relationship between interests and policy, see Michael G. Roskin, *National Interest: From Abstraction to Strategy* (Carlisle, Pa.: US Army Strategic Studies Institute, 1994).

59. In spite of the legal requirement, the George H.W. Bush, Clinton, and George Bush administrations only produced one national security strategy during their first four years in office; John Lewis Gaddis, "A Grand Strategy of Transformation," *Foreign Policy,* 133 (November/December 2002), 53.

60. Glenn Hastedt and Kay Knickrehm, eds., *Toward the Twenty-First Century: A Reader in World Politics* (New York: Prentice Hall, 1994), 142.

61. United States, White House, *National Security Strategy for a New Century* (Washington, D.C.: GPO, 1999), iii.

62. Sam C. Sarkesian, John Allen Williams and Stephen J. Cimbala, *U.S. National Security: Policymakers, Processes, and Politics*, third edition (Boulder: Lynne Rienner, 2002), 5.

63. *Ibid.*

64. United States, White House, *A National Security Strategy for a Global Age* (Washington, D.C.: GPO, December 2000), 9.

65. *Ibid.*

66. Sarkesian, Williams and Cimbala, 6.

67. United States, White House, *National Security Strategy of the United States* (Washington, D.C.: Office of the Press Secretary, 17 September 2002), available online at http://www.whitehouse.gov/nsc/nss5.html.

68. *Ibid.*

69. US, Department of Defense, *Army Modernization Plan 2002* (Washington, D.C.: DOD, 2002), H1.

70. United States, White House, *National Strategy for Homeland Security* (Washington, D.C.: GPO, 2002), 2; available online at http://www.whitehouse.gov/homeland/book/.

71. United States, Department of Defense, *Army Modernization Plan*, H1.

72. Kevin O'Prey, "Homeland Security: Framing the Problem," Speech, Massachusetts Institute of Technology (21 February 2001).

73. US, White House, Office of Management and Budget, *Annual Report to Congress on Combating Terrorism* (July 2001), 6.

74. United States, White House, *National Strategy for Homeland Security*, 2.

75. *Ibid.*

76. *Ibid.*

77. United States, White House, *Analysis for the Department of Homeland Security Act of*

2002: Title 1 (Washington, D.C.: White House, Office of the Press Secretary, 2002); available online at www.whitehouse.gov/deptofhomeland/analysis/title1.html.

78. United States, White House, *National Strategy for Homeland Security*, 2.
79. Ivo Daadler, *et al.*, *Assessing the Department of Homeland Security* (Washington, D.C.: Brookings Institute, 2002), 7.
80. United States. ,White House, *National Strategy for Homeland Security*, 2.
81. United States, White House, *Analysis for the Department of Homeland Security Act of 2002*; available online at www.whitehouse.gov/deptofhomeland/analysis/title1.html.
82. Pinar Bilgin, "Individual and Societal Dimensions of Security," *International Studies Review*, 5 (2003), 203.
83. Andrew Mack, "Human Security Report to Form Key Aspect of 2002 Policy Workshop," *Human Security Network News Bulletin*, 1/1 (December 2001), 2; available online at http://www.hsph.harvard.edu/hpcr/hsn/news_bulletin_v1_i1.pdf.
84. Michael G. Williams, "Words, Images, Enemies: Securitization and International Politics," *International Studies Quarterly* 47 (2003), 513.
85. See, for instance, Barry Buzan and Ole Weaver, "Slippery? Contradictory? Sociologically Untenable?: The Copenhagen School Replies," *Review of International Studies,* 23/2 (1997): 211-250; Barry Buzan, Ole Weaver and J. de Wilde, *Security: A New Framework for Analysis* (Boulder: Lynne Rienner, 1998); or Michael G. Williams, "Modernity, Identity and Security: A Comment on the Copenhagen Controversy," *Review of International Studies*, 24/3 (1998): 135-39.
86. Williams, 528.
87. Ulrich Beck, *World Risk Society* (Cambridge: Polity, 1999), 21.
88. See Russell D. Howard, and Reid Sawyer, eds., *Terrorism and Counterterrorism: Understanding the New Security Environment* (Guilford, Connecticut: The McGraw-Hill Companies, 2002).

Chapter 2

Evolution of Homeland Security

Introduction

The most significant responsibility of the political leadership of any state is to provide for the security of the citizens residing within the territory it governs. Failing to do so has the potential, if not the likelihood, to threaten the welfare of the populace and, in turn, the mandate of the government or regime in power at a particular historical juncture. This is generally the case irrespective of the geographic region of the world or characteristics of the government involved, although the means through which autocracies and democracies attempt to ensure internal security and social and political stability differ markedly. Dictatorial regimes maintain power and stability by repressing their people to such an extent that they are too fearful to rebel despite the dearth of political freedoms and, for most individuals, economic opportunities available. Examples range from Joseph Stalin's Soviet Union to Saddam Hussein's Iraq. Democracies, on the other hand, achieve the same end by creating and preserving a domestic environment conducive to the freedom of expression of a wide range of political viewpoints and the economic capacity to allow the vast majority of the population to prosper. Most prominent and prosperous among contemporary democracies are those situated in the United States and Western Europe. However, states in regions as varied as Central America and Southeast Asia have seen a rise in liberal governance over the past quarter century, and the prospects for democratic reform in the Greater Middle East are now equally promising as a result of elimination of Saddam's regime through the US-led prosecution of the Second Iraq War in the spring of 2003.

An examination of the homeland security concerns of just one of those polities – the United States – is the focal point of the book generally and the balance of this chapter in particular. But in order to engage in a beneficial discussion on that topic, it is first necessary to define the terms security and, more specifically, homeland security. At its most basic level, one could describe security as consistent access to the requisite food, water and shelter to survive on a daily basis and then adapt that definition to account for the characteristics of the environment in which an individual is situated. The basic definition just articulated is suitable as pertains to life in many parts of the developing world in the 2000s. Yet, with respect to the United States, a bit more adaptation is indispensable. For Americans, access to security includes a broad package of needs, ranging from personal protection from those determined to inflict harm on one end of a spectrum to the necessary economic resources to provide for one's individual and family needs and have the requisite funds to expend on leisure pursuits on the other. Personal safety concerns are the most important, especially in the years since Al Qaeda's attacks on the World Trade Center in New York and the Pentagon on the outskirts of Washington, DC, on September 11 2001. But that does not mean that Americans do not remain equally keen on preserving the right to express themselves freely and limit the government's ability to interfere in their private lives.

Defining the concept of homeland security is even more challenging, particularly given that the concept itself was not widely referred to in such terms until after the events of 9/11. Unlike most states around the world, America has traditionally maintained a clear distinction between the defense of the homeland and national security, with the latter pertaining almost exclusively to external threats that can be mitigated, if not eliminated, through economic, military and political action abroad rather than at home.[1] As Stephen Flynn, who served for 20 years in the US Coast Guard and is presently the Jeane J. Kirkpatrick Fellow in National Security Studies at the Council on Foreign Relations, notes, for "virtually every other country on the planet, the term 'national security' does double duty. First, this concept encompasses the protection of the nation. Second, if there is any power left over, it seeks to protect its interests beyond its shores. The United States has historically been just about this second task."[2]

The former task to which Flynn refers now falls under the purview of the US Department of Homeland Security (DHS). The Homeland Security Act of 2002, which gave birth to the department, defines "homeland" in a straightforward manner as encompassing the territory of the United States. Further, that act entrusts the DHS with the responsibility to "prevent terrorist attacks within the United States; reduce the vulnerability of the United States to terrorism; and minimize the damage, and assist in the recovery, from terrorist attacks that do occur in the United States."[3]   In summarizing its mission, the DHS itself stresses, "We will lead the unified national effort to secure America. We will prevent and deter terrorist attacks and protect against and respond to threats and hazards to the nation. We will ensure safe and secure borders, welcome lawful immigrants and visitors, and promote the free flow of commerce."[4]   In light of the shock to all Americans, from federal, state and local government officials to the public they are charged with protecting, it is understandable that the DHS must focus primarily on terrorism. However, the 22 existing agencies that were incorporated into the DHS when it was established and now report to the Secretary of Homeland Security, have responsibilities that extend well beyond the issue area of terrorism. Those responsibilities, for example, range from securing American ports and researching methods to counter biological and chemical attacks to screening passengers at airports and reviewing citizenship applications.[5]

The breadth of the mission of the DHS illustrates the extent to which protecting the American homeland has changed on the basis of emerging threats to the US domestic security agenda. Yet, notwithstanding the scale of the 9/11 attacks and means through which those assaults were prosecuted, the need to adapt to an evolving threat environment at home is certainly not unprecedented in American history. Since the War for Independence from 1776-83 and subsequent establishment of the United

States in 1789, American governments have responded to a perpetually changing series of threats at home concurrent with – and related to – the expansion of the nation's territory, characteristics of its population and political system, and nature of its encounters with outside powers, whether states or, most recently, transnational organizations. Examples include clashes with the British in the War of 1812 and Native Americans associated with the enlargement of America to the West, as well as the Civil War pitting the Union against the Confederacy and concerns over US vulnerability to terrorist attacks by terrorist groups such as Al Qaeda in the post-9/11 era.

With these introductory observations providing a necessary contextual foundation, the balance of the chapter addresses the evolution of homeland security in the United States through the presentation of six sections that unfold in the following manner. The first section discusses the conceptualization of homeland defense from the perspectives of America's Founding Fathers, who engaged in vigorous debates over the extent to which federal and state bodies should be responsible for ensuring domestic security. The second section assesses the impact of the expansion of US territory and the transitory division of the nation during the Civil War years on American perceptions of threats to their individual and collective security. The third section describes the transformation of homeland defense sparked by US involvement in World War I and World War II and the expansion of the responsibilities of the Federal Bureau of Investigation (FBI) prior to and during those conflicts. The fourth section examines American governmental management of civil defense, domestic social unrest and the emergence of international terrorist threats during the half-century-long Cold War pitting the United States against the Soviet Union. The fifth section focuses on the rising dangers associated with domestic and transnational terrorism as America made the transition from the Cold War years to the post-Cold War era in the 1990s. The sixth section puts forward a brief set of conclusions on the domestic shock delivered to the United States by Al Qaeda's attacks on the World Trade Center and the Pentagon on 9/11 and the extent to which the tragic events that unfolded that day set a new agenda for the future of homeland security in America.

Homeland Security and the Founding of the United States

The first requirement to consider with respect to a given political entity's homeland security is that its leaders must have some territory to safeguard. For the Founding Fathers of the United States, the primary concern was thus to seize control over the land they inhabited (namely the 13 American colonies) from Great Britain. Only once the colonists had prevailed in the War of Independence, was it possible for men such as George Washington, John Adams, Benjamin Franklin, Thomas Jefferson, Alexander Hamilton and James Madison to engage in the debate that resulted in the establishment of the United States through the construction and ratification of the Constitution. Simply reaching that point required winning a war that erupted in part over Britain's failure to afford the citizens of an emerging *American homeland* all of the economic and political freedoms and opportunities they desired. Not surprisingly, once the original colonists assumed positions of authority in the United States, they faced comparable challenges in securing the homeland without constraining the rights of their citizens to an extent that would result in internal divisions. Such challenges have proven consistently daunting to American leaders, including current US President George W. Bush and the members of his administration.

Commanded by Washington, who later served as the first President of the United States, the Continental Army drew forces from all 13 colonies and also was supported to a limited extent by locally organized militias in the war against the British. When the conflict ended, with London formally recognizing American independence through the Peace of Paris in 1783, the Founding Fathers set about the task of developing and ratifying the Constitution. During the war and its aftermath, the former colonies were loosely aligned under the auspices of the Articles of Confederation and no more than two-thirds of the individuals living therein had either fought against the British or supported the push for independence. Once independence was assured, even those united in confronting the British were not in agreement on the particulars of the political path the nascent nation should follow in the future.

Central to the debate that ensued was the appropriate division of labor between state and federal officials and institutions in governing American citizens and providing for local, as opposed to national, defense. That debate was driven by two political interest groups – the Federalists and Anti-Federalists – whose members advocated striking balances of power that would tilt in favor of the federal and existing state governments, respectively. The most influential proponents of the Federalist position were Washington, Hamilton, Madison and John Jay, with the latter three articulating many of their arguments publicly through the publication of a series of articles known as the *Federalist Papers* during the debate over the Constitution in 1787-88. Proponents of the anti-Federalist position, on the other hand, included Jefferson, George Mason, John Hancock and Sam Adams.[6]

Two sets of internal developments in the interconnected issue areas of economics, politics and security impressed upon the Federalists and Anti-Federalists generally and the Founding Fathers specifically the need to resolve their differences and institutionalize the resulting compromises as expeditiously as possible in the post-Revolutionary period. First, in bringing the War of Independence to a formal close, the Peace of Paris ceded to the victorious Americans substantial Western territories previously controlled by the British. In the years that followed, many states in the East laid claims to parcels of real estate within a number of new territories that were destined to become states in their own right. Essentially, between the end of the conflict with the British in 1783 and the establishment of a US federal government under the auspices of the Constitution in 1789, the states behaved as wholly sovereign polities, with most behaving as one would expect an independent nation to act rather than interacting as pieces of a coherent and united America. As Paul Johnson, a British scholar of US history, explains, "individual states carried out all kinds of sovereign acts which logically belonged to a central authority – they broke foreign treaties and federal law, made war on Indians, built their own navies, and sometimes did not trouble themselves to send representatives to Congress."[7]

Second, although states often behaved as sovereign entities, they typically lacked the economic and military resources to respond effectively to domestic revolts that could threaten their own ability (and, in some cases, that of their neighbors) to maintain order. An uprising in Western Massachusetts in the fall and winter of 1786-87 – known since as Shays Rebellion – demonstrated as much. Led by a bankrupt farmer and former Continental Army soldier named Daniel Shays, the rebels were protesting direct taxation by the Massachusetts legislature. Although Massachusetts state militiamen repelled the attack by Shays and his followers on the federal armory in Springfield in February 1787, the incident did convince the legislature to back down and eliminate the direct tax it had attempted to impose. More significantly, it served as a warning to the state representatives who gathered at the Constitutional Convention in May 1787 of the clear need to move forward with the establishment of a permanent federal government as expeditiously as possible. As Johnson notes, the uprising "reminded everyone attending in Philadelphia that the Confederation, as it stood, was powerless to protect itself, or any of the states, from large-scale domestic violence, and that this absence of a central power was itself a limitation on state sovereignty as the humiliating climb-down of the Massachusetts legislature demonstrated. The pressure, then, was on to get a federal constitution written and adopted."[8]

The most influential figure in the drive to negotiate a compromise between the Federalists and Anti-Federalists at the Constitutional Convention, one that would result in the establishment of the United States, was Madison. Put simply, Madison set the agenda for debate by promulgating his Virginia Plan. The plan had two principal features. First, it emphasized that the federal government would receive its authority directly from the American people rather than from the assemblies in the individual states in which those people were situated. Johnson explains, for example, that the "sovereign people – it was Madison who coined the majestic phrase 'We, the people' – delegated authority both to the national government and to the states, thereby giving it the authority to act independently in its own sphere, as well as imposing restrictions on the actions of the states."[9] Second, it proposed a three-pronged system of government, with power distributed evenly among the executive, legislative and judicial branches. In general terms, the Virginia Plan served as the basis for the Constitution that was eventually adopted. Complementing the Virginia Plan was a further compromise, which Madison also played an important role in negotiating. That measure, referred to as the Connecticut Compromise, settled differences between states with large and small populations by splitting the legislative branch into a bicameral House of Representatives and Senate, with the membership criteria (proportional vs. equal representation) favoring the former and latter, respectively.[10]

The Constitution formally took effect concurrent with the start of Washington's first term as President and the opening session of the inaugural US Congress in March 1789. At that juncture, it institutionalized a collaborative relationship through which the executive and legislative branches were expected to protect American territory in the future. While responsibility for the development and implementation of policies designed to safeguard American territory rested in the hands of the President and his staff, the Congress was granted the right to accept or reject requests for the use of military force and approval of international treaties. Those measures continue to have an impact on the on the pursuit of US security interests at home and abroad in the 2000s generally and with respect to the prosecution of the war on terror in particular as will be addressed in greater depth in Chapter 3.

The most historically significant piece of business considered by the First Congress was the refinement of the Constitution, which was achieved through the negotiation of 10 amendments known as the Bill of Rights. As suggested by their collective moniker, this initial set of amendments to the Constitution guaranteed a number of fundamental rights to American citizens. Along with basic freedoms of religion, assembly, speech and the press, the Bill of Rights ensured that individuals could legally bear arms to defend themselves and their property. The tenth, and last, of the amendments in the Bill of Rights helped to temper any remaining concerns of states and individuals that the federal government could trample the rights of the people by stressing that "the powers not delegated to the United States by the Constitution, nor prohibited by it to the states, are reserved to the states respectively, or to the people."[11] Above all, in terms of safeguarding the American homeland, which was, at that juncture, an expanding geographical construct, the Constitution and Bill of Rights that followed both reassured citizens that they had the right to defend themselves individually and that the federal government had the responsibility to guarantee their rights and ensure their safety collectively.

The Impact of National Expansion and Division on American Domestic Security

As America's first President, Washington used his two terms in the White House to help build stable economic and political foundations for the future of the United States. In the process, he avoided conflict with foreign powers and minimized internal differences in the American homeland, whether between individual states or pitting states against the federal government. His successors over the ensuing century, on the other hand, dedicated themselves to expanding the size of that homeland in the West, safeguarding it against external threats and, ultimately, waging civil war to ensure it remained whole over the long term.

Historically, US political leaders, Presidents, Congressmen and Senators alike, have deemed it necessary to adapt their philosophical beliefs subtly, if not substantially, in response to the challenges they face while in office. Such was certainly the case for Jefferson, who served as America's third President from 1803-09. During the debate that preceded the adoption of the Constitution and while serving as Secretary of State in the Washington administration, Jefferson was a strong supporter of states rights, especially as pertained to the residents of rural America. Consequently, he was a rival of federalists such as Hamilton and particularly wary of the growing power of the federal government in the 1790s and early 1800s.

Jefferson's approach changed, however, after he defeated incumbent President John Adams in the 1802 national election. Ironically, in fact, Jefferson presided over what was then the largest single geographic expansion of the United States in its history – the Louisiana Purchase – and a concurrent increase in the power and responsibilities of the federal government responsible for securing that territory. By striking a deal with France to purchase approximately 800,000 square miles, including New Orleans, Louisiana and the Mississippi River valley for $15 million, Jefferson doubled the size of the United States.[12] Although negotiating the Louisiana Purchase itself did not involve the use of force, the acquisition of the land therein eventually led the United States into conflict with myriad Native American tribes in the subsequent decades and thus played a part in the evolution of the concept of homeland security. It also demonstrated to the outside world that America was sure to become a continental, if not a hemispheric and global power, in the future. As Johnson asserts, "Not only did it double the size of America, making it a country as large as Europe, it also removed the last doubts about western expansion and made it virtually certain that America would double in size again in the next few decades."[13]

Jefferson's successor as President, his longtime friend and sometimes philosophical rival, Madison, had both to deal with security threats emanating from the territory acquired through the Louisiana Purchase and, more significantly, to defend America against Britain in the War of 1812. With respect to the latter, the United States found itself facing the British on the battlefield for the second time in less than a half century. And, while the Americans ultimately prevailed, essentially eliminating London as a dominant player in Western Hemispheric affairs, they did not do so before the British attacked Washington and burned the White House to the ground in August 1814, an incident that proved to be the most devastating assault on the continental United States until the events of 9/11. Over the long term, the 1814 attack on the nation's capital impressed upon Madison – and the Presidents that followed – the need to continue to reduce America's vulnerability to security threats by strengthening and expanding its power base at home and waging those conflicts against European powers that could not be avoided across the Atlantic rather than in North America. John Lewis Gaddis, one of the most authoritative contemporary scholars of US national security strategy, for instance, notes that:

> Most nations seek safety in the way most animals do: by withdrawing behind defenses, or making themselves inconspicuous, or otherwise avoiding whatever dangers there may be. Americans, in contrast, have generally responded to threats – and particularly to surprise attacks – by taking the offensive, by becoming more conspicuous, by confronting, neutralizing, and if possible overwhelming the sources of danger rather than fleeing from them. Expansion, we have assumed, is the path to security.[14]

The expansion to which Gaddis refers continued at a relatively consistent pace between the end of the War of 1812 in January 1815[15] and the outbreak of the American Civil War in April 1861. In most, albeit not all, cases, the enlargement of

US boundaries during that period occurred peacefully rather than as a direct result of conflict. Examples included land acquired through the Adams-Onis Treaty with Spain in 1819 (East Florida), the Oregon Treaty with Britain in 1846 (the Pacific Northwest south of the 49th parallel), the Texas Cession in 1850 (New Mexico) and the Gadsden Purchase in 1853 (southern Arizona). The latter two measures, as well as the Treaty of Guadalupe Hidalgo in 1848, came in part as a result of the US victory in the Mexican-American War of 1846-47. In each case, save that of the Oregon Treaty, the American government paid the other treaty signatory for the territory it received.[16] And the maintenance of control over that territory required only a minimal federal military commitment as indicated by the fact that the size of the US armed forces between 1816 and 1860 averaged just 20,000.[17]

Notwithstanding the dearth of military power needed to acquire much of the land in the Western half of the continent, administering that territory and eventually incorporating parcels of it into the United States presented much more daunting challenges to American political leaders. Those challenges were associated with two issues: first, the extent to which infringing on the rights of Native Americans was morally, if not legally, defensible under the auspices of the Constitution; and, second, the struggle between the Northern and Southern segments of the Union (more pointedly, the supporters and opponents of slavery, respectively) for allies in the growing West.

While the Constitution and amendments prior to the Civil War did not explicitly afford freedoms to either Native Americans or slaves, the treatment of the latter in particular was a source of rising tensions between individuals and elected officials in the North and the South. Notwithstanding the eruption of small-scale wars between federal forces and Indian tribes such as the Shawnees and Seminoles over the first half of the nineteenth century, they presented only marginal disruptions in maintaining the security of the American homeland. The question of whether a given Western territory would allow or prohibit slavery upon entering the Union proved markedly more divisive and was one of the proverbial sparks that eventually ignited the Civil War in 1861. As Niall Ferguson, a British scholar whose work on the imperial characteristics of US power has drawn considerable acclaim, points out, "By the 1860s the question for which Americans were prepared to fight and die was not how big their republic should be but how free it should be."[18]

The first major compromise negotiated by the North and South with respect to the issue of slavery in the West came with Missouri's admission to the Union as a slave state in 1820. In exchange, in the context of a tradeoff known as the Missouri Compromise, Maine entered the Union as a free state and slavery was subsequently prohibited in all territory north of the 26th parallel. The addition of further territory to the southwest and northwest segments of the United States over the ensuing three decades led to the Compromise of 1850. That compromise resulted in the admission of California to the Union as a free state, a guarantee that no explicit prohibitions on slavery would be put in place in either New Mexico or Utah, and all escaped slaves were to be returned to their owners under the provisions of the Fugitive Slave Act. Subsequent passage of the Kansas Nebraska-Act of 1854 served as a de facto abrogation of the territorial component of the Missouri Compromise favoring the North by allowing the populations of the former two states (both of which were situated above the 26th parallel) to decide whether they would allow slavery.

Seven years later, the North and South commenced the most devastating conflict in American history. Over the course of the Civil War between April 1861 and April 1865, more than a half-million soldiers perished, much of the Confederacy was overrun and, in some cases, physically devastated, and Americans on both sides learned precisely how severe the consequences of domestic conflict can be. In addition to the loss of life, the war was followed by a dozen-year period of Reconstruction that failed to reduce substantially the profound animosity between the winning and losing sides or improve markedly the opportunities afforded to former slaves who continued to reside in the South. What Reconstruction did achieve in the realm of homeland security was passage of the Posse Comitatus Act of 1878. The act was designed to prevent federal troops from supervising elections in former Confederate states and set a precedent that still prohibits American servicemen and women from acting in a law enforcement capacity within the United States unless expressly authorized to do by an act of Congress.[19]

Global Wars, Federal Law Enforcement and Homeland Security

The need to develop and refine American domestic legal, defense and policing institutions increased dramatically over the first half of the twentieth century, concurrent with – and, in some ways, related to – US participation in World War I in 1917-18 and World War II from 1941-45. Central to the evolution of the conceptualization of homeland security in America during that half-century was the creation and evolution of two institutions in particular. The first was a federally controlled National Guard. The second was the FBI. Both have since played important – and, at times, controversial – roles in the defense of American security interests domestically as well as internationally.

By virtue of its resounding victory in the Spanish-American War of 1898, the United States gained control over Guam, the Philippines and Puerto Rico and added to its already growing global influence, further interests and responsibilities, especially in Asia. That triumph also set the stage for an enlargement and adaptation of the American military. While defeating the Spanish was achieved primarily as a result of US naval superiority and thus not particularly taxing on the American Army, which numbered just 30,000 men at that point, the settlement of the conflict through the Treaty of Paris left the administration of President William McKinley with seven million Filipinos to govern. When more than 80,000 of those Filipinos staged an armed rebellion against the United States, 24,000 American soldiers were dispatched to the islands. Three years later, they had subdued the rebellion. However, their deployment thousands of miles from the continental United States in itself demonstrated the need to develop legal provisions to increase the size of the forces available for federal service to defend American interests abroad without mitigating the military's capacity to provide for the security of US citizens at home at a given historical juncture.[20]

In 1903, Senator Charles Dick, a Major General in the Ohio National Guard, sponsored a measure that, following its expeditious passage, provided the federal government with a bit more flexibility in raising forces for national defense. Known formally as the Militia Act and informally as the Dick Act, the measure was a product of the post-Spanish American War military reform and reorganization processes launched by Secretary of War Elihu Root. At its core, the act gave federal status to the organized militia, which would then be incorporated into a National Guard available for deployment both domestically and abroad. Prior to that point, the states had been responsible for funding and administering the militia. The Dick Act provided for a five-year transition period, during which the militia of the states would be required to conform to the standards of the US Army and would, in turn, receive substantial increases in federal funding to achieve that end.[21]

When Congress first allocated federal funds to arm the militia, it put forward $200,000 a year for that purpose, a total that had risen to just $400,000 by 1887. Three years after passage of the Militia Act, $2 million was allocated to arm the militia and the federal government spent a collective $53 million on the National Guard between 1903 and 1916. On the eve of America's entry into World War I, the National Defense Act of 1916 resulted in the permanent transfer of the state militia into a Reserve Component of the US Army. That measure led to the use of National Guardsmen during both World War I and World War II and continues to serve as the basis for the deployment of reservists in places such as Afghanistan and Iraq in the context of the ongoing war on terrorism. During World War II, for example, a collective 19 National Guard Divisions and 29 National Guard Army Air Force observation squadrons saw action in the European and Pacific theatres. That process, in turn, set a necessary precedent for substantial call-ups of guardsmen for service when the United States had to strike a balance in responding to threats to its interests at home and abroad in subsequent decades. The most notable examples prior to the current deployments associated with the war on terror were the 1950-53 Korean War, Vietnam War of the 1960s and 1970s and 1990-91 Persian Gulf War.[22]

The move toward federalization early in the twentieth century was by no means limited to the military arena. It extended into the issue area of law enforcement as well. During the nineteenth century, legal investigations and policing fell almost exclusively under the purview of the states. This was certainly understandable, especially given the divisions between North and South that resulted in the outbreak and conduct of the Civil War and continued to complicate the relationships between those two segments of America during the Reconstruction era and its aftermath. However, North-South differences did not prevent the administration of President Theodore Roosevelt from establishing a federal investigative service within the Department of Justice in 1909 or his successors from expanding that organization's responsibilities over the balance of the twentieth century.

The federalization process commenced with Roosevelt's appointment of a friend and fellow member of the "Progressive" wing of the Republican Party named Charles

Bonaparte as Attorney General in 1905. Three years later, Bonaparte created a corps of Special Agents within the Department of Justice, a force that was renamed the Federal Bureau of Investigation by his successor, Attorney General George Wickersham in 1909. Initially, the FBI dealt primarily with violations involving national banking, bankruptcy, naturalization, antitrust, peonage and land fraud laws. However, its responsibilities increased substantially with passage of the July 1910 Mann Act prohibiting the transportation of women over state lines for immoral purposes and the Espionage, Selective Service and Sabotage Acts resulting from America's entry into World War I in April 1917. Additionally, the FBI was called on to assist the Department of Labor in investigating enemy aliens during the war, a duty that has since fallen to the Immigration and Naturalization Service that is itself now a part of the DHS.[23]

The individual most commonly associated with the evolution of the FBI, J. Edgar Hoover, joined the organization as Assistant Director in 1921. He was named director in 1924 and held that position until his death in 1972. In the 1920s and 1930s, Hoover pressed for – and then oversaw – marked increases in the FBI's responsibilities and resources. The bureau, for example, established 30 field offices in cities across the United States over the course of the 1920s, a number that had risen to 42 by the time the Japanese attacked on Pearl Harbor on 7 December 1941, prompting America's entry into World War II.

Concurrent with that expansion, the FBI responded to criminal threats rooted in both domestic and foreign developments. In addition to investigating and gathering evidence to prosecute leaders of the Mafia and Ku Klux Klan with violations of Prohibition laws and persecution of African-Americans in the 1920s, the bureau's agents had to keep an eye on organizations supporting National Socialist Germany and Fascist Italy such as the German-American Bund and the Silver Shirts in the 1930s. At President Franklin D. Roosevelt's request, Secretary of State Cordell Hull granted the FBI greater authority to investigate foreign subversives in 1936, and Congress strengthened that mandate by passing the Smith Act in 1940. These measures were in part the products of an increased public willingness to give less credence to the rights of minority groups with the perceived potential to threaten US domestic security as war raged abroad.[24] That profound change in public attitude, which allowed for the internment of thousands of Japanese-Americans in relocation camps as the United States mobilized for and prosecuted a devastating war against its adversaries in Tokyo and Berlin from 1941-45, was a direct result of the surprise attack on Pearl Harbor and, more pointedly, its impact on the national psyche. As American historian Victor Davis Hanson explains:

> In the days after Pearl Harbor a dazed American public saw newsreels of victorious Japanese, shouting "Banzai!" with arms outstretched on conquered American outposts, the precursors of suicidal kamikaze pilots who would soon promise the annihilation of our fleet and sailors. What terrible foes, we thought, to hate us so – so adroit at surprising us, so deadly at killing despite our defenses. Yet, the generation of out fathers was not impressed by either images

or rhetoric. In response, a rather innocent and unprepared nation in less than sixty months left both Germany and Japan in smoldering ruins. Both fascism and Japanese militarism were incinerated and have not plagued the world for over a half-century.[25]

Prevailing in the struggle Hanson describes required the collective effort of US military and law enforcement assets at home as well as abroad. It was on the home front, that the FBI played a vital role. In particular, the Roosevelt administration relied on the bureau for two principle tasks that linked the issue areas of domestic and international security during World War II: assistance in the collection of intelligence to help American forces to defeat Germany, Italy and Japan and investigation of efforts by those states to carry out acts of sabotage within the continental United States. The most well-known wartime sabotage operation attempted by Germany on American soil occurred in June 1942 when two U-boats dropped off four operatives along the US east coast – two in Amagansett, Long Island and two in Ponte Vedre Beach, Florida. One of the saboteurs, George Dasch, turned himself in to the FBI, which then located and arrested the remaining three. The bureau's expeditious action helped to reduce American fears of Axis subversion. In addition, the FBI assisted the Office of Strategic Services (OSS) in the collection of intelligence on Axis spies stationed in Latin America by developing a team of Special Intelligence Service (SIS) agents and then deploying its members across that region. Ultimately, the SIS and OSS were forerunners to the Central Intelligence Agency (CIA), which was created to replace the Office of Strategic Services (OSS) in the aftermath of World War II and played the lead role in gathering foreign intelligence to support America in its struggle against the Soviet Union in the ensuing Cold War years.[26]

Nuclear Weapons, Civil Defense and the Bipolar Confrontation

The victory of the United States and its allies over Germany and Japan in the spring and summer of 1945, respectively, produced predictable and very understandable celebrations in America. The two principal threats to the security of the homeland at that juncture had been eliminated and there was good reason to breath a collective sigh of relief. That sense of euphoria, however, was quickly replaced by widespread domestic concerns over foreign ideological infiltration and the threat of nuclear annihilation as the wartime alliance fractured into Western and Eastern blocs, with the United States leading the former and the Soviet Union heading the latter. Americans spent much of the ensuing four decades focusing on the Cold War pitting the United States against the Soviet Union in an international struggle for geopolitical influence and military superiority with spillover effects that presented a range of military and political challenges to domestic security and stability.

The United States and Soviet Union developed spheres of influence in Europe and Asia in the aftermath of World War, with Washington advocating and defending states with governments based on liberal democratic political and capitalist economic values and Moscow imposing communism across the territory it controlled at the end of the conflict. The emerging Cold War abroad, in turn, led to a reorganization of American security institutions at home under the auspices of the Harry S. Truman administration. With respect to the military defense and the collection of intelligence, that reorganization process resulted in the establishment of the CIA, Department of Defense and National Security Council (NSC) through passage of the National Security Act of 1947. The act charged the CIA with the responsibility of conducting foreign intelligence operations to safeguard American interests and provided for the consolidation of the Air Force, Army and Navy into the nascent Department of Defense. The NSC itself evolved into an advisory body housed in the White House under the direction of a National Security Advisor, whose chief duty was to advise the President on threats to the security of the United States. Collectively, the CIA, Department of Defense and NSC spent the subsequent 54 years dealing primarily, albeit not exclusively, with threats based abroad rather than at home, while the FBI focused on domestic security.[27]

The division of labor between the CIA and the FBI, which is addressed in depth in Chapters 3, 4 and 5, left the latter to deal with the domestic byproducts of the conduct of the Cold War between the 1950s and 1980s in addition to maintaining its more traditional law enforcement functions. During the mid- to late-1940s, the FBI focused considerable attention on investigating members of the American Communist Party and other individuals in positions of authority in the US government suspected of displaying any measure of sympathy for, or loyalty to, the Soviet Union. The FBI was authorized to conduct such investigations under the provisions of the 1946 Atomic Energy Act, which gave the bureau "responsibility for determining the loyalty of individuals ... having access to restricted Atomic Energy data," and also through presidential directives from Truman and his successor, Dwight D. Eisenhower.[28] In addition, a very public, although ultimately somewhat discredited, campaign by Wisconsin Republican Senator Joseph McCarthy to expose communists working in American government agencies (most notably the Department of State) contributed to growing public paranoia over the capacity of the Soviet Union to attack the United States from within. In the end, the three most prominent prosecutions were those of Ethel and Julius Rosenberg, who were convicted of passing nuclear secrets to the Soviet Union and executed for their crimes in June 1953; and State Department official Alger Hiss, who was convicted of perjury rather than espionage in January 1950 and spent the subsequent four years in prison.[29] Although one recent study based on Soviet archival evidence released since the end of the Cold War indicates that Hiss and several other officials in the Roosevelt and Truman administrations were indeed on Moscow's payroll, McCarthy's allegations of pervasive Communist penetration of the American government were certainly at least somewhat overblown.[30]

While public concerns over Soviet espionage in the United States had receded by the late 1950s, a much graver threat became openly apparent just under two years into President John F. Kennedy's tenure in the White House. Amidst McCarthy's "Red Scare" of the 1950s, the Eisenhower administration placed an emphasis on the concept of civic defense as a means to defend against and recover from a Soviet nuclear attack.

Americans, for instance, were encouraged to build bomb shelters in their neighborhoods, and schools regularly held "duck and cover" preparatory drills to instruct children how to respond to an atomic explosion. Ironically, the nuclear dangers the United States guarded against during Eisenhower's Presidency, came much closer to realization after he had left office. In October 1962, the Kennedy administration revealed that photographs taken by an American U-2 pilot revealed that the Soviet Union was in the process of installing nuclear missiles on the island of Cuba. Kennedy imposed a naval blockade on the island and demanded that Soviet leader Nikita Khrushchev remove the missiles. Ultimately, after nearly two weeks during which nuclear war appeared possible, albeit certainly not probable, Khrushchev backed down and removed the missiles.[31] The episode was illustrative of the most drastic potential security threat to the homeland of the United States in its history – that posed by the detonation of a nuclear weapon on American soil. It was also one of the reasons that subsequent US efforts to confront the Soviet Union were played out through convention means in the developing world rather than via nuclear brinkmanship. As Gaddis notes, the "missile crisis shocked the United States and its allies into realizing the precariousness of their own security for all the diversity upon which it rested. If only a few inaccurately aimed Soviet nuclear warheads could wreak more havoc than in all previous wars combined, did it really mean all that much to have prevailed economically, ideologically, culturally and even morally."[32]

In the three decades that followed the Cuban Missile Crisis, America faced homeland security threats related to the domestic and foreign policies it implemented and unfavorable reactions to those policies both by adversaries abroad and US citizens at home. The most significant – and controversial – American foreign policy initiative of the 1960s and 1970s was its engagement in the Vietnam War. As the United States increased its commitment to the conflict in an effort to prevent a victory by Communist North Vietnam over Washington's allies in South Vietnam, especially under the auspices of the Lyndon B. Johnson administration from 1962-68, a substantial proportion of Americans began to openly protest the war effort. Coinciding with, and, in some cases, related to, the anti-war protest was a growing push for civil rights by African-Americans. The responsibility for dealing with the potentially destabilizing implications of such protests fell primarily to the FBI. Hoover, for instance, stressed in a 1966 PTA Magazine article that the United States was faced with what he viewed as "a new style in conspiracy – conspiracy that is extremely subtle and devious and hence difficult to understand … a conspiracy reflected by questionable moods and attitudes, by unrestrained individualism, by nonconformism in dress and speech, even by obscene language, rather than by formal membership in specific organizations."[33]

Two of the most serious manifestations of the domestic political and social turbulence that characterized the Vietnam era occurred in 1970. In May of that year, National Guardsmen attempting to put down an antiwar protest at Kent State University of Ohio, killed four students taking part in the demonstrations. And in August, four men in Madison, Wisconsin, including two students, detonated a bomb at Sterling Hall, which housed the Army Math Research Department at the University of Wisconsin. The explosion killed one graduate student.[34] Collectively, these incidents demonstrated the potential domestic security implications of governmental policies that focused on the pursuit of US interests abroad. Such violence subsided with the gradual reduction of the American presence in Vietnam, culminating in the evacuation of the US Embassy in Saigon in April 1975.

Notwithstanding a marginal focus on domestic security affairs through the prosecution of a "war on drugs" designed to stem the flow of illegal narcotics (most notably cocaine) from South America into the United States,[35] President Ronald W. Reagan's principal objective during his tenure in office from 1981-1989 was to roll back Soviet influence across the globe through a massive American defense buildup at home and the provision of support for opposition groups seeking to overthrow the regimes Moscow backed in the developing world.[36] The pursuit of those goals involved the Greater Middle East only tangentially, with the administration concerned almost exclusively with short-term considerations *vis-à-vis* the bipolar confrontation as opposed to the long-term implications of its policies in that region. One example is particularly illustrative of that approach: covert American support for the mujahedeen resistance movement against the Soviet Union in Afghanistan, which Moscow invaded in December 1979.

In Afghanistan, the CIA funneled covert assistance through Pakistan to a coalition of Islamic holy warriors known collectively as the mujahedeen, some of whom were born and raised in the Middle East. US aid included Stinger ground to air missiles, which were first supplied to the mujahedeen in 1986 proved critical in counteracting the use of Hind helicopters in Soviet counterinsurgency operations in the ensuing years preceding Moscow's withdrawal in 1989.[37] Overall, the Soviets spent $75 billion maintaining their military presence in Afghanistan between 1980 and 1988; the cost of American aid to the mujahedeen during that period, by contrast, was a modest $3.3 billion.[38]

Ultimately, the Reagan administration's policy toward Afghanistan had both costs and benefits for the United States in terms of both international and domestic security. Most of the benefits came in the short term, while the primary costs have manifested themselves in the 1990s and 2000s. In the short term, for example, American funding of the mujahedeen led to Moscow's withdrawal from Afghanistan in 1989 and also contributed to the collapse of communist regimes across Central and Eastern Europe in 1989-90 and the implosion of the Soviet Union itself in 1991. Over the longer term, by contrast, the US-backed resistance against the Soviet Union helped lay the foundation for the growth in power and influence of one individual with whom the CIA was aligned – albeit indirectly – at the time: Osama bin Laden, who subsequently founded Al Qaeda.[39]

Domestic and Transnational Terrorism in the Post-Cold War Era

When the William J. Clinton administration entered office in January 1993, the principal security threats it would face in the future were understandably unclear. However, Clinton's failure to mitigate, if not eliminate, one such threat – that posed by

Al Qaeda – to both homeland security and US interests abroad over the ensuing eight years, was arguably his greatest shortcoming as President, particularly given the devastating nature of the attacks that organization staged on 9/11. Ultimately, Clinton and his advisors made two sets of errors with respect to the means through which they chose to confront bin Laden's organization domestically and internationally. First, they were late to recognize the severity of the dangers posed by Al Qaeda, choosing initially to treat terrorism primarily as a law enforcement issue rather than one that should be dealt with via a combination of legal and military tools. Second, even after acknowledging the grave threats presented by bin Laden, they remained reluctant to take decisive military action against either Al Qaeda or those regimes upon which it was suspected of relying for support.

In order to assess the degree to which the Clinton administration should be faulted for its inability to weaken, if not eliminate, Al Qaeda, it is necessary to review the opportunities it had to respond to terrorist acts carried out by bin Laden and his supporters, how effectively or ineffectively it did so and why that was the case in each instance. Given that the relationship between homeland security and national security will be addressed in depth in Chapter 3, a brief review of four examples is sufficient here: the February 1993 bombing of the World Trade Center in New York; a foiled plot to detonate bombs aboard 11 airliners over the Pacific Ocean and subsequent failure to secure bin Laden's extradition from Sudan in 1995-96; the August 1998 bombings of the American Embassies in Nairobi, Kenya, and Dar-es-Salaam, Tanzania; and the October 2000 bombing of the USS *Cole*.[40]

The Clinton administration's first opportunity to deal with an act of terrorism directed against the United States came on 26 February 1993. That morning, a group of terrorists led by a man named Ramzi Yousef parked a rental van packed with explosives in a garage beneath the North Tower of the World Trade Center. They then lit the fuses attached to the bomb and fled. The resulting explosion caused limited damage to the infrastructure of the tower, killing six people and injuring 1,000 more.[41] Yousef, who was traveling on an Iraqi passport at the time and not apprehended until February 1995, later boasted to Federal Bureau of Investigation (FBI) agents that the objective of the operation had been to collapse the foundation of the North Tower, causing it to topple into the adjacent South Tower in hopes of killing up to 250,000, a catastrophe that would have dwarfed the losses in the 9/11 attacks.[42] The subsequent FBI investigation of the bombing uncovered considerable evidence linking Al Qaeda to the operation, a development that proved a indicator of the rising threats bin Laden was to present to US interests in the years to come.[43]

Clinton based his 1992 presidential campaign primarily on domestic rather than foreign policy issues, most notably those associated with economic and social programs. He had minimal experience in international security affairs and the initial foreign policy advisors he chose (Secretary of State Warren Christopher and National Security Advisor Anthony Lake among others) were skeptical of the robust use of military force to back diplomatic overtures. Consequently, Clinton's response to the 1993 bombing of the World Trade Center was hardly surprising. He perceived the attack as an isolated act carried out by a loosely affiliated group of individuals as opposed to a coordinated assault planned and orchestrated by a transnational terrorist organization. As a result, the administration limited its response to a criminal investigation carried out unilaterally by the FBI, an approach that left national security institutions such as the CIA and Department of Defense largely out of the equation. This lack of collaboration reduced the potential to uncover Al Qaeda's misdeeds in an expeditious fashion, costing the administration valuable time in identifying bin Laden as a credible national security threat.[44]

Clinton did eventually recognize the pressing nature of the rising dangers presented by Al Qaeda. As he acknowledges in his memoirs, initially, "bin Laden seemed to be a financier of terrorist operations, but over time we would learn that he was the head of a highly sophisticated terrorist organization, with access to large amounts of money beyond his own fortune, and with operatives in several countries, including Chechnya, Bosnia and the Philippines."[45] Regrettably, though, Clinton remained reluctant to take decisive action to counter those threats, most emphatically so during his initial term. In January 1995, for example, a collaborative effort between US and Filipino domestic law enforcement agencies uncovered a second terrorist plot involving Yousef, an individual named Abdul Hakim Murad and an Al Qaeda member called Khalid Shaikh Mohammed. The plan was designed to facilitate the planting and detonation of bombs aboard 11 commercial airplanes bound from points in Asia to sites in the United States, with the explosions to occur over the Pacific Ocean and result in the deaths of some 4,000 Americans.[46] Fortunately, the plan never came to fruition. Instead, the Filipino police apprehended Murad in Manila in January 1995, and Yousef was taken into custody by Pakistani Special Forces and FBI agents in Islamabad, Pakistan, the next month. Mohammed, on the other hand, remained at large.[47]

Yousef's apprehension and conviction for his role in the World Trade Center bombing in a subsequent trial in New York in 1996 contributed to the development of an increased emphasis within the Clinton administration on dealing with the bin Laden problem. Unfortunately, Clinton and his national security team proceeded to squander repeated opportunities to secure bin Laden's extradition from Sudan to the United States over the course of the 1996 election year. Bin Laden had set up a base of operations in Sudan following his expulsion from Saudi Arabia in the wake of his repeated criticisms of the political leadership in the Kingdom in 1991. Notwithstanding denials by some Clinton administration officials, published reports that have emerged in recent years indicate that Sudan offered to deliver bin Laden to the Americans – either directly or by way of a third country – on repeated occasions during 1996. Such offers were made to contacts in the CIA, the Department of State and in the US private sector.[48] Whether or not the Sudanese would actually have delivered bin Laden remains open to question. What is clear is that the political leadership in Khartoum eventually forced him to leave the country in May 1996, at which point he relocated to Afghanistan, where he reconstituted the Al Qaeda infrastructure he then used to orchestrate the events of 9/11.[49]

Had the Clinton administration elected to engage Sudan more vigorously, at least some of the attacks bin Laden carried out in subsequent years could perhaps have been prevented. One explanation as to why Clinton did not choose to pursue bin Laden any more vigorously at that juncture was that he wanted to maintain a positive focus rather than panic the public prior to the November 1996 Presidential Election, which he won handily over former Republican Senator Robert Dole. Dick Morris, one of Clinton's top domestic political advisors during his initial term, for example, notes that, "on issues of terrorism, defense and foreign affairs, generally, [Clinton] was always too wary of criticism to act decisively."[50] Unfortunately, the trend Morris points out continued throughout Clinton's final four years in the White House as well, a period during which the President had two clear opportunities to respond decisively to attacks carried out by Al Qaeda on American civilian and military targets – the August 1998 African embassy bombings and the October 2000 bombing of the USS *Cole*.

In May 1998, bin Laden called a press conference of sorts near Khost, Afghanistan in territory under the control of the Taliban. He used the occasion to publicly declare war against the United States for the fifth time since October 1996.[51] Three months later, Al Qaeda carried out bombings of the US Embassies in Nairobi, Kenya, and Dar-es-Salaam, Tanzania. The attack in Kenya killed 256 people and injured another 4,500; the strike in Tanzania left 11 dead. Among the fatalities were 12 American diplomats.[52] Clinton responded as forcefully as he had to any previous Al Qaeda assault to that point, authorizing cruise missile strikes on an alleged chemical weapons factory in Khartoum, Sudan (the government of which the administration suspected of collaboration in the embassy bombings) and Al Qaeda training camps in Afghanistan.[53]

In defending the strikes in his memoirs, Clinton recalls stressing in an address to the American people that "our attacks were not aimed against Islam, 'but against fanatics and killers,' and that we had been fighting against them on several fronts for years and would continue to do so, because 'this will be a long, ongoing struggle.'"[54] It remains unclear whether the factory in Khartoum ever actually produced chemical weapons of any sort rather than pharmaceutical supplies (as the Sudanese claimed).[55] And, regrettably, the limited missile strikes directed at the training camps in Afghanistan neither resulted in bin Laden's death nor reduced markedly Al Qaeda's capacity to threaten US interests. In short, pinprick strikes sent the wrong message to bin Laden: that Washington lacked the political will to use the full extent of its military assets against Al Qaeda.

Bin Laden continued to target Americans with tragic repercussions vis-à-vis the attack on the USS *Cole*. Al Qaeda operatives carried out the attack by guiding a small explosives-laden boat across the harbor in the port of Aden, Yemen, to the side of the *Cole*, where they detonated it. The resulting explosion ripped a hole in the side of the vessel, killing 17 US sailors and severely injuring 39 more. Clinton dispatched a team of FBI investigators to Yemen and considered a military response against Al Qaeda once reliable evidence as to its involvement in the attack was uncovered, but ultimately decided not to use force.[56] According to the President, the CIA's inability to pinpoint bin Laden's location in Afghanistan left only two other options: "a larger-scale bombing campaign of all suspected campsites or a sizable invasion. I thought neither was feasible without a [formal US legal] finding of al Qaeda responsibility for the *Cole*."[57]

When President George W. Bush took office in January 2001, he was left with the Clinton administration's legacy of relative inactivity in dealing with the perpetually rising security threats posed by Al Qaeda. Rather than pressure the Taliban, which harbored bin Laden in Afghanistan from 1996-2001, diplomatically or consider the deployment of military forces in that context, Clinton chose to pursue bin Laden primarily through domestic law enforcement bodies and weaken Al Qaeda to the limited extent possible through one flurry of limited cruise missile strikes. As Morris contends, "All our [present] terrorist problems were born during the Clinton years. It was during his eight years in office that [Al] Qaeda began its campaign of bombing and destruction aimed at the United States ... Bill Clinton and his advisors were alerted to the group's power and intentions by these attacks. But they did nothing to stop [Al] Qaeda from building up its resources for the big blow on 9/11."[58] And, regrettably, although perhaps somewhat more understandably, the Bush administration's approach to the issues of terrorism generally and Al Qaeda specifically proved no more robust than Clinton's as the President and his advisors worked to craft an effective foreign and security policy blueprint in the weeks and months preceding the events of 9/11.

Prior to assuming office, Bush joined Vice President-elect Dick Cheney and National Security Advisor to be Condoleezza Rice at a briefing conducted by Clinton's third Director of Central Intelligence, George Tenet. In the context of the briefing, Tenet – who retained his position when Bush took office – warned all three that bin Laden represented a "tremendous threat" to American interests at home and abroad, one that was "immediate."[59] Over the ensuing months, the CIA issued several more warnings, including 34 communications intercepts in the summer of 2001 indicating that Al Qaeda was planning a major operation against the United States by issuing subtly coded statements such as "Zero hour is tomorrow" or "Something spectacular is coming."[60] These warnings stirred the Bush administration to action, albeit of a sort that had not extended beyond the planning stage when Al Qaeda launched its attacks on the World Trade Center and Pentagon. Rice, for example, was in the process of preparing a National Security Directive (NSD) on the issue on September 10, one that built on lower-level National Security Council discussions on the construction of a strategy to eliminate Al Qaeda.[61] That planning, of course, shifted rapidly into concrete military action against both Al Qaeda and the Taliban in the aftermath of 9/11. And the conduct of Operation Enduring Freedom proved to be just the initial battle in the Bush administration's conduct of a broader war against transnational terrorist groups and their state sponsors.

Conclusions

This chapter was designed to review the conceptualization and evolution of homeland security in the United States from its founding to the post-9/11 era. It did so through the presentation of five main sections. The first section discussed the challenges the founding fathers faced in determining the proper balance to strike between the responsibilities of the federal and state governments in providing for the security of the nascent American homeland. The second section described the ways in which the concept of domestic security changed as the United States expanded its territory across the North American continent over the initial half of the nineteenth century, and then struggled to weather the storm of the Civil War. The third section touched on the federalization of the National Guard and examined the creation and expansion of the responsibilities of the FBI concurrent with the prosecution of World War I and World War II. The fourth section focused on the growing confluence between homeland security and national security during the Cold War era. And the fifth section assessed the efforts of the Clinton and Bush administrations to recognize and deal effectively with the threats posed by transnational terrorist organizations to American security interests at home and abroad prior to the events of 9/11.

Collectively, in tracing the evolution of the concept of US homeland security, these five sections serve as a useful bridge between the pre- and post-9/11 eras. Prior to Al Qaeda's attacks on the World Trade Center and Pentagon, it was much easier to make a reasonably clear distinction between homeland security and national security. Past attacks on American soil were undertaken by clearly identifiable states – Britain in 1812 and Japan in 1941. Responding through exclusively military means was necessary, practical and effective. Transnational terrorism, on the other hand, cannot be countered singly by military force, enhanced civil defense measures or legal investigations and trials. Instead, a combination of these variegated tools is essential. Developing that type of an approach, in turn, demands that one first reconsider the relationship between homeland security and national security over the course of US history and determine what combination of the two is most applicable to the pursuit of American interests in the 2000s. The ensuing chapter will attempt to achieve that objective.

Notes

1. This topic, which is just touched on briefly in Chapter 2, will be addressed in depth in Chapter 3.
2. Stephen Flynn, *America the Vulnerable*, 50-51.
3. Excerpted from *Homeland Security Act of 2002*, online at www.dhs.gov/interweb/assetlibrary/hr_5005_enr.pdf.
4. "DHS Organization," Department of Homeland Security (DHS) website, online at http://www.dhs.gov/dhspublic/interapp/editorial/editorial_0413.xml.
5. *Ibid.*
6. For in-depth examinations of the *Federalist Papers*, see Gottfried Dietze, *The Federalist: A Classic on Federalism and Free Government* (Baltimore: The Johns Hopkins Press, 1960) and David F. Epstein, *The Political Theory of the Federalist* (Chicago: University of Chicago Press, 1984).
7. Paul Johnson, *A History of the American People* (New York: Harper Collins Publishers, 1998.
8. *Ibid.*, 187-88.
9. *Ibid.*, 185.

10. David G. Smith, *The Convention and the Constitution: The Political Ideas of the Founding Fathers* (Lanham, MD: University Press of America, 1987), 35-55.
11. Irving Brandt, *The Bill of Rights: Its Origin and Meaning* (Indianapolis: Bobbs-Merrill, 1965). Reference made in Johnson, *A History of the American People*, 195.
12. Richard B. Morris, ed., *Encyclopedia of American History*, 6th ed. (New York: Harper & Row, 1982). Reference made in Niall Ferguson, *Colossus: The Price of America's Empire* (New York: The Penguin Press, 2004), 37, 40.
13. Johnson, *A History of the American People*, 253.
14. John Lewis Gaddis, *Surprise, Security, and the American Experience*, 13.
15. The War of 1812 was formally settled by the negotiation of the Treaty of Ghent in December 1814. However, news of the settlement did not reach North America in time to prevent the Battle of New Orleans between the Americans and the British in January 1815.
16. Charles Arnold-Baker, *The Companion to British History* (New York, Routledge, 2001); Morris, *Encyclopedia of American History*. References made in Ferguson, *Colossus*, 40.
17. Ferguson, *Colossus*, 36. Figures drawn from the University of Michigan Correlates of War database.
18. *Ibid.*, 41.
19. Flynn, *America the Vulnerable*, 39-40.
20. Johnson, *A History of the American People*, 613-14; Max Boot, *The Savage Wars of Peace: Small Wars and the Rise of American Power* (New York: Basic Books, 2002), 99-128.
21. "Militia Act of 1903," Wikipedia Encyclopedia, online at http://enwikipedia.org/wiki/Militia_Act_of_1903.
22. *Ibid.*
23. "History of the FBI," Federal Bureau of Investigation Website, online at www.fbi.gov/libref/historic/history.
24. *Ibid.*
25. Victor Davis Hanson, *An Autumn of War: What America Learned from September 11 and the War on Terrorism* (New York: Anchor Books, 2002), 3.
26. "History of the FBI."
27. Hulnick, *Keeping Us Safe*, 105-07.
28. "History of the FBI."
29. Johnson, *A History of the American People*, 833-37.
30. For an in-depth account of Soviet penetration of the Roosevelt and Truman administrations, see John Earl Haynes and Harvey Klehr, *Venona: Decoding Soviet Espionage in America* (New Haven: Yale University Press, 2002).
31. For in-depth accounts of the Cuban Missile Crisis, see James G. Blight, Bruce J. Allyn and David A. Welch, *Cuba on the Brink: Castro, the Missile Crisis and Soviet the Collapse* (New York: Pantheon, 1992) and James A. Nathan, ed., *The Cuban Missile Crisis Revisited* (New York: St. Martin's Press, 1992).
32. John Lewis Gaddis, *We Now Know: Rethinking Cold War History* (New York: Oxford University Press, 1997), 279.
33. Quoted in "History of the FBI."
34. "History of the FBI."
35. "History of the FBI."
36. For an in-depth examination of the Reagan Doctrine, see Mark P. Lagon, *The Reagan Doctrine: The Sources of American Conduct in the Cold War's Last Chapter* (Westport, CT: Praeger, 1994).
37. Lagon, *The Reagan Doctrine*, 57.

38. Saadet Deger and Somnath Sen, *Military Expenditures: The Political Economy of International Security* (Oxford: Oxford University Press, 1990), 70, 126.

39. While there is no evidence to suggest that the CIA provided directed funding to Osama bin Laden's Arab jihadists in Afghanistan during the 1980s, his group was clearly allied with the Afghan resistance movement. Richard Miniter, *Losing Bin Laden: How Bill Clinton's Failures Unleashed Global Terror* (Washington, D.C.: Regnery Publishing, Inc., 2003), 9-13.

40. The following works provide in-depth examinations of the William J. Clinton administration's handling of the threats posed by Al Qaeda to US interests at home and abroad between January 1993 and January 2001: Kean *et al.*, *9/11 Commission* Report; Miniter, *Losing Bin Laden*; Daniel Benjamin and Steven Simon, *The Age of Sacred Terror* (New York: Random House, 2002); Peter L. Bergen, *Holy War, Inc.: Inside the Secret World of Osama bin Laden* (New York: The Free Press, 2001); and Laurie Mylroie, *Study of Revenge: The First World Trade Center Attack and Saddam Hussein's War against America* (Washington, D.C.: The AEI Press, 2001).

41. Miniter, *Losing Bin Laden*, 1-39; Mylroie, *Study of Revenge*, 78-87; Benjamin and Simon, *Age of Sacred Terror*, 7-26.

42. Mylroie, *Study of Revenge*, 48-50, Miniter, *Losing bin Laden*, 84-85.

43. Miniter, *Losing bin Laden*, 34-39.

44. *Ibid.*, 32-34, 87-92. Complicating matters further, as Miniter notes, was the fact that Clinton never met with Director of the Central Intelligence Agency Director James Woolsey on a one-on-one basis during Woolsey's tenure in that position from 1993-95.

45. Bill Clinton, *My Life* (New York: Alfred A. Knopf, 2004), 797.

46. Miniter, *Losing Bin Laden*, 71-76; Mylroie, *Study of Revenge*, 198-207.

47. Miniter, *Losing Bin Laden*, 83-87.

48. Stephen F. Hayes, *The Connection: How Al Qaeda's Collaboration with Saddam Hussein has Endangered America* (New York: HarperCollins, 2004), 62-77; Miniter, *Losing Bin Laden*, 99-149. For example, Miniter contends that a Pakistani-American businessman by the name of Mansour Ijaz attempted to convince several Clinton administration officials to entertain offers from Sudan to pass bin Laden along to the United States in 1996.

49. Benjamin and Simon, *Age of Sacred* Terror, 131-33.

50. Dick Morris, *Off With Their Heads: Traitors, Crooks & Obstructionists in American Politics, Media & Business* (New York: ReganBooks, 2003), 97-98.

51. Miniter, *Losing Bin Laden*, 161-64.

52. Madeleine Albright, with Bill Woodward, *Madam Secretary: A Memoir* (New York: Mirzmax Books, 2003), 366-67.

53. Albright, *Madam Secretary*, 368; Miniter, *Losing Bin Laden*, 170-86.

54. Clinton, *My Life*, 803-04.

55. Clinton himself still contends that "we did the right thing there. The CIA had soil samples taken at the plant that contained the chemical used to produce VX." Clinton, *My Life*, 805.

56. Miniter, *Losing Bin Laden*, 216-29.

57. Clinton, *My Life*, 925.

58. Morris, *Off With Their Heads*, 70.

59. Bob Woodward, *Bush at War* (New York: Simon & Schuster, 2002), 34-35.

60. *Ibid.*, 4.

61. *Ibid.*, 34-36.

Chapter 3

National Security and Homeland Security

Introduction

In September 2002, American President George W. Bush released his administration's first National Security Strategy (NSS). Formulated in response to Al Qaeda's attacks on the United States on September 11 2001, the document articulated a comprehensive strategy for the prosecution of the Global War on Terrorism. In general, it placed an emphasis on the need to promote democratic values and economic and political reforms abroad as a means to reduce the threats to American security at home. In particular, it focused on the creation of greater opportunities for economic growth and political freedom of expression in the developing world, especially the Greater Middle East, in order to reduce the potential for Al Qaeda to draw recruits from those parts of the world over the long term.

In his introduction to the NSS, Bush stressed that the United States would take advantage of a historic "moment of opportunity" in the wake of the events of 9/11 "to extend the benefits of freedom across the globe. We will actively work to bring the hope of democracy, development, free markets, and free trade to every corner of the world. Poverty does not make people into terrorists and murderers. Yet poverty, weak institutions, and corruption can make weak states vulnerable to terrorist networks and drug cartels within their borders."[1] Furthermore, Bush explained:

> The United States will stand beside any nation determined to build a better future by seeking the rewards of liberty for its people … In building a balance of power that favors freedom, the United States is guided by the conviction that all nations have important responsibilities. Nations that enjoy freedom must actively fight terror. Nations that depend on international stability must help prevent the spread of weapons of mass destruction. Nations that seek international aid must govern themselves wisely, so that aid is well spent. For freedom to thrive, accountability must be expected and required. … Freedom is the non-negotiable demand of human dignity; the birthright of every person – in every civilization. Throughout history, freedom has been threatened by war and terror; it has been challenged by the clashing wills of powerful states and the evil designs of tyrants; and it has been tested by widespread poverty and disease. Today, humanity holds in its hands the opportunity to further freedom's triumph over all these foes. The United States welcomes our responsibility to lead this great mission.[2]

The Bush administration demonstrated its willingness to back the NSS with decisive action by pressing for the removal of one of the Greater Middle East's most ruthless and enduring dictatorial regimes – the Baathist administration of Iraqi President Saddam Hussein. The United States achieved that objective through the conduct of Operation Iraqi Freedom with the assistance of the United Kingdom and a range of other allies, including Australia, Italy, Poland, Portugal and Spain in the spring of 2003. The coalition removed Saddam's regime from power in April 2003 and has since engaged in nation/state-building operations designed to establish a permanent democratic government in Iraq, one that, if it proves viable, has the potential to foster a wider political transformation in the Arab and broader Islamic worlds. As Bernard Lewis, Clifford E. Dodge Professor Emeritus of Near Eastern Studies at Princeton University, notes, "The end of World War II opened the way for democracy in the former Axis powers. The end of the Cold War brought a measure of freedom and a movement toward democracy in much of the former Soviet domains. With steadfastness and patience, it may be possible at last to bring both justice and freedom to the long-tormented peoples of the Middle East."[3]

The cultivation of liberal democratic values to which Lewis refers has been central to the mission of the United States and its allies in an Iraq that has made progress toward the type of political transformation the Bush administration seeks, but continues to face stiff challenges in combating an insurgency fueled by a lethal combination of loyalists to Saddam's former regime and foreign fighters affiliated with Al Qaeda. And, for Bush, the mission in Iraq continues to represent a critical battle in the wider war on terrorism, a conflict on which his own legacy (good or bad) will certainly depend. As the President stressed in his second inaugural address in January 2005 just 10 days prior to the conduct of Iraqi national elections that drew a turnout of nearly 60 percent and resulted in the successful establishment of a transitional government:

> We are led, by events and common sense, to one conclusion: The survival of liberty in our land increasingly depends on the success of liberty in other lands. The best hope for peace in our world is the expansion of freedom in all the world. America's vital interests and our deepest beliefs are now one. From the day of our Founding, we have proclaimed that every man and woman on this earth has rights, and dignity, and matchless values, because they bear the image of the Maker of Heaven and earth. Across the generations we have proclaimed the imperative of self-government, because no one is fit to be a master, and no one deserves to be a slave. Advancing these ideals is the mission that created out nation. It is the honorable achievement of our fathers. Now it is the urgent requirement of our nation's security, and the calling of our time. So it is the policy of the United States to seek and support the growth of democratic movements and institutions in every nation and culture, with the ultimate goal of ending tyranny in our world.[4]

The transformative project the United States has undertaken at Bush's behest is as noble as it is daunting, particularly given the volatility of the Greater Middle East and past American support for a variety of autocratic regimes therein (including Saddam's) in the past. However, the basis for the strategy itself – namely the use of economic, military and political tools abroad to help keep the American homeland secure – is not at all new. Historically, the United States has had a tendency to view the pursuit of national security and homeland security as one, with the former serving as a convenient and effective means to achieve the latter without making unnecessary sacrifices on American soil. As Yale University historian John Lewis Gaddis explains, "Americans … have generally responded to threats – and particularly to surprise attacks – by taking the offensive, by becoming more conspicuous, by confronting neutralizing, and if possible overwhelming the sources of danger rather than fleeing from them. Expansion, we have assumed, is the path to security."[5]

Gaddis' assertion, and the introductory discussion of the Bush administration's NSS, serves as fitting points of departure for a more in-depth analysis of the relationship between national security and homeland security over the course of the history of the United States. The balance of the chapter puts forward precisely such an analysis through the presentation of six sections that unfold in the following manner. The first section engages in a conceptual discussion of the similarities and differences between national security and homeland security in American history, placing emphases on the nineteenth and twentieth centuries. The second section examines the transition of the United States from a Western Hemispheric to a global power in the nineteenth century generally and in the aftermath of its victory in the short-lived Spanish-American War of 1898 specifically. The third section examines the contrasting US tendencies toward isolationism and engagement abroad before, during and after World War I and World War II. The fourth section examines the American emphasis on the maintenance of relative global stability as a means to safeguard domestic security during its bipolar confrontation with the Soviet Union in the Cold War. The fifth section examines the nexus between national security and homeland security in the post-Cold War era. It focuses on the impact of the events of 9/11 on American distinctions between security at home and abroad. The concluding section assesses the extent to which the Bush administration's approach to national security and homeland security represents change as opposed to continuity in US strategy and policy.

National Security vs. Homeland Security: A Conceptual Discussion

The relationship between national security and homeland security in the United States has progressed gradually through a cycle of sorts over the past 230 years. Initially, the two concepts were necessarily inseparable. The United States came into existence as a result of the Revolutionary War of 1776-83, through which the American colonists achieved independence from Britain and the resultant freedom of action to establish their own state. The construction of that state via the conception, negotiation, drafting, revision and formal ratification of the US Constitution between 1783 and 1789 left the American federal and state governments with the responsibility to defend the territory therein. At that juncture, providing for national security entailed federal governmental efforts to maintain control over, and relative stability within, the territory over which the British had previously presided.

However, as the United States expanded its territory over the ensuing decades, the scope of the *homeland* to be secured increased as did the extent of the challenges to be met along the way. In addition to potential threats to American territory emanating from states abroad, US leaders had to contend with Indian revolts in opposition to westward expansion and internal divisions (most notably over slavery) that led to the outbreak and conduct of the Civil War from 1861-65. During the nineteenth century generally and in the last quarter of that time period specifically, the United States expanded its international economic and political interests to a degree that required the commitment of substantial military resources abroad. The conflicts in which America became embroiled, in turn, were fought further and further from US soil. World War I, for example, was contested principally in Western Europe from 1914-18 and World War II in Europe, the islands of the West Pacific and Asia from 1939-45. And, while America's entry in the latter conflict was sparked by the Japanese surprise attack on Pearl Harbor on 7 December 1941, none of the subsequent battles therein were contested inside the United States. Nor did the subsequent Cold War involve any direct assaults on US territory. As a result, American leaders grew ever more comfortable in de-linking national security and homeland security. In short, their sense and that of the general public in the United States was that foreign threats could be countered almost exclusively through the use of military force abroad without incurring significant damage at home. That perception did not change appreciably until after the devastating events of 9/11.

The gravest threat the United States had to confront during its initial quarter-century in existence was posed by a familiar foe: Britain. It came in the form of the War of 1812, which represented what most past and contemporary states in the international system would regard as a traditional national security threat – that is, an attack on the homeland by an external actor. The War of 1812 is particularly germane to a discussion of the nexus between national security and homeland security given that is represents the only direct attack on the continental United States in American history prior to 9/11. From the US perspective, the low point of the above conflict came on 24 August 1814. That day, American forces left Washington, DC, undefended in the wake of a British assault, leading President James Madison and his wife Dolley to abandon the White House and flee the US capital city. The British then occupied the city briefly and set the White House ablaze, a move that was comparable to the events of 9/11 in terms of symbolism rather than casualties.[6] Gaddis, for example, asserts that:

> For Americans at the time … the humiliation was sharp. To sense how much so, consider the now thankfully never sung third verse of *The Star-Spangled Banner*, composed by Francis Scott Key to celebrate the failure of the British to

take Fort McHenry in Baltimore Harbor following their withdrawal from Washington: 'And where is that band who so hauntingly swore. That the havoc of war and the battle's confusion. A home and country shall leave us no more? Their blood has washed out their foul foot step's pollution. No refuge could save the hireling and slave. From the terror of flight or the gloom of the grave.' It was a song intended, rather in the spirit of Dolley Madison, to salvage something from a national embarrassment, and it ought to remind us that security and the self-confidence that comes with it have not always been part of the American experience.[7]

Similarly, historians James Chace and Caleb Carr note that "It would have been difficult to overestimate the effect [of the British attack on Washington. The] threats from abroad that had so long perplexed American leaders had proved grimly real. Thus mindful of the dangers confronting their nation, Americans prepared to commit themselves to the enlarged task of providing for their own safety."[8]

The War of 1812, which had been settled by the end of 1814, came to its practical conclusion with a decisive American victory over the British at the Battle of New Orleans in January 1815 (word from the negotiating table in Ghent, Belgium, did not reach the United States in time to prevent that engagement).[9] However, the conflict's most significant consequences in terms of the formulation and implementation of foreign policy to buttress the security of the American homeland were of a more long-term nature. The United States had already exhibited a penchant for expansion as a means to build its demographic, economic and military power at home and increase its political influence abroad, most notably so through the purchase of the Louisiana Territory from France for $15 million in 1803. It expanded the scope of that approach with the proclamation of what eventually came to be known as the Monroe Doctrine in the context of the December 1823 State of the Union message to Congress by President James Monroe. In his message, Monroe proclaimed, "as a principle ... that the American continents, by the free and independent condition which they have assumed and maintain, are henceforth not to be considered as subjects for future colonization by any European powers."[10] Although, at that juncture, the United States lacked the economic and military resources to back its threat with concrete action if challenged by the Europeans, the statement itself signaled America's determination to forge a place for itself as an influential international player. Establishing predominance in North America and at the broader Western Hemispheric level was part of a process through which the United States would emerge as a global power by the end of the nineteenth century.

The rationale behind the expansion of American power at the hemispheric level was that the exclusion of foreign powers from the neighborhood within which the United States was situated would create a buffer zone and push threats further a field. The Atlantic and Pacific Oceans in particular would mitigate the potential for conflict between America and foreign powers on US soil in the future. As Gaddis explains, "Prior to the War of 1812 ... there was no long-term strategy linking security to expansion. [But] ... if the British could occupy and burn Washington almost as an afterthought while winding up [the Napoleonic Wars] against France that had lasted for almost a quarter of a century, what did that imply about American security once the fighting in Europe had ended."[11]   Creating the buffer zone that would minimize external threats to the United States over the balance of the nineteenth century required the development of a three-pronged foreign policy strategy featuring equally relevant economic, military and political components.   The fashioning of each of those components, in turn, was conditioned primarily by domestic popular attitudes.

All American presidential administrations are charged with the formulation and implementation of foreign policies designed to further US interests, both at home and abroad.   In defining those objectives, policymakers must take into consideration factors ranging from history and geography, culture and religion to economics and politics.   Above all, the foreign policies presidents and their advisors fashion are directed toward three sets of actors – one at the domestic level and two at the international level.   Domestically, an administration must do what is necessary to safeguard the security of the American citizenry while taking into account the interests of the constituents responsible for voting the president into office.   In many cases, the stiffest challenge is in achieving the latter objective without compromising the former.   Internationally, US presidents must design policies that further American interests at the expense of Washington's adversaries without upsetting its allies to an extent that undermines the former goal.   Ultimately, striking a prudential balance between these domestic and international objectives typically determines whether a given administration succeeds or fails in pursuing its foreign policy agenda.   As Walter Russell Mead, the Henry A. Kissinger Senior Fellow in US Foreign Policy at the Council on Foreign Relations, notes:

> American foreign policy may be the most complex subject in the world. Economics, political science, history and the philosophy of history, culture, religion, the nature of human nature: American foreign policy touches on them all.   And while American foreign policy is studied in great detail by professionals and scholars, it must ultimately be debated and decided by tens of millions of voters who have neither the time nor perhaps the inclination to immerse themselves in briefing papers, task force reports, and long scholarly texts.[12]

Developing and implementing policies and explaining them in terms that are decipherable to a broad swath of the American public has led to the characterization of a range of general schools of thought regarding traditions of interaction between the United States and other actors in the international system over the past two centuries. At its core, American foreign policy is perhaps best broken down into three traditions: selective isolationism, unmitigated internationalism and, most common in US history, a balance between the two – at times pragmatic, at others not.   As former Secretary of State Henry Kissinger puts it, "America's journey through international politics has been a triumph of faith over experience ... Torn between nostalgia for a pristine past and yearning for a perfect future, American thought has oscillated between isolationism and commitment."[13]

While somewhat of an oversimplification, the above construct provides plenty of proverbial space to incorporate the more nuanced approaches to foreign policy that have been the rule rather than the exception for American presidents over the years. Mead, for example, provides a four-category description that he characterizes in the following terms: First, a *Hamiltonian* model emphasizing a strong connection between the national government and big business as a means to drive a necessary integration of the United States into the global economy. Second, a *Wilsonian* approach advocating the creation of a peaceful international community by spreading American liberal democratic values abroad. Third, a *Jeffersonian* school stressing a preoccupation with domestic affairs and avoidance of foreign entanglements. And, fourth, a *Jacksonian* construct focusing on the physical security of the United States and an ambivalent attitude toward internationalism broken when necessary with a determination to unleash the unlimited use of military force if provoked by foreign attackers.[14] Distinguishing between these schools, while possible at any temporal juncture in American history between the establishment of the United States and the 2000s, has grown increasingly difficult over time. The reason is simple. Concurrent with America's emergence as a global power over the latter quarter of the nineteenth century, its international interests began to expand in a manner that both required more commitments abroad and thus gradually increased the external threats to domestic security.

America's Transition from Hemispheric to Global Power

In the 2002 NSS, the Bush administration places an emphasis on its willingness to act both preemptively and unilaterally if necessary in order to eliminate emerging threats to US interests before such dangers become imminent and thus unavoidable.[15] While some critics of the NSS have suggested that it is unprecedented, the facts of American history demonstrate otherwise. Prior to the global wars of the twentieth century, the United States acted both unilaterally (that is, without the support of any, let alone multiple, allies) and preemptively via the use of economic, military and political means to safeguard the American homeland. Such measures were applied both within, and outside of, the Western Hemisphere, most decisively so through US intervention in the affairs of states situated in Latin America. As Gaddis explains, "Concerns about 'failed' or 'derelict' states ... are nothing new in the history of United States foreign relations, nor are strategies of preemption in dealing with them."[16]

A decisive victory in the Spanish-American War of 1896 signaled America's arrival as a global rather than regional power on the world stage. However, prior to discussing that conflict and its consequences in greater depth, it is instructive to examine some of the US economic, military and political initiatives that preceded it and served as a preview of American ambition. Between the conclusion of the War of 1812 in January 1815 and the commencement of the Spanish-American War in April

1898, the United States employed a combination of direct payments, subtler economic inducements, military interventions and diplomacy to both enlarge – and pacify adversaries within – its own territory and minimize the potential for instability along its borders and at the broader regional level. Essentially, America took it upon itself to maintain stability in Western Hemisphere and, with each initiative it took to achieve that objective, it reduced further European influence therein. As Gaddis contends, "Security could best be assured ... by making certain that no other great power gained sovereignty within geographic proximity of the United States. The fact that small powers dominated regions to the south was thought not to be a threat as long as Europeans refrained from exploiting their weakness."[17]

Economically, the Louisiana Purchase was by no means the only American initiative designed to enhance US security through territorial expansion in the nineteenth century. In 1819, the American government paid Spain $15 million for more than 46 million acres in East Florida under the auspices of the Adams-Onis Treaty. Subsequent acquisitions, similar primarily in that the United States paid no more than 53 cents an acre and as little as just 2 cents an acre, included the following deals: the Gadsden Purchase of nearly 19 million acres in Southern Arizona from Mexico for $10 million in 1853 and the Alaska Purchase of the 375 million acres that now constitutes the state by the same name from Russia for a paltry $7.2 million in 1867.[18] In each of these cases, the United States acquired territory that provided living space for its expanding population, natural resources such as gold and petroleum deposits or a combination of the two for a fraction of their long-term worth.

Along with the aforementioned direct purchases, America acquired additional territory in the southwest and Pacific northwest through a complementary blend of diplomacy and the occasional use of military force. In 1846, for instance, the administration of President James K. Polk negotiated the cession of 192 million acres in the Pacific Northwest from London to Washington under the auspices of the Oregon Treaty.[19] That negotiation of that treaty was a purely diplomatic affair between an established global power (Britain) and a regional power with nascent global ambitions (the United States) that had fought twice between 1776 and 1815 and were content to settle their subsequent differences at the bargaining table. America's differences with Mexico, on the other hand, required a military resolution, one that ultimately left the United States with more than 338,000 acres in Texas, New Mexico and California in exchange for $20 million via the Treaty of Guadalupe Hildalgo that brought the Mexican-American War to a conclusion in 1848.[20] The conflict was sparked two years earlier by the Polk administration's decision to annex Texas, a former Mexican territory populated primarily by American settlers.[21] Geographically, as historians Michael Allen and Larry Schweikart point out, "Mexico and Oregon form bookends, a pair of the most spectacular foreign policy triumphs in American history."[22]

In addition to territorial enlargement in the North American continental context, the United States spent much of the nineteenth century expanding its international trade interests within, and increasingly, outside of, the Western Hemisphere. Mead's categorization of foreign policy schools is instructive in this regard. Those with a Hamiltonian bent in policy matters placed an emphasis on boosting America's global influence through overseas trade to the south, east and west. Their approach mirrored that of Britain. As Mead notes:

> British policy was more commercial and less militaristic than Continental [European] policies; American policy could and would be more commercial still. Indeed, the importance of trade would determine the Hamiltonian definitions of US security interests. If the United States was isolated from European armies, it was also potentially isolated from European trade. The weakest point of the United States was its sea link across the Atlantic to Europe. Access to trade with the rest of the world would clearly be a paramount American interest. It was an interruption of trade, rather than the loss of territory to rivals, that would most worry American foreign policy intellectuals through the first 150 years of national independence.[23]

Given America's colonial roots, it was natural that the United States initially developed trade linkages across the Atlantic to the states of Europe, most notably Britain and France. The idea was to cultivate mutually beneficial economic relationships that would gradually reduce the potential for conflict with America's European rivals, with an eye toward turning those rivals into partners over the long term. As the United States expanded its territory to the west, resulting in the acquisition of a Pacific Coast, the prospect of trade with Asia grew increasingly attractive. The most significant example of efforts to expand America's trade interests in the Pacific was Commodore Matthew C. Perry's expedition to Asia in 1853, which led to the negotiation and signing of a treaty that opened Japan to US-based commerce in March 1854.

Coinciding with and driven to a considerable extent by the expansion of America's economic interests overseas, the United States spent much of the latter half of the nineteenth century in particular expanding its navy and establishing military bases abroad to support its commercial ventures. The first such America base in the Pacific was established on the atoll of Midway, which Washington annexed in 1867. The United States also secured the right to use the harbor of Pago Pago on the Samoan island of Tutuila in 1877, two years after signing a free trade treaty with the eight-island chain of Hawaii that represented the first step toward the eventual colonization and annexation of that entity.[24] These Pacific bases added a greater sense of permanence to the global reach of American sea power, which was itself already manifested in the formation of permanent squadrons in the Mediterranean (1815), West India and the Pacific (1822), Brazil and the South Atlantic (1826), East India (1835) and West Africa (1843). Each of these developments demonstrated the depth of the US commitment to enhancing domestic power and security through expansion during a period when America was considered by its rivals abroad as more of an isolated Western Hemispheric state rather than a challenger for global economic, military and political influence. As Mead asserts, "In other words, during the period of American innocence and isolation, the United States had forces stationed on or near every major continent in the world; its navy was active in virtually every ocean, its troops saw combat on virtually every continent, and its foreign relations were in a perpetual state of crisis and turmoil."[25]

The concerns to which Mead refers grew out of the fact that establishing buffer zones to safeguard the American homeland entailed military costs abroad, initially in Latin America and, in time, further a field as well. Over the first half of the nineteenth century, for instance, US military forces engaged in combat missions abroad in an effort to further American commercial and political interests in the Falkland Islands (1832), Haiti (1800, 1817-21), Tripoli (1815), the Marquesas Islands (1813-14), Spanish Florida (1806-10, 1812, 1813, 1814, 1816-18), the Dominican Republic (1800), Curacao (1800), the Galapagos Islands (1813), Cuba (1822), Puerto Rico (1824), Argentina (1833) and Peru (1835-36).[26] Other examples included marine operations in Liberia on the West African Coast and Canton, China, in 1843, Japan and Panama as the Civil War raged at home in 1863 and Korea in 1871.[27] Collectively, these episodes paved the path to the proverbial coming out party for United States as a global power, which it achieved by way of the prosecution of the Spanish-American War in 1898.

Sparked by the sinking of the USS Maine in the Havana Harbor on 15 February 1898 at a cost of 260 lives by what was then deemed a Spanish mine but may have been the result of an accidental explosion in the ship's coal bunker,[28] the Spanish-American War lasted less than four months between April and June 1898.[29] A decisive US victory resulted in the establishment of an independent Cuba free of Spanish influence and under an American security umbrella and the handover of the Philippines from Madrid to Washington in exchange for a payment of $20 million.[30] Symbolically, it served notice to the states of Europe that the United States had arrived as a global power capable of occupying a substantial chunk of territory and exerting considerable economic and political influence backed by credible military force far from its borders. However, it would also demonstrate to Americans the limits of their power and the challenges associated with attempting to govern a foreign people, in this case the Filipinos.

After occupying the Philippines in May 1898 and assisting the natives in overthrowing the Spanish colonial regime, the United States set about establishing an American-style democratic government over the islands. The process did not proceed smoothly. Instead, an insurgency erupted in 1899, which the United States spent nearly three years subduing at a cost of the lives of 4,234 American servicemen.[31] The insurgency, which was carried out primarily, if not exclusively, by the Muslims inhabiting the southern half of the archipelago, served as a lesson that US expansion, while generally beneficial for American domestic security would always come with a price. Ultimately, the extent to which the US public was willing to pay that price in exchange for the benefits it entailed at home shaped America's role in the global wars of the twentieth century that followed.

Disengagement vs. Commitment: America, Europe and Global War

America's experience with the insurgency in the Philippines at the turn of the twentieth century proved unsettling to the public and helped to impress upon present and future leaders in Washington the need to proceed with at least some caution in the pursuit of national interests abroad, especially beyond the Western Hemisphere. Above all, the episode left Americans torn over the extent to which it would be beneficial for the United States to play a central role in global affairs in the future, particularly in those cases demanding substantial military commitments in foreign lands. It was an issue that would remain unsettled until two global wars had been fought at the cost of hundreds of thousands of American lives between 1914 and 1945.

In August 1914, World War I erupted among Europe's Great Powers, with France, Britain and Russia on one side and Germany and Austria-Hungary on the other.[32] The initial response from the administration of President Woodrow Wilson was to emphasis America's neutral stance on the conflict, which reflected the attitude of the US public at that juncture. Although Wilson had a penchant for internationalism, one fueled by the vision of a global collective security system based on the development of cooperative multilateral institutions, intervention in 1914 would have been imprudent given the lack of threats the war presented to American interests, whether at home or abroad. In short, there was no danger that the war would extend across the Atlantic to the United States nor any expectations that the conflict would continue long enough to undermine American commercial interests in Europe to a considerable extent. In short, the dangers presented by the war were not nearly significant enough to develop a consensus for US entry among proponents of the Wilsonian, Hamiltonian, Jeffersonian and Jacksonian foreign policy schools. Until that changed, which it did over the ensuing 2½ years, America would remain outside of the conflict.

By the start of 1917, the political atmosphere in the United States had shifted to an extent that led Wilson to make a strong case for America's entry into World War I on the side of the British and French (Russia was on the brink of a communist revolution at that point and formally withdrew from the conflict in March 1918). The United States declared war on Germany in April 1917 and American troops began arriving to support the British and French on the Western Front in July. A number of things had changed between 1914 and 1917, including the following four particularly significant developments. First, in May 1915, a German U-boat attacked the passenger ocean liner *Lusitania* off the coast of Britain, sinking the ship and killing 1,198 civilians, including 128 US citizens. Second, in January 1917, Germany announced publicly that its U-boats would carry out unrestricted submarine warfare on all ships whose paths they might cross, whether military vessels of their enemies, neutral powers or civilian vessels. Third, German Foreign Minister Alfred von Zimmerman sent a coded letter to Mexican President Venustiano Carranza urging him to declare war against the United States in exchange for Berlin's recognition of an eventual reconquest of Arizona, New Mexico and other parts of the American southwest by Mexico. The message was intercepted, decoded and revealed to the US public.[33] Fourth, American bankers had an interest in recouping the loans they had made to Britain and France to help those states finance the war effort.[34]

Collectively, these developments produced a general consensus among the Wilsonians, Hamiltonians, Jeffersonians and Jacksonians that dispatching troops to Europe to assist the British and French was in the best interest of the United States. American bankers put forward the Hamiltonian argument, while the threats posed by German U-boats and the Zimmerman telegram provided the necessary motivations for the Jeffersonians and Jacksonians. And, for his part, Wilson used the emerging consensus to lobby for support for the development of a global collective security system under the auspices of a League of Nations once the war had ended. Ultimately, US intervention tipped the balance in the war in favor of the British and French. By the end of the war in November 1918, America had lost 112,432 servicemen and Wilson was prepared to present his idealistic plan for the future when the victors met in Paris in 1919 to fashion a settlement that became known as the Treaty of Versailles.[35]

Wilson presented his vision for the League of Nations in the context of his "Fourteen Points," calling on the British and French to deal mercifully with the defeated Germany, which would then be invited to play a productive role in the new world order. British Prime Minister David Lloyd George and French Prime Minister Georges Clemenceau, however, were determined to impose a punitive peace on Germany and did so by demanding reparations that Berlin was unable to pay and excluding it from the postwar order. Disheartened at the British and French rejection of his vision, Wilson returned home, where the Republican-controlled US Senate refused to approve the treaty and America declined to play an enduring role in European security affairs over the ensuing two decades.[36] Lacking the incentive collective incentives that prompted approval of the entry in the war, the United States was content to focus on domestic affairs in the 1920s and obligated to do so during the Great Depression of the 1930s. As British scholar Niall Ferguson notes, in the end, the "Europeans wanted the Americans to bind themselves to the new postwar order. The Americans preferred to retain their freedom of action."[37]

Just 20 years after the conclusion of World War I, Europe was again embroiled in conflict, with National Socialist Germany aligned with Italy against France, Britain and an array of less power neighbors, including Belgium and the Netherlands, while the Soviet Union remained temporarily on the sidelines. Initially, the administration of President Franklin D. Roosevelt reacted in a manner similar to that of the Wilson administration in 1914 – remaining neutral with a gradual but steady shift to the side of Britain and its allies across the Atlantic. In particular, Roosevelt instituted a Lend-Lease Program to support the British and, following Germany's attack on the Soviet Union in June 1941, Moscow as well. In this case, however, there was no need for the confluence of a complex range of motives to convince the United States to commit itself fully to the war. One such motive was sufficient. On 7 December 1941, Japan carried out a surprise air assault on the US fleet stationed at Pearl Harbor, Hawaii. The attack left 2,403 Americans dead and prompted an American declaration of war against Japan. Four days later, Germany and Italy declared war on the United States, which led Washington to focus on a two-front war in Europe and the Pacific over the ensuing three years and nine months.[38] Above all, the attack on Pearl Harbor removed the sense of invulnerability that Americans generally took for granted. That alone was more than enough to ensure unequivocal public support for the war, irrespective of an individual's specific foreign policy inclinations. It helped Roosevelt justify the need to confront enemies in order to both preserve the American way of life at home and ensure that US values would provide hope for those fighting for freedom against the Germans and Japanese abroad. As Gaddis explains, it "forced a reconsideration of American grand strategy, but not of the conviction that empire and liberty could coexist. The military and economic strength of the United States would be deployed now, not just to dominate North America or even the western hemisphere, but to restore an international balance of power in which democracies would be free."[39]

Joining Britain and the Soviet Union in the struggle against Germany, Japan and Italy, the United States helped to turn the tide of the conflict decisively in favor of the allies. America's economic might provided the requisite fuel for the prosecution of an unlimited war that had forced Italy out of the war by the end of 1944 and left both Germany and Japan in ruins and allied forces in control of what remained of those states by August 1945. And, ultimately, the war's conclusion was ensured by an unprecedented use of military technology that could certainly be described as preventative, if not unambiguously preemptive, in character. As the war in the Pacific proceeded through its final months in the spring and summer of 1945, it became increasing apparent to the Harry S. Truman administration that the Japanese were not likely to surrender without organizing and staging a stalwart defense of their home islands. More pointedly, US military leaders viewed Tokyo's defense of Okinawa from April-June 1945, in the context of which 100,000 Japanese and 7,000 Americans perished, as a preview of what they anticipated would be a considerably more brutal struggle for the home islands.[40] At least in part as a result of that assessment, Truman elected to force the Japanese into submission by dropping atomic bombs on Hiroshima and Nagasaki on 6 and 9 August, respectively, which led to Tokyo's decision to surrender on 10 August. While those bombings killed nearly 200,000 civilians, they also rendered unnecessary a conventional invasion that would likely have produced the deaths of millions of Americans and Japanese. In that sense, the bombings were preemptive to the extent that they prevented an extraordinary loss of life that would, in all probability, otherwise have occurred. As American historian Victor Davis Hanson notes, the "plan of homeland defense (ketsu-go) was predicated on the idea that every Japanese civilian and soldier alike would kill as many Americans as possible – resulting in either a fitting genocide for a still unconquered and unoccupied people or such mayhem for the enemy that the Americans, not the Japanese would seek negotiations. So the holocaust on Okinawa led to the dropping of the bombs, which led to a surrender rather than greater carnage for both sides."[41]

Stability and Security During the Cold War Years

At the conclusion of World War II, Western European leaders faced two fundamental challenges, one immediate and the other of a more long-term nature. First, they had to rebuild the infrastructures of cities and towns within and the economies of states across the continent. Second, they had to develop a new systemic model governing inter-state behavior to replace the outdated balance-of-power framework that contributed to the outbreak and conduct of two global conflicts from 1914-45 and the alienation and subsequent appeasement of the continent's largest state during the inter-war years. These challenges were related in two ways. First, none of the states of Western Europe possessed the requisite physical resources and political will to overcome either hurdle unilaterally. Second, because of such shortcomings, they needed assistance from an outside power with an interest in cultivating political stability and economic prosperity across the region.[42]

Put simply, after World War II, two nascent hegemons controlled the continent's geopolitical future. At the heart of a physically destroyed, economically bankrupt and emotionally exhausted Europe in need of regional redefinition, the United States and Soviet Union occupied what remained of the once mighty but now prostrate German colossus. The former presided over the Western half with Britain and France; the latter was in charge of the Eastern half (aside from collective Allied administration of Berlin). Each side possessed fundamentally different political and economic systems, with Washington and Moscow married to the philosophies of liberal democracy and capitalism, and totalitarianism and communism, respectively. Ultimately, the transformation of Western European identity came in the context of and had a profound impact upon the development and subsequent conduct of a global Cold War pitting the United States against the Soviet Union over a period lasting more than four decades. As Walter Laqueur notes, the "old European balance of power was replaced by the global balance of power between America and Russia. Europe paid a terrible price for its disunity: the division into so many nation-states with conflicting intensity. The fate of the continent was now being decided in Moscow and Washington."[43]

In order to prevent Soviet advances beyond Moscow's control of the Eastern slab of Germany and the states of Central and Eastern Europe, the United States needed the support of a cohesive Western Europe. The creation of such an entity would entail economic, political and military cooperation and thus the willingness of Western Europeans to overcome bitter inter-state animosities, particularly with respect to the Germans. For their part, the Western Europeans required economic assistance for the reconstruction that would necessarily precede the process of reconciliation.[44] As Old Dominion University Eminent Professor Simon Serfaty argues, "[u]nity among the nation-states of Europe was a precondition for economic reconstruction not from one but two world wars; reconstruction was also the precondition for political unity not only within each European nation-state but among all of them as well. Without reconstruction first, the states of Europe could be saved neither from themselves nor from each other. Reconciliation would come next."[45]

American support for Western European reconstruction, which was manifested in the provision of more than $12 billion in economic assistance through the Marshall Plan between 1948 and 1952, was part of a multi-step bargaining process between the United States and its allies across the Atlantic. First, the administration of American President Harry S. Truman proposed and the Western Europeans accepted the Marshall Plan in exchange for a pledge to administer the aid multilaterally as the first step in a long-term regional integration project. Second, the Western Europeans requested that the United States maintain a long-term military presence on the continent in order to mitigate if not eliminate any security threats posed by their Soviet adversaries and recently reformed but still innately distrusted German partners. Third, Washington complied by establishing the North Atlantic Treaty Organization (NATO) in April 1949, with the guarantee of collective defense serving as a proverbial security blanket under the cover of which the Western Europeans could deepen and widen the integration process in the future.[46]

These agreements were necessarily connected, each serving to reinforce transatlantic and inter- and intra-European linkages at the intergovernmental level and change popular perceptions of past foes domestically. Serfaty, for example, explains that postwar:

> European policies were guided by complementary goals; to foster a peaceful community of democratic states on the continent and to build a strong security alliance with the United States ... Both sides of the Atlantic understood that neither goal could be achieved without the other. Europe's will to unite had to be credible before the United States would accept the European 'invitation' to make an unprecedented peacetime commitment to the continent.[47]

By committing itself to the defense of Western Europe through the establishment of NATO, the United States essentially placed the central front in the Cold War thousands of miles from the American homeland. Thus, the historical US emphasis on safeguarding domestic security by confronting adversaries abroad remained firmly in place.

During the Cold War, the United States developed and implemented foreign policies that responded primarily, if not always exclusively, to its bipolar struggle against the Soviet Union. Notwithstanding their individual particularities, the presidential administrations serving in office between the conclusion of World War II in August 1945 and the implosion of the Soviet Union in December 1991 each defined American interests relative to those pursued by the leadership in Moscow at a given point. Most such policies were based at least in part on the containment doctrine outlined by seminal Cold War strategist George F. Kennan in the aftermath of World War II. The Truman administration, for example, opened the Cold War by committing itself to the economic prosperity, political integration and military security of Western Europe (through Marshall Plan grants and the establishment of the North Atlantic Treaty Organization [NATO], respectively) in order to limit the Soviet sphere of influence to Eastern and Central Europe. The Ronald W. Reagan administration, by contrast, successfully pursued the rollback of Soviet influence at the global level by increasing US military spending during the 1980s to a level at which Moscow could no longer compete and elected to release the vice grip it had previously held on its sphere of influence. And the George H.W. Bush administration was left to orchestrate, if not preside over, the opening act of the restoration of democracy across Eastern and Central Europe in 1989-90 culminating in the reunification of Germany in October 1990. While by no means unchallenging, the policies each of these leaders and their advisors crafted were a product of an all but identically structured international system. In short, they each had a familiar bipolar model to use as a point of departure in developing and implementing their respective policies.

Over the course of the Cold War, American presidents used a variety of preemptive military and non-military means to further US interests relative to those of the Soviet Union and enhance American domestic security in the process. Examinations of the efforts of the administrations headed by two particularly charismatic leaders – John F. Kennedy and Reagan – are especially useful in illustrating that point. The firm yet prudential management of the Cuban Missile Crisis by the former and the rollback of Soviet global influence by the latter were each demonstrative of the utility of the employment of proactive rather than strictly reactive policymaking tools in eliminating threats to the United States posed by a dangerous adversary.

The stiffest test Kennedy faced during his presidency came in October 1962 when American reconnaissance photos revealed an ongoing Soviet initiative to install nuclear-tipped missiles on the island of Cuba with the acquiescence, if not at the behest of, Communist dictator Fidel Castro. After considering a range of options that included a preemptive military invasion of Cuba to remove those missiles that had already arrived, Kennedy decided to impose a naval blockade of the island, which could technically be deemed an act of war under international law. Ultimately, Soviet leader Nikita Khrushchev backed down and removed the missiles from Cuba.[48] At its core, Kennedy's action was preemptive in that it prevented the Soviet Union from increasing markedly the threats it already posed to the continental United States and did so before the missiles were fully operational and the potential for their use was *imminent*. It was also illustrative of the fact that any administration typically has a range of preemptive and preventive means at its disposal when required to deal with the escalation of an existing threat to its interests or the sudden emergence of a new one.

Similar to Kennedy, Reagan took a proactive stance in US-Soviet relations and he did so in the aftermath of Moscow's most aggressive foreign policy initiative since the 1962 episode in Cuba – its invasion of Afghanistan on the eve of the start of the 1980 Presidential race in December 1979. After defeating President Jimmy Carter in the ensuing election, Reagan crafted and implemented a strategy that sought to confront the Soviet Union and "roll back" its global influence through two means. First, the Reagan administration engaged in a massive military buildup that included the proposed development of a Strategic Defense Initiative to safeguard the United States against the threat of Soviet intercontinental missiles via space-based lasers. Second, it challenged Moscow by supporting insurgencies fighting Soviet-backed regimes in developing world states ranging from Afghanistan to Nicaragua and spent much less money that the Soviet Union in the process. Collectively, these initiatives helped to convince Soviet leader Mikhail Gorbachev that his state could no longer compete with the United States in terms of either economic vitality – and related conventional military reach – or political influence. As a result, Moscow gradually reduced its control over the Warsaw Pact, which led to the proverbial closing act of the Cold War, one that was managed by the George H.W. Bush administration from 1989-1992 and left the Clinton administration facing a new set of threats over the balance of the 1990s.[49]

Put simply, Reagan recognized that he could prevent unnecessary American – and, for that matter, Central and Eastern European – sacrifices, whether in terms of military outlays or the limitation of economic opportunity and political freedom over the long term through the implementation of a range of proactive (and, to some extent, preemptive) policies in the short term. As Max Boot, a senior fellow at the Council on Foreign Relations, asserts, "Ronald Reagan waged political, economic, and moral warfare on the 'evil empire,' and even sponsored proxy wars, but he prudently refrained from direct military attacks. His is a preemptive strategy we can and should apply around the world today."[50]

The Post-Cold War Era, 9/11 and the Doctrine of Preemption

As opposed to its Cold War counterparts, the first post-Cold War administration – that run by President William J. Clinton and his advisors – did not have a clear foreign policy blueprint to consult. Instead, Clinton's foreign policy team (along with, for that matter, myriad scholars of international relations) struggled to develop a model to fit a system no longer conditioned by the actions of two superpowers grappling for power and influence across the world. For their part, scholars offered five general paradigms with potential applicability to the emerging post-Cold War order. The first model, of which Francis Fukuyama was the principal advocate, predicted a diminution of, if not an end to, conflict as a byproduct of the victory of the American-led West over the Soviet-sponsored East in the Cold War.[51] The second, put forward by Samuel P. Huntington, mirrored the Cold War system but replaced the ideological confrontation pitting the United States against the Soviet Union with cleavages rooted in religious, economic and cultural differences, which, he predicted, would divide the world between North and South, Christianity and Islam, and Orient and Occident.[52] The third reflected the self-help world of neo-realists such as Kenneth Waltz and John Mearsheimer, with states striving to advance their interests unilaterally in an anarchical international environment.[53] The fourth, proposed by Zbigniew Brzezinski and Robert Kaplan among others, focused on the intensification of ethnic conflict manifested in a proliferation of failed states in regions as geographically diverse as Central Africa and the former Yugoslavia.[54]

Above all else, the promulgation of such a dissimilar set of models reflected the uncertainty prevalent within the international system in the aftermath of the Cold War.

That uncertainty complicated the foreign policy construction process to such an extent that the Clinton administration failed to develop a clear blueprint to help guide American engagement abroad during either of its two terms. Rather than prioritize US interests consistently on the basis of a particular region of the globe or issue area, the administration launched and pursued a wide variety of initiatives, ranging from military intervention in the Balkans to often overbearing mediation in the context of the Israeli-Palestinian peace process, few of which it followed through to completion. As Richard Haass, President of the Council on Foreign Relations and former head of policy planning under Secretary of State Colin Powell, has argued, "Clinton inherited a world of unprecedented American advantage and opportunity and did little with it ... A foreign legacy can result either from achieving something great on the ground (defeating major rivals or building major institutions, for example) or from changing the way people at home or abroad think about international relations. Clinton did neither."[55]

Regrettably, neither Clinton nor George W. Bush acted either early or proactively enough to prevent the occurrence of the events of 9/11. The attacks on the World Trade Center and Pentagon did, however, impress upon the Bush administration and the American public at large that the United States was not nearly so invulnerable to the sudden infliction of massive civilian casualties by an external adversary as was previously believed. That realization led correctly to a fundamental re-evaluation not only of American national security strategy but also of the way in which it should be articulated publicly. To treat the attacks as a criminal matter and leave the subsequent investigation and response to the Justice Department – Clinton's method choice after the February 1993 bombing of the garage of the North Tower of the World Trade Center – would have been inconceivable morally as well as politically. Yet, drafting and issuing a new NSS in the short term, would have been equally impractical and thus imprudent.

Instead, the Bush administration began by defining the fundamental challenges the United States would face in waging a war against terrorism of indeterminate length, one generally comparable in its global scope, if not in the monolithic nature of the adversary, to the five decade long Cold War that had defined American foreign policy over the latter half of the previous century. It then planned and conducted Operation Enduring Freedom against Al Qaeda and its Taliban sponsors in Afghanistan from October-December 2001 as a means both to weaken bin Laden's network and serve notice to those regimes that chose to support terrorist groups that their actions would entail serious consequences. Next, it used much of 2002 to identify and issue overt warnings to those states it perceived as the most stalwart and, consequently, the most threatening, pursuers of weapons of mass destruction (WMD) and sponsors of terrorism – most notably Iraq, Iran and North Korea. Lastly, it incorporated a range of military and non-military preemptive and preventative means to safeguard US interests at home and abroad into the NSS that Bush promulgated that September.

American presidents have employed a variety of means in conducting foreign policy throughout US history. The particulars of their approaches were in the past and are presently conditioned by the contemporary circumstances and events to which they have had to respond. Yet, irrespective of the temporal context, three rules have always proven indispensable to effective presidential policymaking and decision taking. It is first necessary to determine and prioritize the nation's interests, second to assess the capabilities at one's disposal to use in safeguarding those interests and third to formulate and implement national security policy and strategy accordingly. Above all, given those rules, the Bush administration's NSS is demonstrative of a keen understanding of the need to consider the interconnected relationship between interests, commitments and capabilities in responding to unanticipated changes in the international security environment.[56]

Most indispensably, Bush's NSS recognizes the increased vulnerability of the United States to attacks by transnational terrorist organizations and their supporters (whether state or non-state actors) as was so clearly – and tragically – demonstrated by the events of 9/11. In particular, the document defines three fundamental national interests – the defense, preservation and extension of the peace through collaboration with the world's great powers at the expense of its terrorists and tyrants – on behalf of which Bush promises to utilize America's unparalleled economic, military and political assets. However, it cleverly frames those interest-based objectives in principled rhetoric, noting that the United States seeks to promote a "balance of power that favors ... political and economic freedom, peaceful relations with other states and respect for human dignity" and also stressing that "today, the international community has the best chance since the rise of the nation-state in the seventeenth century to build a world where great powers compete in peace instead of continually preparing for war. Today, the world's great powers find ourselves on the same side."[57]

Domestic and foreign opponents of the Bush administration, along with some of America's European allies (France and Germany in particular), have derided its NSS as one based all but exclusively on the preemptive use of military force, whether employed unilaterally or multilaterally. But even a cursory reading of the document reveals such criticism to be misguided. It is 40 pages in length and the discussion of preemption encompasses just two sentences in one of its eight sections. Granted, Bush and his advisors placed an emphasis on the use of preemptive measures in light of the dire threats posed by terrorist groups and their state sponsors and heightened public sensitivities to those dangers as a result of the 9/11 attacks, but when taken as a whole, the NSS represents a considerably more wide ranging strategy. As Secretary of State Colin Powell has pointed out:

> The NSS made the concept of preemption explicit in the heady aftermath of September 11, and it did so for obvious reasons. One reason was to reassure the American people that the government possessed common sense. As President Bush has said – and as any sensible person understands – if you recognize a clear and present threat that is undeterrable by the means you have at hand, then you must deal with it. You do not wait for it to strike; you do not allow future attacks to happen before you take action. A second reason for including the notion of preemption in the NSS was to convey to our adversaries that they were in big trouble ... Sensible as these reasons were, some observers have

exaggerated both the scope of preemption in foreign policy and the centrality of preemption in US strategy as a whole.[58]

Justifiably, Bush cedes primacy to hard-core security issues over the low politics of the environment favored by his immediate predecessor in the White House (President Bill Clinton) and his opponent in the 2000 Presidential Election (Albert Gore). However, Bush does so by laying out the White House's strategy in terms of the proactive pursuit of eight separate goals, five of which relate directly to hard-core security issues and three more than pertain to efforts to foster economic growth and the construction of enduring democratic institutions in the developing world in general and across the Greater Middle East in particular. Specifically, the administration pledges that the United States will:

- Champion aspirations for human dignity.
- Strengthen alliances to defeat global terrorism and work to prevent attacks against us and our friends.
- Work with others to defuse regional conflicts.
- Prevent our enemies from threatening us, our allies, and our friends, with weapons of mass destruction.
- Ignite a new era of global economic growth through free markets and free trade.
- Expand the circle of development by opening societies and building the infrastructure of democracy.
- Develop agendas for cooperative action with other main centers of global power.
- Transform America's national security institutions to meet the challenges and opportunities of the twenty-first century."[59]

In light of the historical discussion of US foreign policy and strategy in the preceding sections, Bush's strategy appears not as a rash reaction to the 9/11 assaults, but as a comprehensive blueprint that takes into account the successes and failures of his predecessors in the White House over the past two centuries. One of the means the United States used to weaken the Soviet Union's grip over its Warsaw Pact satellites over the long term, for instance, was by "opening societies and building the infrastructure of democracy" throughout Central and Eastern Europe. Most significantly, Reagan's willingness to push the Soviets to loosen and then release their control over the Warsaw Pact once the arms buildup of the early 1980s put Washington in a position of relative strength vis-à-vis Moscow, triggered the subsequent collapse of Communist regimes from Bucharest to East Berlin in the fall and winter of 1989-90. The Bush NSS is designed to eventually produce a similar democratization of the Islamic world. In that sense, it is both flexible and visionary rather than ill conceived and illogical. As Powell concludes, "Together, [its eight] parts add up to a strategy that is broad and deep, far ranging and forward looking, attuned as much to opportunities for the United States as to the dangers it faces."[60]

What is most instructive about the Bush administration's NSS is the extent to which it takes an assertive but multilateral stance in discussing the economic, political and military means the United States is prepared to use to preempt threats to American security at home and abroad.[61] The NSS suggests that such threats – most notably the acquisition, production and proliferation of WMD by dictatorial regimes – are best mitigated and eventually eliminated multilaterally through the organization of "coalitions – as broad as practicable – of states able and willing to promote a balance of power that favors freedom."[62] Furthermore, it renders critics' characterizations of the Bush administration's supposed aversion to working with the UN under any circumstances considerably less credible by justifying its doctrine of preemption in globally acceptable legal terms pertaining to a state's right to defend itself.[63]

Much of the criticism of Bush's foreign policy before, as well as during and after, the conduct of the Second Iraq War, rests primarily on the premise that he has acted unilaterally more often than not. Responding effectively to that criticism is relatively easy so long as one defines the term unilateralism first. The narrowest definition of the term would suggest that a given state is acting alone – that is, without the support, of any allies whatsoever, let alone the blessing of the UN Security Council or wider international community. A broader definition, by contrast, might indicate a coalition of less than 10 states acting without the authority of a formal Security Council resolution. Yet, neither of these definitions applies to US action in the contexts of either Operation Enduring Freedom or Operation Iraqi Freedom. In each case, the United States acted with the direct or indirect military, logistical and political support of no less than 50 states. In addition, the Security Council acceded to the former, albeit not to the latter. As Powell explains, "Partnership is the watchword of US strategy in this administration. Partnership is not about deferring to others; it is about working with them."[64]

Moving beyond its general and specific characterizations of the potential security threats the United States must confront (most notably the arming of terrorist organizations with WMD by tyrannical regimes) and the means to use in preempting those threats (collective diplomacy if possible; the multilateral or unilateral use of force if necessary), the NSS also prioritizes American interests regionally. Not unexpectedly, that prioritization places an emphasis on Greater Middle Eastern and South Asian security affairs generally and such long-standing imbroglios as the Israeli-Palestinian conflict and troubled Indian-Pakistani relationship in particular. Significantly, in addressing each of these contentious relationships, the NSS acknowledges the need for the United States to strike a balance between the interests of the disparate ethnic and religious groups involved.[65] It does so in large part in order to avoid deepening the anti-American sentiments that have in the past – and continue at present – to make members of the lower classes of the Islamic world susceptible to the recruitment efforts of regional and global terrorist organizations. Rice, for example, has pointed out, that the Bush administration "rejects the condescending view that freedom will not grow in the soil of the Middle East – or that Muslims somehow do not share in the desire to be free."[66]

Conclusions

At its core, this chapter was designed to address the evolution of the relationship between homeland security and national security by examining five issue areas. First, it presented a primer on the extent to which, historically, American policymakers have sought to achieve security at home by expanding the extent of US territory in the Western Hemisphere while increasing Washington's economic and politically influence and military reach at the global level. Second, it described America's transition from a regional power to a globally influential actor over the course of the nineteenth century. Third, it discussed the differences in the roles of the United States in World Wars I and II and the unwillingness and willingness, respectively, of Americans to support long-term commitments to European security following those conflicts. Fourth, it assessed US policies during the Cold War, placing an emphasis on the achievement of stability in the American-Soviet relationship (and thus security at home) via containment and the more revolutionary approach of rollback by challenging Moscow abroad. Fifth, it examined the George W. Bush administration's response to the 9/11 attacks and the extent to which promoting liberal democracy abroad is an effective means to safeguard American domestic interests.

Above all, the evidence presented in the five main sections of the chapter suggest strains of both continuity and change in the relationship between homeland security and national security in the United States prior to and after the events of 9/11, with the proverbial balance favoring the former rather than the latter. Although Al Qaeda's attacks on the World Trade Center and Pentagon on 9/11 was unprecedented in terms of the method utilized and extent of casualties and economic impact, the American response was reflective of continuity in two principal respects. First, as in the past, the United States has confronted the aggressors responsible for their attacks, along with their supporters (most notably so with respect to Al Qaeda on one hand and the Taliban and Iraq on the other) primarily by seeking them out abroad. The two clearest examples of this were the prosecution of Operation Enduring Freedom in Afghanistan in the fall of 2001 and Operation Iraqi Freedom in the spring of 2003. Second, the use of the above operations as a point of departure for a liberal democratic transformation of the Greater Middle East mirrors America's determination to defeat the Soviet Union and allow the peoples of Central and Eastern Europe the freedom of expression denied to them by Moscow for nearly a half-century.

Since the events of 9/11, Al Qaeda has yet to carry out another direct attack on America at home. That fact reflects the utility of the Bush administration's present strategy in the war on terrorism. Yet, it has also contributed to a growing sense of complacency among a substantial proportion of the US public. America faced comparable challenges in the latter stages and aftermath of the Vietnam War during the 1960s and 1970s, before rallying in support of the proactive approach through which the Reagan administration rolled back Soviet influence across the world and thus brought the Cold War to a successful conclusion. There was no such similar lack of resolve between the Japanese attack on Pearl Harbor in December 1941 and the end of World War II nearly four years later. The threats the United States faces now from Al

Qaeda and its myriad affiliates are equally grave, but, on balance, are perhaps not perceived as such by many Americans. One must hope that future presidents, their staffs and congressmen and women on both side of the political aisle maintain their focus on safeguarding US interests at home and overseas from the continuing dangers of terrorists and their sponsors with vigor that equals that of the Bush administration.

Notes

1.   George W. Bush, "National Security Strategy of the United States," 17 September 2003, *White House Office of the Press Secretary* (www.whitehouse.gov).
2.   *Ibid.*
3.   Bernard Lewis, "Freedom and Justice in the Modern Middle East," *Foreign Affairs*, 84/3 (May/June2005): 51.
4.   George W. Bush, "Inaugural Address," 20 January 2005, *White House Office of the Press Secretary.*
5.   Gaddis, *Surprise, Security and the American Experience*, 13.
6.   Larry Schweikart and Michael Allen, *A Patriot's History of the United States: From Columbus's Great Discovery to the War on Terror* (New York: Sentinel, 2005).
7.   Gaddis, *Surprise, Security and the American Experience*, 11-12.
8.   James Chace and Caleb Carr, *America Invulnerable: The Quest for Absolute Security from 1812 to State Wars* (New York: Summit Books, 1988), 37. Reference made in Gaddis, *Surprise, Security and the American Experience*, 12.
9.   Schweikart and Allen, *A Patriot's History*, 176-77.
10. Joseph Freeman and Joseph Nearing, *Dollar Diplomacy: A Study in American Imperialism* (New York: Monthly Review Press, 1928), 236f. Reference made in Ferguson, *Colossus*, 42.
11. Gaddis, *Surprise, Security and the American Experience*, 14-15.
12. Mead, *Power, Terror, Peace and War*, 8.
13. Henry A. Kissinger, *Diplomacy* (New York: Simon & Shuster, 1994), 18.
14. For a detailed description of these four foreign policy schools, please see Walter Russell Mead, *Special Providence: American Foreign Policy and How it Changed the World* (New York: Routledge, 2002).
15. Bush, "National Security Strategy of the United States."
16. Gaddis, *Surprise, Security and the American Experience*, 21.
17. *Ibid.*, 29.
18. Morris, *Encyclopedia of American History*, 599. Reference made in Ferguson, *Colossus*, 40.
19. Baker, *The Politics of Diplomacy: Revolution, War and Peace, 1989-1992*. Reference made in Ferguson, *Colossus*, 40.
20. Morris, *Encyclopedia of American History*, 599. Reference made in Ferguson, *Colossus*, 40.
21. Schweikart and Allen, *Patriot's History of the United States*, 239-45.
22. *Ibid.*, 245.

23. Mead, *Special Providence*, 102.
24. Ferguson, *Colossus*, 45-46.
25. Mead, *Special Providence*, 26.
26. House Committee on International Relations [now Foreign Affairs], Subcommittee on International Security and Scientific Affairs, *Background Information on the Use of U.S. Armed Forces in Foreign Countries, 1975 Revision.* Committee Print, 94th Congress, 1st Session, 1995, prepared by the Foreign Affairs Division, Congressional Research Service, Library of Congress, 84. Reference made in Mead, *Special Providence*, 24.
27. Mead, *Special Providence*, 25.
28. For the Naval *Historical Center*'s assessment, please see http://www.history. navy.mil/faqs/faq71-1.htm. Reference made in Gaddis, *Surprise, Security and the American Experience*, 124.
29. Schweikart and Allen, *Patriot's History of the United States*, 467.
30. Morris, *Encyclopedia of American History*, 599. Reference made in Ferguson, *Colossus*, 40.
31. Max Boot, *The Savage Wars of Peace*, 99-128; Robert D. Kaplan, *Imperial Grunts: The American Military on the Ground* (New York: Random House, 2005), 136-42.
32. For an in-depth study of the road to World War I in Europe, please see Barbara Tuchman, *The Guns of August* (New York: Random House, 1962).
33. Schweikart and Allen, *A Patriot's History of the United States*, 510-15.
34. Ferguson, *Colossus*, 63.
35. Schweikart and Allen, *A Patriot's History of the United States*, 520-21.
36. *Ibid.*, 522-26.
37. Ferguson, *Colossus*, 64.
38. Schweikart and Allen, *A Patriot's History of the United States*, 593-97; Ferguson, *Colossus*, 61-62.
39. Gaddis, *Surprise, Security and the American Experience*, 109.
40. Victor Davis Hanson, *Ripples of Battle*, 44-45.
41. *Ibid.*, 56-57.
42. William Wallace, *The Transformation of Western Europe* (New York: Council on Foreign Relations Press, 1990), 35-45; Joan Hoff and Richard K. Vedder, eds., *The European Union: From Jean Monnet to the Euro* (Athens: Ohio University Press, 2000), 57-78.
43. Walter Laqueur, *Europe in Our Time: A History, 1945-1992* (New York: Penguin, 1992), 21.
44. Wallace, *Transformation of Western Europe*, 28-34.
45. Simon Serfaty, *Stay the Course: European Unity and Atlantic Solidarity* (Westport, Conn.: Praeger, 1997), 53.
46. Paul Graham Taylor, *The European Union in the 1990s* (New York: Oxford University Press, 1996), 8-57; Dusan Sjdjanski, *The Federal Future of Europe: From the European Community to the European Union* (Ann Arbor: University of Michigan Press, 2000), 7-25.
47. Serfaty, *Stay the Course*, 52.
48. For a detailed account of the crisis from one of those directly involved at the time, please see Robert F. Kennedy, *Thirteen Days: A Memoir of the Cuban Missile Crisis* (New York:

W.W. Norton & Company, 1969).

49. For a detailed examination of the Reagan Doctrine, see Lagon, *The Reagan Doctrine.*
50. Max Boot, "The Bush Doctrine Lives," *The Weekly Standard*, 16 February 2004, 25.
51. See Francis Fukuyama, *The End of History and the Last Man* (New York: Avon, 1993).
52. See Samuel P. Huntington, *The Clash of Civilizations and the Remaking of World Order* (New York: Simon & Schuster, 1996).
53. See Kenneth N. Waltz, "The Emerging Structure of International Politics," *International Security* 18 (Fall 1993): 44-79; John J. Mearsheimer, "Back to the Future: Instability in Europe After the Cold War," *International Security* 15 (Summer 1990): 5-56.
54. See Zbigniew Brzezinski, *Out of Control: Global Turmoil on the Eve of the Twenty-first Century* (New York: Touchstone Books, 1993); Robert D. Kaplan, "The Coming Anarchy," *Atlantic Monthly* 281 (Summer 1994).
55. Richard N. Haass, "The Squandered Presidency: Demanding More From the Commander-in-Chief," *Foreign Affairs*, 79/3 (May/June 2000): 137.
56. For a more in-depth discussion of these issues, please see Lansford and Pauly, *Strategic Preemption.*
57. Bush, "National Security Strategy."
58. Colin L. Powell, "A Strategy of Partnerships," *Foreign Affairs*, 83/1 (January/February 2004): 24.
59. Bush, "National Security Strategy."
60. Powell, "A Strategy of Partnerships," 23.
61. Bush, "National Security Strategy." In particular, the NSS states that "[w]e must be prepared to stop rogue states and their terrorist clients before they are able to threaten or use weapons of mass destruction against the United States and our allies and friends."
62. *Ibid.*, 15.
63. *Ibid.*, 9.
64. Powell, "A Strategy of Partnerships," 25-26.
65. Bush, "National Security Strategy."
66. Condoleezza Rice, "2002 Wriston Lecture at the Manhattan Institute," 10 October 2002, *White House Office of the Press Secretary* (www.whitehouse.gov).

Chapter 4

Structure of Homeland Security

Introduction

The United States has some 87,000 jurisdictions at the federal, state, and local level with homeland security responsibilities.[1] The coordination of the many groups, agencies and governments within this framework is a multilayered and overlapping enterprise that exists on an often need-based, but sometimes arbitrary, system developed in an ad-hoc fashion to counter a specific event. With the creation of the Department of Homeland Security in 2002, the process of streamlining this framework to meet the merging needs of the nation commenced in earnest as it became increasingly obvious that the existing system was incapable of adequately handling large scale domestic emergencies. While the September 11 2001 terrorist attacks were the impetus for a shuffling of the nation's homeland security structure, incidents such as Hurricane Katrina and Rita in the summer and fall of 2005 forced the government into taking positive steps in refocusing homeland security toward a broad based effort, instead of one designed just to counter terrorism. All domestic emergencies, both man made and natural, have once again been placed on the agenda, instead of just the politically expedient effort at counter terrorism.

With that said, a glance at the structure of homeland security as it exists today within the United States is still an act of cursory confusion with few single points of control or contact and no overall authority granted outside of the Presidential office. The formation of the Department of Homeland Security was an important first step in granting authority for action; however, as the confusion around Hurricane Katrina demonstrated, the coordination between federal, state, and local resources still leaves much to be desired. The coordination between federal agencies was not much better.

Examples of these failures were seen in the pre and post hurricane operations that occurred. The failures of the state and local governments to adequently warn and prepare for a tragedy of this nature, as demonstrated in the lack of sufficient National Guard call ups or the issuance and enforcement of mandatory evacuations in a timely manner, contributed as much to the disaster as the failure of the local and state governments in pleading its case before a federal system geared toward support and not control. The system of state requests for federal support was not adequately understood at either level. The reduced capacity of FEMA, due to a thinning budget and a progressively expanded mandate, coupled with a lack of firm command and control capabilities, hampered the response of federal, state, and private organizations. In essence, the failure of Katrina was partly one of bureaucracy. With no one taking over all authority and no one having access to all levels, everyone's hands were tied. State authorities were reluctant to give control to federal authorities even while federal authorities did not seem to understand exactly what their role entailed.[2]

Of course, one must use caution in blaming any one entity for failures of US homeland security efforts as it is a relatively new concept and has many road blocks to integration built within because of the federal system that exists with strong levels of state authority that sometimes counteract the ability of the federal government to make broad sweeping changes. In addition, the bureaucratic hurdles of sweeping away entanglements and pre existing homeland security institutions is difficult at best and practically impossible when taking into account the many heads of decision making represented in the congress, in the executive branch, in the territorial federal departments, and in a very open and often hostile political system. Big changes do not come easy and the status quo often only shifts when these decision making authorities are embarrassed or forced into action by events.

While Chapter Five will address some of the issues involved in formulating policy, this chapter describes a number of positive changes towards greater integration have occurred in the past few years. The formation of the Director of National Intelligence is a positive step in the intelligence community towards US efforts at developing a broad picture of the threats the nation faces. The refocus of FEMA and the reorganization of the Department of Homeland Security show promise in the nation's efforts towards preparedness and mitigation issues.[3] The formation of the US Northern Command by the military should help streamline military assistance to civilian authorities as well as provide a single coordinated effort for homeland defense operations. The US Congress has made great strides in consolidating the number of oversight committees that oversee homeland security concerns.[4] This chapter will offer an overview of the main agencies that play a role in US Homeland Security efforts.

The Presidential Office

In the United States, the President is viewed as the final authority and the final level of coordination for homeland security at all levels. Granted, much of this power is delegated throughout the executive branch of government and into the hands of the many officers and Secretaries within the department structure. However, the President wields a great deal of personal power in terms of what picture is presented to the public and what polices will be followed. In addition, the President has the power to declare national emergencies and activate processes through which federal resources are funneled into the state and local levels.

In order to assist the President in his role as head of the Executive Branch of government, the National Security Council (NSC) was formed as "the principal forum for considering national security and foreign policy matters with his senior national security advisors and cabinet officials … the Council also serves as the President's principal arm for coordinating these polices among various agencies."[5] This council is composed of the President and Vice President, the Secretaries of State, Treasury and

Defense, the National Security Advisor,[6] the Chairman of the Joint Chiefs of Staff, the Director of National Intelligence, the Chief of Staff to the President, Counsel to the President and the Assistant to the President for Economic Policy. In addition, other agency or department heads are invited when appropriate. The NSC has a number of committees and working groups under its guidance in order to assist the Council and the President in their functions. For example, the Counterterrorism Security Group is specifically tasked with exploring terrorism issues.[7]

In addition, the President created, through executive order, the Office of Homeland Security, consisting of an Assistant to the President for Homeland Security and a Homeland Security Council, on 8 October 2001. The Homeland Security Council is structured similarly to the NSC with the Assistant to the President for Homeland Security playing a comparable role as the National Security Advisor. The establishment of DHS has significantly diminished the role of the Office of Homeland Security with no budget allotted to the office all together in 2005.[8]

Department of Homeland Security

The principal organization within the US government tasked with homeland security concerns is the Department of Homeland Security (DHS), formed under the administration of President George W. Bush through the Homeland Security Act of 2002.[9] DHS represents the ongoing reorganization of the US government's response to the growing threat of international terrorism and the perceived failure of the federal response to natural disasters such as Hurricane Katrina. Officially beginning operations on 24 January 2003, the original formation was the largest restructuring of the federal government since the formation of the US Department of Defense into its current reiteration after World War II.

The initial formulation of DHS divided a number of agencies into four broad directorates: Border and Transportation Security; Emergency Preparedness and Response; Science and Technology; and Information Analysis and Infrastructure Protection. Under these four directorates, organizations from throughout the government were housed in order to focus the nation's energies toward its new post-9/11 role. In addition to the Secret Service and the Coast Guard being wholly moved into DHS, the department was formed from the following.[10]

Border and Transportation Security Directorate

The US Customs Service from the Department of the Treasury; parts of the Immigration and Naturalization Service from the Department of Justice; the Federal Protective Service; the Transportation and Security Administration from the Department of Transportation; parts of the Animal and Plan Health Inspection Service from the Department of Agriculture; and the Office of Domestic Preparedness from the Department of Justice.

Emergency Preparedness and Response Directorate

The Federal Emergency Management Agency; Strategic National Stockpile and the National Disaster Medical System from the Department of Health and Human Services; the Nuclear Incident Response Team from the Department of Energy; Domestic Emergency Support Teams from the Department of Justice; and the FBI's National Domestic Preparedness Office.

Science and Technology Directorate

The CBRN Countermeasures Programs and the Environmental Measurements Laboratory from the Department of Energy; the National BW Defense Analysis Center from the Department of Defense; and the Plum Island Animal Disease Center from the Department of Agriculture.

Information Analysis and Infrastructure Protection

The Federal Computer Response Center from the US Government Service Administration; the National Communications System from the Department of Defense; the National Infrastructure Protection Center from the FBI and; the Energy Security and Assurance Program from the Department of Energy.

To lead this new agency, former Congressman and Governor from Pennsylvania, and the then Assistant to the President for Homeland Security, Tom Ridge, was tasked at organizing and developing DHS and turning the many separate agencies into a competent structure.[11] Some 23 months after his arrival, he resigned, leaving DHS as a functioning department; however, a number of issues with the original plan have been pointed out as in need of addressing. Specifically, the need for a central policy component and the need for a strengthened intelligence component were highlighted in a department that was described as "in need of a midcourse correction."[12]

Soon after assuming his role on 15 February 2005 as the second DHS Secretary in its young history, Secretary Michael Chertoff ordered a review of the department's practices, which was released in July 2005.[13] As of the time of this writing, DHS Secretary Chertoff has authorized a number of organizational and policy changes within the department to reflect the most recent proposals in DHS' ongoing efforts to develop an effective and viable organization.[14] His six point agenda for the transformation of DHS came before the crippling effects of Hurricane Katrina and Rita in August 2005. However, it is worth noting that the department was well aware of the need for greater focus on preparing for catastrophic man made and natural disasters.

A number of primary components are represented under the DHS umbrella, including the US Secret Service and the Federal Law Enforcement Training Center, as well as the administrative offices of the Secretary. In addition, DHS includes the following components.

Advisory Committees

DHS has two primary advisory committees that have been stood up in order to assist the Secretary in his role in managing the department. The Homeland Security Advisory Council and the National Infrastructure Advisory Council are both comprised of leaders from various emergency services and leaders at the state and local level, as well as distinguished citizens in the private sector and in academia. Neither panel has any regulatory authority.

The Homeland Security Advisory Council provides "organizationally independent advice and recommendations to the Secretary of the Department, aiding in the creation and implementation of critical and actionable policy relating to the security of the American homeland."[15] For example, the Council has focused on such issues as information sharing between federal agencies and state and local authorities, as well as issues ranging from funding to education.[16] The National Infrastructure Advisory Council provides advice "on the security of information systems for the public and private institutions that constitute the critical infrastructure of our Nation's economy."[17] For example, this council has previously focused on issues such as protecting the internet.[18]

Directorate for Preparedness

In order to assist DHS and the US federal government in preparing for homeland security threats, the Directorate for Preparedness was formed in order to facilitate federal, state, and local efforts.[19] The Directorate has a number of functions that include: 1) Consolidating preparedness assets across DHS; 2) Facilitating grants and overseeing nationwide preparedness efforts by supporting first responder training, citizen awareness, public health, infrastructure and cyber security and ensures proper steps are taken to protect high-risk targets; 3) Focusing on cyber security and telecommunications; and 4) Coordinating efforts in regard to public health and biological threats.[20]

Under the Directorate of Preparedness are a number of sub components, including the Cyber and Telecommunications component, which is tasked with "identifying and assessing the vulnerability of critical telecommunications infrastructure and assets; providing timely, actionable and valuable threat information; and leading the national response to cyber and telecommunications attacks."[21] The Chief Medical Officer is tasked with coordinating DHS's efforts on all medical matters associated with Homeland Security, including preparing against and preventing biological attacks and coordinating DHS efforts along these lines with other federal efforts across departments.[22] The US Fire Administration (USFA) mission is to "reduce life and economic loss due to fire and related emergencies, through advocacy, coordination, and support."[23] Under the USFA are a number of entities, including the National Fire Academy and the National Fire Data Center. The Assistant Secretary for Grants and Training facilitates the dispersion of federal funds to local and state agencies as well as coordinates a number of exercises for homeland security efforts.[24]

The Assistant Secretary for Infrastructure Protection identifies and develops broad based recommendations for the protection of the nation's critical infrastructure and the Office of National Capital Region Coordination coordinates preparedness activities in the 6,000 square miles surrounding Washington DC.[25]

Formed after the Second Stage Review process, the Preparedness Directorate took elements from across the department that had preparedness taskings and placed them in one location. The directorate is responsible for such issues as risk analysis, training, and exercise support.

Directorate for Science and Technology

The principal task for coordinating the nation's efforts at developing the technology used in homeland security rests with the Directorate for Science and Technology. This directorate's primary mission is as follows:

- Develop and deploy state-of-the art, high-performance, low-operating-cost systems to prevent, detect, and mitigate the consequences of chemical, biological, radiological, nuclear, and explosive attacks.
- Develop equipment, protocols, and training procedures for response to and recovery from chemical, biological, radiological, nuclear, and explosive attacks.
- Enhance the technical capabilities of the Department's operational elements and other Federal, State, local, and tribal agencies to fulfill their homeland security related missions.
- Develop methods and capabilities to test and assess threats and vulnerabilities, and prevent technology surprise and anticipate emerging threats.
- Develop technical standards and establish certified laboratories to evaluate homeland security and emergency responder technologies.[26]

The Directorate for Science and Technology houses the Homeland Security Advanced Research Projects Agency (HSARPA), which provides grants and directs homeland security related technological research for industry and academia.[27] The Office of Research and Development (ORD), which is responsible for various governmental research facilities as well as the direction of DHS's various university programs, and the Office of Systems Engineering and Development (SED), which facilitates the transition of engineering technologies from testing into production, are also housed within this directorate.[28]

Office of Intelligence and Analysis

Led by the Chief Intelligence Officer, the Office of Intelligence and Analysis (OIA) is the key intelligence analysis and coordination center for DHS. As one of two entities of DHS within the broader United States Intelligence Community (the Coast Guard being the other), the organization supports DHS, local and state intelligence needs as relates to homeland security. The Office of Intelligence Analysis is designed to be a one stop location for gathering state, local, and federal intelligence in order to present an overall picture of homeland security threats. The Office does not have collection assets of its own. Instead, it relies on the other components within DHS, as well as the 14 other federal agencies with intelligence capabilities to supply it with intelligence. The Chief Intelligence Officer reports to the Secretary and is appointed by the President.[29]

Originally, the office was part of the now defunct Information Analysis and Infrastructure Protection Directorate (IAIP). As part of this broader directorate, it had been described as "marginalized and deprived of leadership, resources and a clear, full fledged role in the US intelligence community."[30] In the final report of the 9/11 commission, IAIP was described as "embryonic" and having not taken control of the intelligence capabilities needed in order to understand the intelligence picture needed to detect and deter terrorist activity.[31] A 2005 statement by Richard Ben-Veniste, of the original 9/11 Commission, blamed this failure on three key issues: 1) Intelligence in the department did not have a clear mission; 2) The Terrorist Threat Integration Center was outside of DHS and was tasked at essentially the same role; 3) It did not have access to status, resources or support and was not respected within the nations' intelligence community; and 4) It did not unify the efforts of the various intelligence gathering components found in other areas of DHS.[32]

As of this writing, not much is known on exactly what shape the newly formed OIA will have. However, DHS's first Chief Intelligence Officer, Charles Allen, has given a hint of what role the organization will assume.[33] He has organized a Homeland Security Intelligence Council consisting of representative from the various components of DHS. In addition, he intends on establishing a reports officer program in which elements of his office will be disseminated into the various operational components of DHS and the various regional, state and local intelligence centers. He also intends to act as a hub for matching state and local intelligence requirements with the relevant national intelligence program.

Office of Operations Coordination

Perhaps the most visible office within DHS, the Office of Operations Coordination houses the Homeland Security Operations Center (HSOC) as well as controls the nation's Homeland Security Advisory System. The office monitors the threats to the United States and coordinates and informs the activities of various state homeland security assets as well as various law enforcement entities at the state and federal level. The Director of Operations Coordination reports to the Secretary.

HSOC is a multi agency operations center that acts as the primary national facility for incident management and coordination activities associated with homeland security threats.[34] In addition, HSOC disseminates recommendations to federal, state, and local partners for threat mitigation in the form of informational bulletins as well as houses DHS' Interagency Incident Management Group, a senior level policy and strategy group; the National Response Coordination Center (NRCC), which provides overall federal response coordination; and Regional Response Coordination Centers (RRCC), which coordinates regional responses and implements local federal support.[35]

Policy Directorate

The function of the Policy Directorate is to establish departmental wide regulatory and initiative coordination in order to assure consistency in long range and strategic planning. The office takes over many of the policy functions from the former Border and Transportation Security Directorate, now defunct after the 2005 reorganization. The policy development tools previous to the formation of this directorate were very compartmentalized and largely holdovers from the formation of DHS in 2003 from existing agencies and programs.[36] Having an overall policy coordination component should assure consistency throughout the department.

The Policy Directorate is broken down into five key components.[37] The Office of Policy coordinates the activities of the other offices within the directorate as well as formulates and sets broad policy goals for DHS. The other four offices focus on specific aspects of policy development. The Office of Immigration Statistics develops and disseminates statistical data on immigration issues. The Office of International Affairs focuses on policies that affect the international community. The Office of the Private Sector acts as the primary system of communication between the private sector and the department in terms of the potential impact of policy goals. The Office of Strategic Planning works on the long range planning for the department. The Senior Asylum Officer focuses on the policies and procedures that affect the many refugees and asylum seekers in the nation.

Domestic Nuclear Detection Office (DNDO)

This office is responsible for all levels of the nation's efforts to detect and regulate the unauthorized importation, development, or possession of nuclear related materials.[38] Established by the President with NSPD-43 and HSPD-14 on 15 April 2005, the DNDO acts as a "single accountable organization with dedicated responsibilities to develop the global nuclear detection architecture, and acquire, and support the deployment of the domestic detection system to detect and report attempts to import or transport a nuclear device or fissile or radiological material intended for illicit use."[39]

In order to accomplish this mission, DNDO has seven principal offices.[40] The Office of the Director coordinates the activities of the other components of DNDO and develops, in coordination with other departments and agencies, the integrated global and domestic nuclear detection architecture. The Office of Systems Engineering and the Office of Systems Architect develops a master engineering plan and the global detection architecture. The Office of System Development and Acquisition coordinates research from determining requirements to deployment. The Office of Assessments tests equipment and procedures to assure effectiveness. The Office of Transformational Research and Development identifies existing technology and develops them for the DNDO mission. The Office of Operations Support observes the existing detection structure and suggests improvements to deployed systems.

Federal Emergency Management Agency (FEMA)

FEMA is the principal agency responsible for preparing against and mitigating the effects of man made and natural disasters. Its primary function is the coordination of federal, state, and local efforts in responding to various disasters by offering training and financial relief assets as well as a number of specialized skills at the federal level. FEMA is divided into ten regional offices with approximately 2,600 full time employees.

FEMA came into existence in 1979 by executive order in order to integrate the many different programs that had existed previously. Originally, the organization had two primary responsibilities, disaster relief and civil defense. Throughout the 1990s the civil defense aspect of its mission was a distant second place to its disaster relief efforts. In 1993, President Bill Clinton made FEMA a cabinet level position. By the September 11 2001 terrorist attacks, the FEMA role was firmly in the disaster and recover relief role. However, FEMA was absorbed into DHS in 2003 whose counter terrorist role completely overshadowed FEMA and disaster recovery.[41] In addition, during the 9/11 disaster, FEMA was not hampered by the additional layers of bureaucracy and increased directions of responsibility that it was encumbered with under the yoke of DHS. With the Second Stage Review, reinforced by the lesson of Hurricane Katrina, FEMA is once again the nation's response and recovery agency with an increased stature in DHS.

FEMA is responsible for 28 Urban Search and Rescue task forces manned by at least 70 trained individuals distributed throughout the United States.[42] These specialized units are organized at the local level but receive funding, training and accreditation from the federal government. They must be capable of deploying at full force within six hours of activations and able to sustain themselves for three days without relief. Federal funds for these task forces have increased substantially over the past several years, rising from $4 million to a high of $60 million in 2004 with at least some of the increased funding going towards upgrading their capabilities for working within a WMD contaminated environment. State and local authorities are responsible for about 80 percent of their long term costs.

The National Disaster Medical System, also under the FEMA umbrella, organizes and supports the development of specialized medical teams that are capable of independently responding to and sustaining operations in an emergency and the assets to coordinate the medical evacuation of victims of natural and technological disasters, major transportation accidents and acts of terrorism, including WMD events.[43] Sponsored at the local level by major medical centers and hospitals, teams of volunteer doctors, nurses and other medical oriented professionals train to deploy when needed.[44] NDMS has more than 9,000 personnel organized into 107 teams with a budget of approximately $20 million.[45]

The National Incident Management System (NIMS) "establishes standardized incident management processes, protocols, and procedures that all responders – federal, state, tribal, and local – will use to coordinate and conduct response actions."[46] Through federal statute, all federal agencies must take part. In addition, state and local agencies are required to take part in order to receive federal funding. FEMA coordinates the Mobile Emergency Response System, which operates communication equipment for local and state efforts during an emergency, as well as the Office of National Security Coordination Overview, which plans for continuity of operations of vital governmental functions during emergencies.

Border Security

A number of components of DHS are responsible for protecting the nation's borders, including the Transportation Security Administration (TSA), Customs and Border Protection (CBP), Immigration and Customs Enforcement (ICE), and the US Coast Guard (USCG). Combined, they comprise the bulk of DHS' man power and financial outlays with some 154,777 employees.

TSA is primarily tasked with securing the nation's transportation network.[47] The bulk of efforts are seen in the efforts within the nation's airports as screeners and also with the Federal Air Marshal program. However, TSA is also responsible for implementing the program that allows the arming of flight crews as well as the security of air cargo and airports. In addition, TSA operates a number of programs that deal with such diverse tasks as securing pipelines, railways, and other forms of mass transit. TSA has some 52,615 employees with a budget of $2.75 billion.[48]

CBP is comprised of some 42,000 employees with a budget of $6.7 billion in its efforts of protecting the borders of the United States. Its primary mission is "preventing terrorists and terrorist weapons from entering the United States, while also facilitating the flow of legitimate trade and travel."[49] In order to accomplish this mission, CBP deploys a vast array of technological and physical barriers that once were constituted within the former agencies of the US Customs, US Immigration, the Animal and Plant Health Inspection Service, and the US Border Patrol.

ICE is the primary investigation component of DHS and is comprised of approximately 15,000 employees and a budget of $3.65 billion[50] within an administrative section and four operational components – the Federal Protective Service, Office of Investigations, Office of Detention and Removal, and the Office of Intelligence. The Office of Investigations focuses on a broad assortment of illegal activities including narcotics and weapons smuggling, human trafficking, money laundering and terrorist financing, as well as other cross border crimes. The Federal Protective Service provides protection to governmental buildings. The Office of Detention and Removal investigates and deports illegal aliens within the United States. The Office of Intelligence provides broad based intelligence assets to ICE and DHS in general. The overall mission of ICE is to "detect and prevent terrorist and criminal acts by targeting the people, money, and materials that support terrorist and criminal networks."[51]

The last border security agency within DHS discussed here is the USCG. In addition to its role in search and rescue operations, the USCG is the primary maritime law enforcement and border security agency and the lead federal agency for maritime homeland security. USCG is tasked with, by the Homeland Security Act of 2002, port, waterways, and coastal security; drug interdiction; migrant interdiction; defense readiness and; other law enforcement activities (environmental protections, marine safety, aids to navigation, etc.).[52]

The USCG is composed of approximately 47,000 employees with a budget of $7.58 billion.[53] Since its pre 9/11 status as part of the Department of Transportation, the Coast Guard has undergone a fundamental shift as represented in its transition to DHS and its increased role in homeland security operations. Prior to the terrorist attacks, port security operations amounted to less than 2 percent of its activities whereas immediately after port security consumed 56 percent of its operations.[54] In addition, the Coast Guard has had to increase its operational tempo to take on new homeland security taskings.[55]

Department of Defense

While DHS is the primary department responsible for homeland security within the nation, DOD has the second largest role and houses a number of key components that are important to the overall goal of protecting the homeland from terrorist threats as well as assisting in the recovery from national disasters. This role is an important one, particularly after the events of September 11 2001 and the devastation left by Hurricane Katrina and Rita in 2005. Often, DOD is the only agency within the US government capable of ramping up operations within the time frame required to forestall further damage and assuring domestic safety. However, because of the role assigned to DOD by US Law and the sensitive nature of operating military forces domestically, DOD is constrained a great deal in what it can and cannot do.

The Posse Comitatus Act is the principal legal impediment to the use of the armed forces in performing the task of civilian government. A number of exceptions are legislated within the laws, however. For example, the military can share equipment and intelligence, as well as training, with civilian authorities. The military has also been used for the enforcement of immigration, drug and border laws. The military can be used to suppress insurrection or assist state governments, upon request by the governor, to perform emergency work. What the act prohibits is the use of the Army or the Air Force to execute the law. This has been interpreted to mean that the military should not participate in searches, seizures, arrests or other civilian police functions except under exceptional circumstances during national emergency. The court test of violation of the act rests on the concept of "active" or "passive" support by the military. Active functions are prohibited whereas passive are not.

The Department of Defense has extended this tradition to cover the Navy and the Marine Corps in the spirit of the act. Thus, the true nature of DOD's limitations is more of tradition and over time interpretation of these limitations in the courts and through congressional legislation have increasingly become less stringent. For example, the erosion of posse comitatus is demonstrated in the use of federal troops in the security of major sporting events, or through the Stafford Act. As DOD's role in homeland security has become more pronounced so has the abandonment of these limitations.[56]

The primary mission of DOD, in a homeland security sense, is to confront the nation's enemies away from its shores; however, this is not always possible. Internal to the United States, DOD's role can be broken down into two components – Homeland defense and Military Assistance to Civilian Authorities (MACA).[57] Homeland defense involves what one would consider the traditional role of military forces in protecting the homeland. The Combat Air Patrols over major cities within the United States and the deployment of troops within the nation's airports after the September 11 attacks is probably the most readily recalled example of the homeland defense role in action.

Homeland security within the United States is considered the domain of civilian federal, state, and local entities, thus relegating DOD's role as a support component to the civilian effort. It is in this role that the military's MACA protocols come into play. Most of the efforts in this regard have largely been weighted towards specialized units designed to manage the consequences of CBR and/or terrorist attacks.[58] However, the call up of DOD units to support civilian authorities can occur for a multitude of reasons, including disaster relief, counter drug and counter terrorism, as well as any other contingency that may require the specialized and disciplined forces the military has to offer. As a general role, DOD provides resources to state and local efforts only when requested and with the understanding that state and local resources cannot handle the contingency requirements.[59] National Guard forces, under Title 32 status, are not included within this general rule.

US Northern Command

As part of DOD's response to the renewed emphasis on homeland security, the US Northern Command was created to: 1) "conduct operations to deter, prevent, and defeat threats and aggression aimed at the United States, its territories and interest within assigned areas of responsibility;" 2) "as directed by the President or Secretary of Defense, provides military assistance to civil authorities, including consequence management operations."[60] NORTHCOM is designed to facilitate the use of US forces within the continental United States as required and thus has few operational forces attached to its command; however, it brings units as needed from other commands in order to fulfill its mission.

The headquarters unit for NORTHCOM is co-located and co- led, with NORAD in Colorado Springs thus utilizing NORAD's functions as part of its overall mission. In addition to the some 1,200 personnel that comprise the headquarters staff, the Domestic Watch Center, "the commands eyes and ears, detecting and assessing land and maritime threats and reporting them,"[61] is also located here. In addition, Standing Joint Forces Headquarters North, Joint Task Force North, Joint Task Force Civil

Support and Joint Force Headquarters National Capital Region fall under the umbrella of NORTHCOM.[62] All together, these resources represent approximately 6,800 civilian and military employees.

NORTHCOM works through a joint interagency coordination group (JIACG) in order to facilitate its role within the broader homeland security structure.[63] This group is comprised of representative from various DOD commands as well as pertinent federal agencies. In addition, NORTHCOM has permanently assigned personnel within DHS.

National Guard

The National Guard within the United States has a unique role that provides unique abilities not available to other DOD components. As both a state asset, under Title 32, and a national asset, under Title 10, the guard can operate at the state level, at the behest of the governor, or it can operate within the federal system when required. Operating at the state level places Guard units in the familiar territory of their home states and under state jurisdiction – not under the confines of the Posse Comitatus Act. With some 3,000 locations throughout the United States, the Guard is well placed to react in case of emergency. Total Guard levels are approximately 353,000 in the Army National Guard and 108,000 in the Air National Guard.[64]

Intelligence

The United States has 15 intelligence components that all have a role in homeland security to various levels. These include components in the four branches of the military and the Coast Guard, the Central Intelligence Agency, Defense Intelligence Agency, elements within DHS, Energy Department, FBI, National Geospatial Intelligence Agency, National Reconnaissance Office, National Security Agency, the State Department and Treasury Department. While federal statutes regulate the intrusion of these components into domestic society at various levels, the coordinated efforts of the whole are important to the overall efforts at protecting the nation.

The Intelligence Reform and Terrorism Prevention Act of 2004 created the position of Director of National Intelligence (DNI) with the responsibility of coordinating the efforts of the intelligence community and acting as the principal intelligence advisor to the President and the National Security Council.[65] However, the debate over the creation of the position had been an ongoing one since at least the second Hoover Commission in 1955.[66] Over the years, a number of Commissions and Congressional proposals have surfaced including a thwarted effort at legislation to that effect in 1992.[67] The 9/11 Commission recommended its formation, as well as the formation of the National Counterterrorism Center, in its final report. This appeared to be the impetus for change within the overall intelligence system.

The most recent, and ultimately successful, public debate for the formation of the DNI began with the 107th Congress and ended with the passage of Public Law 108-458

– The Intelligence Reform and Terrorism Prevention Act of 2004. Arguments in favor of the position centered on the need for coordination across the intelligence committee and the inability of the Director of Central Intelligence to exert the level of control over the other communities, particularly DOD.[68] Arguments against the formation of the DNI ranged from the added bureaucracy that the position would entail to the fact that the role would have had no affect on the outcome of the September 11 2001 attacks.

The DNI was granted a great deal of authority above what the Director of Central Intelligence wielded as the head of the nation's Intelligence agencies.[69] Perhaps most importantly, the DNI can determine how money is budgeted, allotted and disbursed amongst the agencies. In addition, the DNI can transfer money and personnel between agencies as well as limited appointment, acquisition and tasking authority over the various agencies within his purview. The DNI wields a great deal of control over the National Counterterrorism Center which was formed at the same time.

National Counterterrorism Center (NCTC)

Formed in 2004, NCTC:

> serves as the primary organization in the US Government for analyzing and integrating all intelligence possessed or acquired by the US Government pertaining to terrorism and counter terrorism, excepting intelligence pertaining exclusively to domestic terrorists and domestic counterterrorism. The NCTC also conducts strategic operational planning for counterterrorism activities, integrating all instruments of national power, including diplomatic, financial, military, intelligence, homeland security, and law enforcement activities within and among agencies."[70]

Members of the NCTC come from throughout the government.

The formation of the NCTC began as a recommendation of the 9/11 Commission final report. The Commission recommended an agency that would combine intelligence and joint operational planning across the intelligence community in order to correct some of the pre 9/11 issues of disjointness of effort that was the hallmark of intelligence up until that point.[71] Particularly, there was perceived to be a lack of communication between domestic and foreign intelligence efforts that was exacerbated by agencies jealous of their territory. In addition, because of the relative weakness of the Director of Central Intelligence over the other intelligence agencies, little or no coordination of effort existed on an operational or analytical side.

In order to remedy these issues President George W. Bush signed executive order 13354 in August of 2004 and the US Congress included provisions for the NCTC in the Intelligence Reform and Terrorism Prevention Act of 2004. The NCTC was given a broad mandate as outlined by the White House:

1) Support the development and coordination of US Government action plans, ensuring that individual departments and agencies receive the all-source intelligence support needed to execute their plans to counter terrorist threats against the US and US interests.

2) Serve as the principal US Government coordinator for plans and monitor action plans of the agencies and departments for the collection of terror-related intelligence and to counter terror threats against the United States and its interests and, as appropriate, the interests of its friends and allies.

3) Concentrate analytical expertise on foreign and domestic terrorism in one location and assure the flow of alternative analytic views, to the extent they exist in the Center and among agencies and departments, to policymakers, including to the President. Agencies and departments are to retain sufficient analytic expertise on counterterrorism to support their unique operational missions.

4) Prepare the President's Terrorist Threat Report (PTTR) and a range of other Integrated analytic products on terrorism.

5) Support the National Security Council's preparation of the national counterterrorism strategy, which will be coordinated with the Homeland Security Council.

6) Help identify and coordinate intelligence requirements on terror targets both overseas and at home.

7) Serve as the US Government's central and shared knowledge bank on known and suspected terrorists and international terror groups, as well as their goals, strategies, capabilities, and networks of contacts and support.

8) Coordinate counterterrorism plans and ensure all source intelligence support for counterterrorism operational planning efforts underway in the departments and agencies of government.

9) As necessary, coordinate the prioritization of and interagency law enforcement or counterterrorism response to terrorist threats, and de-conflict and track the actions of the United States Government as currently done by the interagency Counterterrorism Security Group.[72]

State and Local Roles

State and local officials are considered the primary responders for any homeland security issues. It is the police, medical and fire services that are usually the first on the scene and first to know if an incident is beyond their ability to handle. The National Response plan recognizes the role that state and local officials play, as well as the role of the governor and local elected officials during an emergency.[73] The Governor of each state is responsible for "the public safety and welfare of the people of that State or territory. The Governor is responsible for coordinating State resources to address the full spectrum of actions to prevent, prepare for, respond to, and recover from incidents in an all-hazards context to include terrorism, natural disasters, accidents, and other contingencies."[74] As such, each state has an agency responsible for homeland security concerns. In addition to coordinating state and local efforts, these state agencies often act as the primary conduit for appropriating federal grants into specific state and local efforts.

Likewise, the mayors and local leaders within the state act as the principal leaders for assuring their communities are prepared for homeland security related incidents by developing and implementing the recommendations and resources that are handed down from federal and state levels.

Conclusion

Since the September 11 2001 terrorist attacks against the United States, the structure and focus of homeland security has shifted significantly from primarily counter terrorism to one of a more all hazards approach to the concept. Thus, the evolution of homeland security from its pre-9/11 disjointed effort to the post 9/11 coordinated focus for all hazards has created an effective yet still evolving and sometimes misunderstood system. The many disparate parts that were pieced together in the post 9/11 environment have been forced to coordinate efforts.

Prior to 9/11, the homeland security efforts within the United States were performed by many different agencies across departments in a competitive environment rich with territorial mentality and no real history of coordinated efforts. The example for how this situation may have contributed to the failure to detect an impending attack cited most perhaps is the inability of the nation's intelligence agencies to "connect the dots" before the terrorists could attack.

After the attacks, the nation was understandable focused on how to protect against further events. Thus, the formation of first, the Office of Homeland Security and finally, the Department of Homeland Security was a concerted effort to place all of the assets of the United States under a common umbrella. This was apparently effective except the nature of the system dampened efforts outside of counter terrorism leaving a weakened FEMA to face the worst natural disaster in the history of the United States, as represented by Hurricane Katrina in August of 2005. Further, a number of recommendations that were made in the 9/11 final report were left out of the Homeland Security Act of 2002. Most notably, DHS had no broad policy component and the Intelligence capabilities of DHS were not capable of performing their intended tasks.

With the Second Stage Review process in early 2005 and in reflection of the weakness of FEMA, DHS has once again been reformed in order to better represent an all hazards approach to homeland security. In addition to the formation of the position of Director of National Intelligence, DHS has separated its intelligence component in order to allow a more focused effort in that regard. DHS has also formed a policy directorate and separated FEMA from preparedness, tasking more toward a focus on response and recovery. These changes, coupled with the formation of the military's Northern Command, should ease the bureaucratic hurdles faced immediately after 9/11 and Hurricane Katrina.

The problem, of course, is that the best test for these many changes will be another terrorist attack or natural disaster. Until that point, we can only hope the nation has adequately prepared to the best of its abilities. As discussed in Chapter Five, the federal system that exists today means that there are broad differences between how states prepare for homeland security threats. While the government can recommend and lure states into compliance with federal grants, the ability to coordinate across federal-state lines often means elected governors must show apparent weakness in the face of potential tragedy. Likewise, federal agencies have often been hesitant to step out of the support role and into the lead role because of tradition and the assumed primacy of the state in all matters of domestic emergency management. Much of the federal and state systems for meeting emergencies has been planned and worked out. What is in question at times is leadership and the willingness to act.

Notes

1. National Strategy for Homeland Security, *DHS*, July 2002, includes a section on organizing for homeland security.
2. For further reading see Ronald J. Daniels, Donald F. Kettl and Howard Kunreuther (eds), *On Risk and Disaster: Lessons from Hurricane Katrina* (Philadelphia, PA: University of Pennsylvania Press, 2006); Evan Thomas, "The Lost City; What Went Wrong: Devastating a Swath of the South, Katrina Plunged New Orleans into Agony. The story or a storm – and a disastrously slow rescue," *Newsweek* 12 September 2005; John Brown Childs (ed.), *Hurricane Katrina: Response and Responsibilities* (Santa Cruz, CA: New Pacific Press, 2005).
3. "Department of Homeland Security Reorganization: The 2SR Initiative," *CRS Report RL33042*, 19 August 2005.
4. "Homeland Security Oversight," *The Washington Post*, 28 December 2004;
5. "National Security Council," http://www.whitehouse.gov/nsc/; The National Security Council was established by the National Security Act of 1947 (PL 235 – 61 Stat. 496; U.S.C. 402) and amended by the National Security Act Amendments of 1949 (63 Stat. 579; 50 U.S.C. 401 et seq.).
6. Officially titled the Assistant to the President for National Security Affairs.
7. Raphael Perl, "Terrorism and National Security: Issues and Trends," *CRS Issue Brief IB1011*, 21 December 2004.
8. Harold C. Relyea, "Homeland Security: The Presidential Coordination Office," *CRS Report RL31148*, 30 March 2004.
9. Homeland Security Act of 2002, P.L. 107-296.
10. "History: Who Became Part of the Department," as viewed at http://www.dhs.gov/dhspublic/ interapp/editorial/ editorial_0133.xml.
11. Harold C. Relyea, "Homeland Security: Department Organization and Management-Implementation Phase," *CRS Report RL31751*, 3 January 2005. Describes the transition from legislation to active department.

12. Susan B. Glasser and Michael Grunwald, "Department Mission Was Undermined From Start," *The Washington Post*, 22 December 2005.

13. "Secretary Michael Chertoff U.S. Department of Homeland Security Second Stage Review Remarks," *DHS Press Release* 13 July 2005.

14. DHS issued a six point agenda for the ongoing refinement of the department that included the following: 1) Increase overall preparedness, particularly for catastrophic events; 2) Create better transportation security systems to move people and cargo more securely and efficiently; 3) Strengthen border security and interior enforcement and reform immigration processes; 4) Enhance information sharing with our partners; 5) Improve DHS financial management, human resource development, procurement and information technology; 6) Realign the DHS organization to maximize mission performance. Available at *www.dhs.gov.*

15. "Homeland Security Advisory Council Charter," available at http://www.dhs.gov/ interweb/assetlibrary/HSAC_Charter.pdf.

16. A list of the reports of the Homeland Security Advisory Council is at http://www.dhs.gov/ dhspublic/interapp/editorial/editorial_0331.xml.

17. "Charter of the National Infrastructure Advisory Council," available at http://www.dhs.gov/interweb/assetlibrary/NIAC_Charter.pdf.

18. A list of the reports from the National Infrastructure Advisory Council is found at http://www.dhs.gov/dhspublic/interapp/editorial/editorial_0353.xml.

19. Originally the Information Analysis and Infrastructure Protection Directorate, this component of DHS was renamed as well as retooled in 2005 as per the second stage review.

20. "Directorate for Preparedness", As viewed at http://www.dhs.gov/dhspublic/ interapp/editorial/editorial_0794.xml.

21. "Secretary Michael Chertoff U.S. Department of Homeland Security Second Stage Review Remarks," *DHS Press Release* 13 July 2005.

22. Matt Pueschel, "New National Medical Chief Will Lead Homeland Bioterrorism Defense Expert," *U.S. Medicine* September 2005; "Directorate for Preparedness", As viewed at http://www.dhs.gov/dhspublic/interapp/editorial/editorial_0794.xml.

23. As viewed at http://www.usfa.fema.gov/about/.

24. This task was originally part of the Office of Domestic Preparedness.

25. Robert B. Stephan, "Statement of Assistant Secretary for Infrastructure Protection Robert B. Stephan U.S. Department of Homeland Security Before the Economic Security, Infrastructure Protection, and Cyber Security Subcommittee of the House Homeland Security Committee", 20 October 2005, http://homeland.house.gov/ files/Testimony Stephan.pdf; "Office of National Capital Region Coordination," http://www.dhs.gov.

26. As listed at http://www.dhs.gov/dhspublic/interapp/editorial/editorial_0530.xml.

27. http://www.hsarpabaa.com/.

28. The two offices work on such technologies as communications and biodefense; they operate the US nuclear labs and develop the protocols for CBR response.

29. Charles Allen, "Written Statement of Charles Allen Chief Intelligence Officer of Department of Homeland Security House Committee on Homeland Security Subcommittee on Intelligence, Information Sharing and Terrorism Risk Assessment and House Permanent Select Committee on Intelligence Subcommittee on Terrorism/HUMINT,

Analysis and Counterintelligence, 19 October 2005; this office was formed when the directorate of intelligence analysis and infrastructure protection was split upon recommendation of the second stage review in July of 2005.

30. "Allen: Chief Intelligence Officer," *The Washington Post*, 11 January 2006.

31. p. 427.

32. "Intelligence and Information Analysis within the Department of Homeland Security," Prepared Statement of Richard Ben-Veniste, Member of the 9/11 Commission, *US House of Representatives*, 19 October 2005.

33. Charles Allen written statement, 19 October 2005.

34. "National Response Plan," *DHS*, December 2004.

35. "Fact sheet: Homeland Security Operations Center," http://www.dhs.gov/dhspublic/ display?content=3814; "National Response Plan."

36. James Jay Carafano, Richard Weitz, and Alan Kochens, "Department of Homeland Security Needs Under Secretary for Policy," *The Heritage Foundation*, Backgrounder #1788, 17 August 2004.

37. Available online at http://www.dhs.gov/dhspublic/interapp/editorial/editorial_0795.xml.

38. "Domestic Nuclear Detection Office," available athttp://www.dhs.gov/ dhspublic/interapp/ editorial/_editorial_0766.xml; "Domestic Nuclear Detection Office," *Statement by the Honorable Fred C. Ikle before the Committee on Homeland Security Subcommittee on the Prevention of Nuclear and Biological Attack House of Representatives*, 19 April 2005. Because of the voluntary nature of cooperation amongst departments in this area, Ikle has testified that while the creation of the DNDO is a good step more is needed in order to make sure that it does not turn into a purely discussion orientated platform.

39. NSPD-43; HSPD-14.

40. "Domestic Nuclear Detection Office Organization," http://www.dhs.gov/ dhspublic/ interapp/ editorial/editorial_0767.xml.

41. James Jay Carafano, "The Truth About FEMA: Analysis and Proposal," *The Heritage Foundation*, Backgrounder #1901, 7 December 2005.

42. Keith Bea, "Urban Search and Rescue Task Forces: Facts and Issues," *CRS Report RS21073*, 10 January 2005.

43. As viewed at http://www.ndms.fema.gov/.

44. According to several reports, NDMS is seriously under budgeted for its mission and lacks key abilities. Jeffrey A. Lowell, "Medical Readiness Responsibilities and Capabilities: A Strategy for Realigning and Strengthening the Federal Medical Response," *DHS*, 3 January 2005.

45. "Mitigating Catastrophic Events Through Effective Medical Response," Testimony of Roy L. Alson, Ph.D., MD, FACEP Before the House Committee on Homeland Security Subcommitte on Prevention of Nuclear and Biological Attack.

46. "National Incident Management System," *DHS*, 1 March 2004.

47. TSA was formed with the Aviation and Transportation Security Act, Public Law 107-71, 19 November 2001.

48. Blas Nunez-Neto, "Border Security: Key Agencies and Their Missions," *CRS Report RS21899*, 9 May 2005.

49. "Protecting Our Borders Against Terrorism," *US Customs and Border Security,* http://www.cbp.gov/xp/cgov/toolbox/about/mission/cbp.xml.

50. *CRS Report RS21899.*

51. *Ibid.*

52. Ronald O'Rourke, "Homeland Security: Coast Guard Operations-Background and Issues for Congress," *CRS Report RS21125,* 30 June 2005..

53. *Ibid.* USCG has a reserve component of approximately 33,000.

54. Bruce Stubbs, "Where to Place the U.S. Coast Guard for Success in the Department of Homeland Security," *The Heritage Foundation,* Backgrounder #1586, 11 September 2002.

55. Ronald O'Rourke, "Homeland Security: Coast Guard Operations – Background and Issues for Congress," *CRS Report RS21125.*

56. Craig T. Trebilcock, "The Myth of Posse Comitatus," *Journal of Homeland Security* (October 2000); John R. Brinkerhoff, "The Posse Comitatus Act and Homeland Security," *Journal of Homeland Security* (February 2002); Charles Doyle and Jennifer Elsea, "Terrorism: Some Legal Restrictions on Military Assistance to Domestic Authorities Following a Terrorist Attack," *CRS Report RS21012,* 27 May 2005.

57. For the relevant directives dealing with the Militaries role in homeland security see appendix c and d of Eric V. Larson and John E. Peters, *Preparing the U.S. Army for Homeland Security: Concepts, Issues, and Options,* Rand Corporation, report MR-1251-A, 2001.

58. Steven J. Tomisek, "Homeland Security: The New Role for Defense," *Strategic Forum,* 189 (February 2002).

59. "DoD Roles and Missions in Homeland Security: Volume II-A: Supporting Reports," *Defense Science Board 2003 Summer Study,* May 2004; The three mechanism by which DOD supports domestic operations are 1) at the direction of the president; 2) Secretary of Homeland Security declares an Incident of National Significance; 3) Request of a Governor in accordance with the Stafford Act. Scott Shepherd and Steve Bowman, "Homeland Security: Establishment and Implementation of the United States Northern Command," *CRS Report RS21322,* 10 February 2005.

60. "Who We Are~ Mission: http://www.northcom.mil.

61. Merrie Schilter-Lowe, "USNORTHCOM and NORAD-Parners in Defending the Homeland," *Homeland Defense Journal* 2:11 (December 2004).

62. Scott Shepherd and Steve Bowman, "Homeland Security."

63. Harold Kennedy, "U.S. Northern Command Actively Enlisting Partners," *National Defense* (June 2004).

64. This does not include the Reserves as they are not Title 32 forces.

65. "Appendix C: An Intelligence Community Primer," http://www.gpoaccess.gov/wmd/pdf/appendix_c_fm.pdf.

66. Alfred Cumming, "The Position of Director of National Intelligence: Issues for Congress," *CRS Report RL32506,* 12 August 2004.

67. *Ibid.*

68. *Ibid.*

69. Richard Best, Jr., Alfred Cumming, and Todd Masse, "Director of National Intelligence: Statutory Authorities," *CRS Report RS22112,* 11 April 2005.

70. Appendix C: An Intelligence Community Primer.
71. Todd Masse, "The 9/11 Commission and a National Counterterrorism Center: Issues and Options for Congress," *CRS Report RL32558*, 3 September 2004.
72. "Fact Sheet: Making America Safer by Strengthening Our Intelligence Capabilities," *White House Press Release*, 2 August 2004.
73. "National Response Plan," *DHS*, October 2004.
74. *Ibid.*

Chapter 5

Homeland Security Policies and Processes

Introduction

The framers of the US Constitution sought to develop a governmental system that forestalled the rise of tyranny. From experiences related to the American Revolution and the broad political philosophy which undergirded the drive for independence from Great Britain, early US leaders imbued the nation's politics with a deep and abiding mistrust of government. One manifestation of this trend was the division of powers among the three main branches of the federal government and the broader division of authority between the national and state governments. Indeed, the early history of the United States was marked by a constant struggle to define the relationship and division of power between the national government and the states.[1] As noted in Chapter Two, "Evolution of Homeland Security," the constant territorial expansion of the United States further complicated the security relationship between the federal government and the states, even though the Supremacy Clause of the Constitution established the primacy of the federal government. By reserving powers not expressly granted to the central government for the states, the Tenth Amendment continued to serve as a means to ensure a state role in domestic security.

In the modern period of the American history, questions over role and scope of federal, state and local authorities in domestic security continue to bedevil policymakers. Efforts to establish clear and coherent counterterrorism policies, and implement effective homeland security measures, remain complicated by varying capabilities and priorities among the different levels of government within the United States. In addition, the balance between local autonomy and national goals has added an further complication in the quest to develop capable homeland security polices and resources. In the immediate aftermath of the September 11 attacks, wide disparities among states and localities emerged (just as there were revealed great variations among federal agencies). On the federal level, the creation of the Department of Homeland Security was the first major post-September 11 initiative to coordinate across federal agencies and state and local bodies. Concurrently, there were a range of proposals and legislation which sought to ensure that states had adequate homeland security resources and planning and that these capabilities matched the often unique challenges facing states. However, it quickly became apparent that state and local homeland security infrastructure would remain uneven and subject to the ongoing complications of federalism and vagrancies of local politics. The ultimate result in the

US has been the evolution of a homeland security system that at its best is highly flexible and capable of responding to the specific local challenges of individual states and cities, but at its worst is marked by disparate planning, leadership and abilities to respond to threats, whether those threats are manifested through international terrorism or even natural disasters.

The First Line of Defense

Local law enforcement and emergency response personnel, commonly referred to as "first responders," are described by the Department of Homeland Security as the nation's "first line of defense in any terrorist attack."[2]   Given the nature of superterrorist strikes such as those of 11 September, local and state law enforcement are the most likely actors to forestall attacks, while local and state emergency responders would provide the initial governmental reaction. The National Commission on Terrorist Attacks Upon the United States (commonly known as the 9/11 Commission) stated that "On the morning of September 11, 2001, the last best hope for the community of people working in or visiting the World Trade Center rested not with national policymakers but with private firms and local public servants, especially the first responders: fire, police, emergency medical service, and building safety professionals."[3]   For instance, the Commission reports that the New York Fire Department's response to the attacks began within "five seconds of the crash" of the first plane.[4] In a summary of the New York City's first responder response, the Commission noted the accomplishments of the city's emergency response workers: "In the 17-minute period between 8:46 and 9:03 A.M. on September 11, New York City and the Port Authority of New York and New Jersey had mobilized the largest rescue operation in the city's history. Well over a thousand first responders had been deployed, an evacuation had begun, and the critical decision that the fire could not be fought had been made."[5]

Few local emergency response systems had, or have, the capabilities of New York. In addition, the New York system had undergone a series of reforms in the wake of the first World Trade Center bombings in February 1993. That attack revealed problems with the communications abilities of first responders and command and control issues. Furthermore, the city's evacuation plans and such basic necessities as power sources and fire suppression equipment were found to be inadequate. To address these issues, $100 million was spent on infrastructure upgrades to the area and new positions were created to better coordinate command and control issues.[6] The magnitude of the 2001 attacks would identify further flaws, but in many regards, those attacks occurred in the US city that was best capable of responding.

The result of the combination of system and planning improvements, the high skill levels and bravery of the city's first responders, and the exceptional leadership among the city government and first response system, significantly reduced the casualties. For instance, the 9/11 Commission concludes that the improvements undertaken after the initial attacks in 1993, reduced the evacuation time from the buildings from four hours to under one hour for most civilians not specifically trapped.[7] In overall terms, the Commission affirmed that the evacuation worked very well:

> The National Institute of Standards and Technology has provided a preliminary estimation that between 16,400 and 18,800 civilians were in the WTC complex as of 8:46 A.M. on September 11. At most 2,152 individuals died at the WTC complex who were not (1) fire or police first responders, (2) security or fire safety personnel of the WTC or individual companies, (3) volunteer civilians who ran to the WTC after the planes' impact to help others, or (4) on the two planes that crashed into the Twin Towers. Out of this total number of fatalities, we can account for the workplace location of 2,052 individuals, or 95.35 percent. Of this number, 1,942 or 94.64 percent either worked or were supposed to attend a meeting at or above the respective impact zones of the Twin Towers; only 110, or 5.36 percent of those who died, worked below the impact zone. While a given person's office location at the WTC does not definitively indicate where that individual died that morning or whether he or she could have evacuated, these data strongly suggest that the evacuation was a success for civilians below the impact zone.[8]

New York City has resources and personnel which exceed those of any other local government in the United States. In September 2001, the city's regular police department numbered 40,000 (there were an additional 1,300 Port Authority police officers divided among nine areas, including the World Trade Center), while there were 11,000 firefighters divided into 205 engine companies and 133 ladder companies.[9] After 11 September, the city created a deputy commissioner of intelligence to oversee counterterrorism programs.[10] It also implemented new training and emergency response systems, including initiatives designed to enhance communications and command and control. For example, in July 2001, Mayor Rudolf ("Rudy") Giuliani issued a memo to clarify the roles of the police and fire departments in the event of terrorist attacks.[11] The city also has a counterterrorism task force with more than 130 officers. This body is closely integrated with federal agencies and its personnel are routinely sent overseas for training with international bodies and to study the anti-terrorism methods and tactics utilized by other countries.[12]

Resources and Capabilities

Few municipalities (and more than a few states) do not have the resources or capabilities of New York to respond to a disaster, whether that incident is a terrorist strike or a natural disaster. The Department of Homeland Security reports that in the United States there are more than one million firefighters (including about 750,000 volunteers), local or municipal police agencies have 556,000 personnel (of which 436,000 are police officers). In addition, sheriff's departments have approximately 291,000 personnel (of which 186,000 are sworn officers). There are also more than 155,000 registered Emergency Medical Technicians (EMTs) out of an estimated

900,000 full- and part-time EMTs and paramedics.[13] These first responders must protect and manage crises in 75 major metropolitan areas and 3,540,000 square miles of territory (along with 12,383 miles of coastline) and the "responsibility" for homeland security will, as Brookings Institution Senior Fellow Pietro S. Nivola noted in a report, "rest in large part with local agencies that are closest, so to speak, to the facts on the ground."[14]

Prior to 11 September, many of these first responders were already overworked and tasked with a variety of missions and operations that strained capabilities. Following the attack, a range of additional duties and responsibilities were added to all state and local agencies. Although some missions were not entirely new, the potential for catastrophic terrorism gave new impetus, or new responsibilities, to the state and local governments. Among the increased responsibilities were new emphases on: 1) border security; 2) transportation security; 3) maritime security; 4) the identification and management of potential biological, chemical or nuclear attacks; and finally; 5) enhanced emergency management planning and disaster response.[15]

As new directives and national plans were developed to improve homeland security, local and state governments needed additional personnel and resources to accomplish the increased responsibilities. For instance, after the attacks on New York and Washington, the added security costs borne by major cities were enormous. Boston spent $100,000 more per week on overtime, while Baltimore had an unanticipated $2.6 million in security expenditures. By year's end, Dallas had spent an additional $6 million and New Orleans an extra $10 million.[16] In the first year after the attacks, estimates are that the 50 states spent a combined $650 million on homeland security, while individual cities spent approximately $525 million.[17]

Federal Mandates and Local Resources

Only the federal government possessed the resources necessary to enact the improvements in homeland security called for by the public and government officials following the 2001 terrorist strikes. In the days after the attacks, Congress spared little expense in both the effort to recover from the attacks and the concurrent struggle against Al Qaeda. In a chapter on the evolution of terrorism, John Weinzierl points out that the US reaction to the terrorist strikes was unmatched. He writes that:

> This unprecedented national response to the modern terrorist threat represents a new course for US security. Congress appropriated a $40 billion Emergency Response Fund to wage war against al-Qaeda, help efforts to rebuild New York and Virginia, compensate victim, and strengthen home defenses. A total of $10 billion was dedicated to homeland security for such things as increased security for airports, nuclear facilities, dams, and bridges; employment of sky marshals on airlines; production of vaccines; installation of detection equipment in major mail sorting facilities; and many other measures.[18]

Comprehensive estimates of spending on homeland security are difficult to finalize. Figures from the Government Accounting Office (GAO) estimate that the US spent about $11 billion in 2004 to fund non-military counterterrorism efforts around the world. For fiscal 2006, the Department of Homeland Security was given appropriations of $30.8 billion.[19] In 2006, the Department will distribute $3.6 billion (about 11 percent of its total budget) to states in the form of Homeland Security grants and assistance. To put this in perspective, in 1995, the US spent about $9 billion for homeland security. That figure steadily increased, rising to $10.5 billion 1998, $13.2 billion in 2000 and $16 billion in 2001 (the budget prior to the attacks).[20]

In spite of the increased federal funding, states and localities are hard-pressed to meet the additional spending requirements of homeland security. A 2004 study of localities in Florida revealed that the financial costs of homeland security mandates and polices was the number one concern of officials, followed by the administrative burdens created by new missions and policies.[21] Many state and local officials argue that the increased expenditures necessitated by homeland security legislation amount to an unfair burden from the federal government. One continuing source of tension between state and local governments on the one hand, and the national government on the other, is the issue of unfunded mandates. Unfunded mandates are laws or policies enacted by Congress which require states or localities to adopt policies but fail to provide funding, or adequate funding, to cover the costs of the programs.

In 1995, Congress enacted the Unfunded Mandates Reform Act which required the Legislature to debate whether the costs were worth the benefits of any mandate passed on to state and local governments if the costs to those entities would exceed $50 million over a five-year period. Officially, since the passage of the bill, only five mandates have been passed on to the states. However, David Broder notes that Congress often sidesteps the law by simply declaring that federal programs are outside of the requirement. As a result, programs such as Medicaid and the No Child Left Behind initiative, both of which require significant local funding, are not subject to the Unfunded Mandates Reform Act.[22] In an analysis of the legislation, the General Accounting Office (GAO) found that since 2001 43 laws and 65 rules have funding requirements that would be considered unfunded mandates.[23] One result is that the National Conference of State Legislatures has identified some $29 billion in unfunded mandates, including requirements for spending on homeland security.[24] For instance, some aspects of the USA Patriot Act contained components which preempted some state liability laws and restricted the ability of states to issue licenses to transport hazardous materials (including transport by state bodies).[25] Local officials have also complained that required security improvements to airports and ports amount to unfunded mandates since Congress has not allocated sufficient funds to cover the costs of the upgrades.

A principal example of homeland security costs borne by state and local entities involves overtime pay for first responders during periods of heightened security. In 2003, the Department of Homeland Security provided the states with $1.5 billion "to help state and local law enforcement personnel pay for equipment, planning, training and exercises and to offset costs associated with enhanced security measures deployed during heightened threat periods."[26] Under the current federal guidelines, the Department of Homeland Security allocates about 40 percent of its first responder grant budget so that each state receives 0.75 percent of the total (territories and dependencies receive a smaller percentage) funding distributed to the states. The remaining 60 percent of the total is divided by population. The Congressional Research Service highlights the disparities created under the current system. In 2005, Wyoming received $13.9 million in homeland security funding (which with a population of 498,703 meant that that state received $27.80 per capita). Meanwhile, New York received $298.3 million (but with a population of 19,157,532, that equated to $15.54 per capita).[27] Other examples of such imbalances would be North Dakota with $14.3 million in homeland security funding, or $23.83 per capita, versus Florida with $101.3 million, or $6.07 per capita.[28]

Several proposals for revisions of the grant system have been advocated. For instance, there have been calls for the 0.75 percent aid figure to be reduced and the excess funds remaining be distributed based on risk. Other proposals include targeting funding for "high-risk urban areas deemed at higher risk and at a greater threat of terrorist attacks."[29]

A range of officials at the national, state or local levels have repeatedly urged that homeland security funding be tied to risk. In its final report, the 9/11 Commission recommended that state funding be linked to vulnerabilities, including critical infrastructure, and to broader measures such as population density and economic resources. This recommendation was also echoed by various congressional committees.[30] However, proponents of the current system point to the inability of either the federal or state governments to create an accurate or useful risk assessment tool as justification to avoid a risk-based system. In addition, arguments against grant criteria being based on vulnerabilities include the assertion that efforts to strengthen one geographic area (without concurrent distribution of resources to other areas) would lead terrorists to seek out "other, softer, targets."[31]

Homeland Security Grant Programs

The Office for Domestic Preparedness (ODP) is the body within the Department of Homeland Security that is responsible for overseeing grants and assistance to states and localities. Initially, aid was dispensed to the states through six grant initiatives: 1) the State Homeland Security Grant Program (SHSGP); 2) the Law Enforcement Terrorism Prevention Program (LETPP); 3) the Urban Area Security Initiative (UASI); 4) the Metropolitan Medical Response System (MMRS); 5) Emergency Management Performance Grants (EMPG); and 6) the Citizen Corps Programs (CCP).[32] Each of these programs was designed to assist states in meeting specific needs. However, the disparate nature of the programs led to criticism that the grants were often disjointed and discouraged initiatives to improve capabilities across the broad spectrum. In addition, the six programs were seen as encouraging repetition and redundancy. In response, the ODP recommended and then Homeland Security Secretary Tom Ridge approved the consolidation of the six grants into a single program, the Homeland Security Grant Program (HSGP).[33] In past years, some states did not receive any funding through certain grant programs. For example, in 2005, Delaware, the District of Columbia, Idaho, Maine, Montana, New Mexico, North Dakota, South Dakota, Vermont, West Virginia and Wyoming did not receive any funding through the MMRS program. Furthermore, Alabama, Alaska, Arkansas, Connecticut, Delaware, Idaho, Iowa, Kansas, Maine, Mississippi, Montana, New Hampshire, New Mexico, North Dakota, Rhode Island, South Carolina, South Dakota, Utah, Vermont, Virginia, West Virginia and Wyoming did not receive funding through UASI.[34]

Yet the states and cities note that such funding comes in the form of grants and is often both less than what they spend during the alert periods and requires the local entities to choose among funding priorities. In addition, some funding has come at the costs of other programs, such as the Community-Oriented Policing Services (COPS) program (this Clinton-era program had provided money to hire 110,000 additional law enforcement personnel since 1995). In 2004, funding for the COPS program was reduced from $1.01 billion to $756 million. In 2005, the administration proposed for fiscal year 2006 further reductions in the COPS initiative and the elimination of a second grant program to hire police officers and fire fighters, the Justice Assistance Grant (JAG) program.[35]

In addition, there has been a steady decline in the total assistance provided to states for homeland security assistance. In 2003, states received $3.820 billion, but that figure declined to $3.795 billion in 2004 and $3.610 billion in 2005 (with a budget request by the Bush administration of $3.360 billion for fiscal year 2006).[36] At the federal level, there is widespread sentiment that large appropriations were appropriate in the immediate aftermath of the 2001 terrorist attacks, but as time as progressed, states and localities have been able to upgrade equipment and put in place the necessary assets to improve homeland security capabilities. However, reductions in assistance will likely impair the ability of states to meet goals set at the federal level (and encourage resistance by state and local leaders to continuing mandates from Washington).[37]

Homeland Security and State and Local Government

In the wake of the 1993 World Trade Center Bombing and the 1995 Oklahoma City Bombing, governors across the United States recognized terrorism as their main security concern.[38] In 1996, the National Governors Association (NGA) began including terrorism and response to terrorist attacks as part of their agenda during their regular meetings. A succession of commissions and reports forewarned of the potential for acts of catastrophic terrorism (sometimes referred to as "superterrorism").[39] Consequently, the 9/11 attacks were not entirely unique or unexpected, but rather the climax of a series of attacks through the decade of the 1990s. These earlier attacks led policymakers and officials to begin rethinking the notion of homeland security and the relationship between the states and the federal government on domestic security.[40]

Among the areas identified by state officials as a major problem was the divide between national security and state and local law enforcement. Writing in a joint-authored essay prior to the September 11 attacks, National Security Council member Philip Zelikow noted that:

> The law enforcement/national security divide is especially significant, carved deeply into the topography of the American government. The national security paradigm fosters aggressive, active intelligence gathering. It anticipates the threat before it arises and plans preventive action against suspected targets. In contrast, the law enforcement paradigm fosters reactions to information provided voluntarily, uses ex post facto arrests and trials governed by rules of evidence, and protects the rights of citizens.[41]

The NGA reported that the September 11 attacks, when combined with the subsequent domestic anthrax attacks, "led Governors to initiate unprecedented efforts to implement a comprehensive state-based strategy to prepare, prevent, respond and recover from terrorist attacks within their borders."[42] In addition to the loss of life and economic costs of the attacks, Deil S. Wright notes that the terrorist strikes "marked a tectonic shift, an off-the scale earthquake, that altered and continues to reshape developments in federalism/intergovernmental relations."[43]

By 2005, 50 percent of the states had made the head of the state homeland security system a cabinet-level position (although 26 percent of the state homeland security advisors have dual roles as the head of another agency or body in addition to being the leader of the homeland security department).[44] Among the most significant accomplishments cited by governors was the creation of state emergency response centers (done in 100 percent of the states) and the implementation of "mutual assistance agreements" with bordering states to share National Guard units and other homeland security assets (done by 94 percent of the states).[45] In addition, nearly all states have developed exercises to prepare for chemical, biological or nuclear attacks and a majority of states report finalizing plans to protect and recover critical infrastructure assets that are privately owned (ranging from power stations and refineries to telecommunications equipment to port facilities).[46] Overall, nine of every ten state chief executives report feeling comfortable with the structure and authority of their state homeland security agencies.[47]

Nonetheless, there remain a number of challenges and unmet needs among the states. Deil points out that the attacks occurred simultaneously with a significant downturn in the financial revenues of many states. For instance, in 2003, states faced combined revenue shortfalls of $50 billion. These declines were the culmination of broad-based tax reductions enacted by states in the 1990s, which reduced tax revenues by $40 billion and the economic slowdown that had preceded (but was accelerated by) the 11 September attacks. The tax reductions had been enacted during a period of spiraling growth so that even with the tax cuts, revenue from income taxes grew at an average of 9.1 percent between 1995 and 2000. However, in 2002, the revenues declined by 12 percent. Meanwhile, sales tax revenues had grown an average of 5.7

percent during this period, while in 2002, the increase was just 0.5 percent.[48] The constraints on state revenues were made much worse by the growth in entitlement programs, mainly Medicaid.[49] For instance, in 2001, Medicaid expenditures accounted for the largest growth items in city and state budgets (about 20 percent of total state expenditures, with predictions that the percentage will increase to 25 percent by 2008 and 30 percent by 2013).[50] Medicaid grew by 11 percent and outpaced expectations in 31 states. The following year, the program expanded by a further 13 percent and exceeded the budget projections in 36 states.[51] In light of the potential for catastrophic terrorism and the budget constraints faced by the individual states, the nation's governors sought to guide the evolution of homeland security in such a fashion as to ensure greater federal assistance to states and localities, especially through increased financial aid.

Both the federal and sub-federal levels of government share a common vision in which one of the national government's main functions in homeland security is as a coordinating body. The cornerstone of this coordination function has become the National Response Plan (NRP). Promulgated in December 2004, the NRP was designed to "to establish a comprehensive, national, all hazards approach to domestic incident management."[52] Simply put, the NRP was the federal government's plan to coordinate national, state, local and sub-local governments in the event of a major attack or natural disaster.

In addition to grants, the federal government has also provided a range of assistance to state and local governments. The Department of Homeland Security's Office of State and Local Government Coordination has overseen more than 400 training exercises and drills for state and local first responders. The Department has also worked to standardize training. The Department created the National Incident Management System (NIMS) curriculum in order to provide a standardized training regimen for first responders. Some 725,000 first responders at the national, state and local levels have completed MINS training and certification. NIMS training is in addition to general counterterrorism training which the Department has provided to some 1.2 million personnel across the country. The federal government has also initiated a series of programs to improve intelligence sharing and facilitate communications about terrorism and other homeland security threats. For instance, the Department reports that it conveyed some 1,260 "intelligence information products on threat information and protective measures that can be taken to remain vigilant."[53]

The States' Priorities

The NGA subsequently served as a coordinating body for the governors to develop joint planning and resource utilization efforts and to develop consensus in response to the Office (and later Department) of Homeland Security initiatives. The NGA's efforts occurred at the level of state chief executives (the governors) and through the various state offices overseeing homeland security or emergency management.[54] Ultimately, through the NGA, governors and state homeland security directors identified ten main goals and issue-areas that required greater federal and state cooperation:

1) Coordination must involve all levels of government.
2) The federal government must disseminate timely intelligence information to the states.
3) States must work with local governments to develop interoperable communications between first responders and adequate wireless spectrum must be put aside to do the job.
4) State and local governments need help and technical assistance to identify and protect critical infrastructure.
5) Both the states and federal government must focus on enhancing bioterrorism preparedness and rebuilding the nation's public health system to address twenty-first century threats.
6) The federal government should provide adequate federal funding and support to ensure that homeland security needs are met.
7) The federal government should work with states to protect sensitive security information including restricting access to information available through "freedom of information" requests.
8) An effective system must be developed that secures points of entry at borders, airports, and seaports without placing an undue burden on commerce.
9) The National Guard has proven itself to be an effective force during emergencies and crises. The mission of the National Guard should remain flexible, and Guard units should primarily remain under the control of the governor during crises.
10) Federal agencies should integrate their command systems into existing state and local incident command systems (ICS) rather than requiring state and local agencies to adapt to federal command systems.[55]

Central to the governors' goals was an increase in federal coordination with state and local entities. State and local officials noted that majority of law enforcement and emergency responders were employed at the state and local level. Nonetheless, the aftermath of the 11 September attacks led to a system in which federal agencies played a major role in determining the priorities and actions of the various state and local first responders. For instance, one of the first initiatives undertaken by the Office/Department of Homeland Security, was the creation of a color-coded system of national alert.[56] The threat level is determined at the federal level, even though increases in the threat level result in extra deployments of first responders, as well as state and local security forces. Furthermore, different states have responded to the heightened security alert in different fashions. In the pervious alerts, 16 states simply enhanced protective measures that were already in place, while six implemented new measures and five did not add any significant new measures (the remaining states employed some mix of new actions and enhancements of exiting protocols). States reported that the variation in response was often due to the lack of specific information about the threat.[57] State officials also contend that the federal government must do a better job of facilitating communications about terrorist threats. Ronald Marks echoes the calls of many state officials when he points out that the:

the Department of Homeland Security must reach out in a comprehensive way to the 17,000-plus state and local police departments to understand their needs and provide them information accordingly. Also, DHS must be able to acquire from state and local authorities the kind of information the "cops on the beat" get about what is going on in their area. The relative success of the British in dealing with the July 7 bombing has to do with local authorities and national intelligence working together closely and quickly.[58]

When federal coordination is required, governors want to ensure local command and control systems remain in place. They seek equal access to intelligence and resources. Nonetheless, the governors do view such heightened coordination as best achieved through greater sharing of information and more resources (hence the tenth point which called for federal integration into local and state command structures). Instead, governors want to maximize their authority and minimize federal control of the emerging national homeland security system.

The Cities' Priorities

The United States Conference of Mayors (USCM) met one month after the 2001 attacks and subsequently developed a comprehensive plan which highlighted the needs of municipalities and localities and the preferred role of the federal government, as seen by the chief executives of the nation's largest cities. Many of the recommendations of the mayors' group paralleled those of federal bodies and the states. For example, immediately after the attacks, New Orleans Mayor Mark Morial, then President of the USCM, called for the federalization of airport security.[59] The group identified four major areas which needed to be addressed in order to bolster homeland security and better prepare cities and towns for catastrophic terrorism and recovery efforts. The four priorities for the mayors were: 1) transportation security; 2) emergency preparedness; 3) federal-local law enforcement; and 4) economic security.

While airline security was the immediate focus of the mayors, they also wanted improvements in security on rail, road and mass transit systems. This included a call to integrate security planning and features into future highway projects (including evacuation planning) and recommendations on port security and Amtrak, the nation's passenger rail system.[60] The mayors also backed calls for increased training and funding for first responders and better intelligence sharing and coordination between local and federal law enforcement agencies.[61] Of particular concern was that of the initial $10 billion allocated for homeland security, only 4.9 percent was designated for use by local and state first responders. They sought federal block grants, which would provide localities with discretion in spending on security needs at the local level. This would allow some localities to focus on port security while others focused on border control and immigration and still other groups could devote the majority of resources to protecting critical infrastructure. The mayors also sought a greater role in determining the mission and scope of the Department of Homeland Security through closer federal-local integration and cooperation.

Finally, the local chief executives wanted the economic ramifications of homeland security threats recognized and incorporated into planning. The 2001 attacks had an estimated cost of some $4 billion to the City of New York. Most localities would not have the economic resources to recover quickly in the event of a major homeland security incident. Consequently, the mayors called for the federal government to enact a range of programs related to economic recovery. For instance, the mayors argued in favor of worker assistance initiatives, including the extension of unemployment benefits from 26 to 78 weeks, temporary free or low-cost health insurance and worker retraining and relocation. The USCM also called for better "strategic public investment" such as a prepackaged series of tax breaks to encourage investment and aid recovery (the idea being that in the event of an incident, these tax breaks could be put in place quickly without the usual delays). Once in place, the USCM recommended that the tax incentives be left in place for 12-18 months. Among the specific tax recommendations were "lifting the cap on state and local tax exempt bonds to spur stalled development; doubling the allocation of low income housing tax credits to advance housing construction; and providing a tax credit to low and moderate income families who purchase computers to boost technology literacy."[62]

A year after the attacks on New York and Washington, the USCM issued a call for a stronger "federal-local partnership in areas such as aviation security, information sharing, and bio-terrorism preparedness."[63] A study by the USCM found that cities were spending an additional $2.6 billion in unanticipated homeland security costs in the year after the 2001 attacks. Central to continuing homeland security improvements would be federal block grants which would provide cities with the flexibility to cover costs based on locally-identified needs. The mayors also highlighted a range of accomplishments at the local level. Foremost among the homeland security measures undertaken in cities and towns were increased security at public buildings, improvements in airport security, enhanced chemical and biological detection capabilities and more equipment (including better communications gear).

The USCM also pointed out a range of areas in which the federal-local partnership has fallen short. In spite of promises and legislation, most major cities remain woefully under-equipped to deal with biological attacks or incidents. The USCM points out that the majority of assistance to prepare for a biological attack (including equipment and training) has been provided through the states and not federal agencies.[64] As a result, only about half of the nation's EMTs and paramedics have had more than one hour of training in responding to chemical or biological attacks (20 percent have had not training in these WMD situations) and only one-third of medical first responders have participated in a drill or simulation of a chemical or biological attack. Overall, local emergency management systems have received only about 4 percent of the Homeland Security grants funds that have been provided to states.[65]

Other accomplishments were better public-private security cooperation (for instance, Las Vegas expanded security cooperation and coordination between the municipal and county police and private security agencies at casinos).[66] Cities have undertaken a variety of training exercises and simulations to improve local capabilities and enhance state and local cooperation. Mayors have also ordered risk assessments to identify potential targets within their jurisdictions and studies to determine methods to protect vulnerable areas. For example, Los Angeles undertook a 6 month study, which ultimately identified more than $133 million in potential homeland security upgrades.[67]

The USCM went on to refine its key priorities in federal-local homeland security relations. Most of the current priorities reflect the early assessment and highlight lingering areas of tension between the different levels of government. The USCM has five main homeland security priorities:

1) Direct funding to cities for first responders to help reimburse expenses already incurred for planning, training, equipment and overtime, and additional future needs in this area.
2) Full funding for existing law enforcement resources such as COPS programs and Local Law Enforcement Block Grant. Local law officers are our first line of defense against domestic terrorism, and we must continue our aggressive efforts against traditional crime.
3) Reimbursement for airport security improvements as mandated under the Transportation Security Act.
4) Continued improvement in federal information sharing.
5) An improved border inspection system.[68]

In some cases, the nexus between local and national policy continues to create friction between the priorities of localities and the goals of the national government. Some localities have complained that increased border security has led to economic damage through border crossing delays and the "federal insistence on locating transportation inspection stations literally at the border crossing points."[69] Cities and states assert that the inability of the federal government to develop a comprehensive and effective immigration policy creates additional burdens on localities and states.[70] Underlying the goals and priorities of both states and localities are two main areas, personnel and communications, in which both levels of government continue to seek significant federal assistance.

Personnel and Communications

Ultimately, the two most pressing homeland security needs cited by state and local officials are personnel and communications. For instance, the International Association of Fire Fighters (IAFF), which represents 90 percent of the fire departments in the United States, estimated that the country needed an additional 75,000 professional firefighters.[71] Meanwhile, the number of volunteer firefighters has decreased by 20 percent over the past decade and among many departments there is a annual turnover rate as high as 25 percent. E. James Monihan, the Director of New Jersey's chapter of the National Volunteer Fire Council (and past chairman of the national body) noted that the high turnover rate "equates to tremendous loss of talent each year, thus departments are less able to meet their staffing needs and advanced training is rarely offered because members are consumed with basic functions."[72]

Monihan also noted that "Personnel shortages are another large concern of America's fire service. Many departments, in communities of all sizes, struggle on a daily basis to adequately staff local fire stations and respond to calls. Personnel shortfalls endanger the safety of firefighters and hinder the ability of first responders to effectively protect the public from fire and other hazards."[73]

Under current law, hiring and retention of first responders is not an authorized use of federal homeland security funds. Some grant funds are eligible for use as overtime pay in response to increased security needs when the national threat level is elevated. However, in testimony in 2003, former Homeland Security Secretary Tom Ridge insisted adamantly that it was not the role of the federal government to fund the hire and pay of state or local first responders.[74] Ridge's successor. Michael Chertoff, continues to support the prohibition on the use of homeland security funds to employ first responders. This is in spite of efforts by state and local officials to increase federal block grants for personnel and the support of members of Congress for such action. For instance, some 50 members of the House of Representatives, from both parties, in January 2005 sent a letter to President George W. Bush requesting funding for 2006 so that states and localities could hire additional first responders.[75] In Congressional testimony, Alexander Knopp, the Mayor of Norwalk Connecticut, noted that federal funding was essential in order for cities to meet the additional missions of homeland security, including preparation and training for catastrophic terrorist attacks or major natural disasters.[76] A range of alternatives to direct federal funding of salaries exist, including:

> funding for national and local recruitment campaigns; tax credits and deductions for volunteers; funding for length of service award programs and other pension programs for volunteers; incentives for employers to allow employees, who are volunteers, time off for training or emergency calls; tuition assistance for higher education and increased proliferation of on-line training on-demand for volunteers.[77]

Behind hiring and personnel retention, communications interoperability is cited as a critical need for state and local governments. In August 2004, only 22 percent of the states reported that they had achieved statewide interoperability in communications, while the remaining 73 percent were still working to integrate emergency management services, law enforcement and their disparate localities. The report noted that "much of the communications equipment used by emergency responders is incompatible, which inhibits communication between state and local governments and between neighboring local jurisdictions."[78] In assessing the ranking for communications within the hierarchy of needs, the NGA noted that

> Developing statewide interoperability for emergency responders is the chief priority, and states are working diligently to bolster this capacity. Many are struggling with the dual challenges of funding and time. States must either

replace outdated equipment with new models, or install software that allows incompatible equipment throughout the state to communicate with each other.[79]

The Department of Homeland Security does allow states to purchase communications equipment through its grant program. It does not offer special incentives or funding to deal with interoperability issues. Instead, state homeland security officials must factor interoperability into other equations, including costs, capabilities and availability.[80] Meanwhile, 66 percent of all fire departments in the United States report they are in need of better communications equipment (adding to the interoperability problem).[81]

Homeland Security and Partisan Politics

Homeland security policy in the United States is also complicated by party politics. In the initial aftermath of the 11 September there was remarkable unity between the Republican and Democratic Parties. Randell J. Larsen, a retired Air Force Colonel and homeland security consultant, noted that "it used to be said that in war, partisan politics ended at the water's edge, but that was when the battlefields were overseas. Now the battlefields are here, and we don't know where to draw the lines."[82] The Republicans effectively used homeland security in the 2002 congressional elections to win a historic midterm victory. In the aftermath of the elections, one poll found that 57 percent of American thought the Republicans would do a better job on homeland security as compared with 17 percent who perceived that Democrats would do a better job (the same poll found 62 percent of the public approved of Bush's handing of the war on terror).[83] The Democrats were hurt when congressional leaders stalled legislation creating the Department of Homeland Security in an effort to ensure union protections for workers being transferred into the newly created organization. Paul Glatris, the editor of the pro-Democratic *Washington Monthly*, noted that:

> Even if Democrats believed that worker protections were more important to the country than the flexibility the president requested – a debatable proposition – it was devastatingly shortsighted of them not to give into the president's demands in order to pass the homeland security bill. To have done so would have enabled them to legitimately claim leadership on an important national security matter. They could have spent the fall campaign season bashing the GOP for underfunding the new department.[84]

In the 2004 presidential election, both candidates, Bush and John F. Kerry, used homeland security as an issue to gain political superiority over the other. In fact, both accused the other of not supporting strong measures in homeland security and argued that they could do a better job of protecting the nation than could the opposing candidate.[85]

After the presidential election, both parties continued to endeavor to use homeland security as a political wedge issue. For instance in 2005, Democratic members of the House of Representatives charged in a report that the Republican Bush administration had failed to keep 33 pledges related to homeland security.[86] The Ranking Democratic member of the House Committee on Homeland Security, Representative Bennie Thompson of Mississippi, stated that "it would be one thing if the department [Homeland Security] didn't identify security lapses in the first place, but a more troubling situation when they make promises to the American people and then leave them unfulfilled."[87] The Democratic members cited a range of problems, including the failure of the Department to "create a comprehensive plan to identify and protect critical infrastructure," and the inability of the Department to do more to coordinate with private industry to ameliorate "cybersecurity threats and vulnerabilities."[88]

Especially in the absence of immediate terrorist threats to the nation, homeland security is increasingly becoming just one of a range of divisive political issues between the two parties in the United States. One result is that the bipartisan consensus on security that had marked Cold War US policy and homeland security policy in the post-11 September era has evaporated. Instead, both parties increasingly seek to use domestic security as a means to gain political advantage. Significantly, neither party has yet to identify significant differences in policies or priorities, instead, the main differences are in funding emphases.

Conclusions

The nature of American federalism has created additional complications in the effort to develop comprehensive homeland security strategies. Federalism at its finest provides a high degree of flexibility at the state and local level and ensures a degree of local influence in national policy and decisions. At its worst, federalism prevents the development of uniform policies and slows the policy process. Within the context of homeland security, or any broad national policies, there is a continuum through which the merits of federalism can be assessed. Those who favor a more significant role for the federal government, at the expense of state and local bodies, are likely to charge the national government with failure to expend an adequate amount of resources to ensure the safety and protection of the homeland. Conversely, those who oppose an expanded role for the national government, assert that state and local government are best suited to determine the needs and vulnerabilities of individual areas. These divisions are further exacerbated by the growing partisanship that marks domestic politics in the US.

States and cities remain the front line of defense in the national counterterrorism effort. The two levels of government have fairly similar homeland security priorities. Personnel hiring and retention and communications interoperability are cited as the most significant needs for cities and states. State and local governments also seek more coordination and information-sharing from the federal government. While there has been significant progress in homeland security infrastructure and preparations, as a report from the National Governors' Association was titled: "Much Progress, More Work."[89]

Notes

1. See Smith, *The Convention and the Constitution*.
2. US, Department of Homeland Security, *Emergencies and Disasters: First Responders*, online at http://www.dhs.gov/dhspublic/interapp/editorial/editorial_0197.xml.
3. US, National Commission on Terrorist Attacks on the United States, "The 9/11 Commission Report" (Washington, D.C.: GPO, 2004), online at http://www.9-11commission.gov/report/911Report_Ch9.htm.
4. *Ibid.*
5. *Ibid.*
6. *Ibid.*
7. *Ibid.*
8. *Ibid.* The Commission Report cites the following for its analysis: CNN, "September 11: A Memorial," (updated 2004), online at: www.cnn.com/SPECIALS/2001/memorial /index.html; "Company Contacts" (29 June 2004), online at: http://worldtrade aftermath.com/wta/contacts/companies_list.asp?letter=a; CNN, "WTC Tenants, 2001," online at: www.cnn.com/SPECIALS/2001/trade.center/tenants1.html); "September 11 Personal Tributes" (19 June 2004), online at www.legacy.com/LegacyTribute/Sept11.asp); "September 11 Personal Profiles, 11 October 2003), online at www.september11 victims.com/september11Victims; New York Times, *Portraits: 9/11/01: The Collected "Portraits of Grief"* (New York: Times Books, 2002).
9. *Ibid.*
10. Dave Siff, "Despite Top Rank, New York Keeps Preparing," *CNN.com* (6 September 2002), online at http://edition.cnn.com/2002/US/09/06/prepared.cities.newyork/.
11. Specifically, Giuliani tasked the Police Department as the lead agency in dealing with the threat of a conventional, biological, chemical or nuclear attack; however, the Fire Department would be the lead agency in dealing with the initial response to an attack, while the Police Department then took over the investigation following an incident; Office of the Mayor, New York City, "Direction and Control of Emergencies in the City of New York" (New York: Office of the Mayor, July 2001).
12. Anya Sostek, "Taking Action: New York's State of Mind: Out of the Twin Towers' Ashes, NY is building a World Class Terror-Fighting Machine," *Securing the Homeland: A Special Report From Governing Magazine and Congressional Quarterly*, online at http://www.manhattan-institute.org/html/_govmag-out_of_the_twin_towers.htm.
13. US, Department of Homeland Security, *Emergencies and Disasters: First Responders*.
14. Pietro S. Nivola, "Reflections on Homeland Security and American Federalism," Brookings Institution Working Paper (13 May 2003), online at http://www.brookings.edu/ views/papers/nivola/20020513.htm.
15. Shawn Reese, "State and Local Homeland Security: Unresolved Issues for the 109th Congress," Congressional Research Service Report RL 32941 (Washington, D.C.: Library of Congress, 9 June 2005), 2.
16. *Ibid.*
17. The United States Conference on Mayors estimated that the homeland security costs for cities would rise to $2.1 billion in 2003; White House, *Securing the Homeland, Strengthening the Nation* (Washington, D.C.: White House, 2002), online at http://www.whitehouse.gov/homeland/homeland_security_book.html.
18. John Weinzierl, "Terrorism: Its Origin and History," in Akorlie A. Nyatepe-Coo and Dorothy Zeisler-Vralsted, eds, *Understanding Terrorism: Threats in an Uncertain World* (Upper Saddle, NJ: Pearson, 2004), 45.

19. Raphael Perl, "Combating Terrorism: The Challenge of Measuring Effectiveness," Congressional Research Service Report RL 33160 (Washington, D.C.: Library of Congress, 23 November 2005), 2.

20. White House, *Securing the Homeland.*

21. In the study conducted by researchers at the University of South Florida, 52 percent of respondents rated the financial burdens of new homeland security mandates as their main concern, while 31 percent cited the added administrative responsibilities; Kiki Caruson and Susan A. MacManus, "Homeland Security Preparedness: Federal and State Mandates and Local Government," *Spectrum: The Journal of State Government* (Spring 2005), 26. Among the added administrative responsibilities is additional planning. The study cites the 2004 state requirement that Florida localities develop plans for 15 separate disaster scenarios by year's end; *ibid.*

22. David Broder, "Those Unfunded Mandates," *The Washington Post* (17 March 2005), A25.

23. US, General Accounting Office, *Unfunded Mandates: Analysis of Reform Act Coverage* (Washington, D.C.: GPO, May 2004), 4; online at http://www.gao.gov/new.items /d04637.pdf.

24. Broder, "Those Unfunded Mandates."

25. US, General Accounting Office, *Unfunded Mandates*, 43; the National League of Cities cites the following examples as being of the most pressing concern to municipalities: "Recent issues of focus include the preemption of local taxing authority on internet access and imposition of unfunded mandates such as the MTBE liability waiver, as well as less-than-full funding of the No Child Left Behind Act;" National League of Cities, "Issues: Federalism and Unfunded Mandates," online at http://www.nlc.org/Issues/ Federalism___Unfunded_Mandates/.

26. US, Department of Homeland Security, "Fact Sheet: Department of Homeland Security Funding for States and Cities," Press Release (21 May 2003), online at http://www.dhs.gov/dhspublic/display?content=755.

27. The CRS reports also notes that New York would be a "more likely target for terrorist attacks;" Shawn Reese, "Fiscal Year 2005 Homeland Security Grant Program: State Allocations and Issues for Congressional Oversight," Congressional Research Service Report RL 32696 (Washington, D.C.: Library of Congress, 16 February 2005), 9.

28. *Ibid.*, 14-16.

29. *Ibid.*, 11.

30. *Ibid.*, 8-9.

31. John Furry, "Heartland Logical Target," *The Columbus Dispatch* (16 June 2004), A1; quoted in *ibid.*, 10.

32. *Ibid.*, 1.

33. The six original grants remain as distinct categories (or "sub-grants") within the major HSGP grants; *ibid.*

34. In all some $854.8 million was distributed to urban areas through the USAI. This included funding for the National Capital Region (including a range of territories around Washington, such as the District of Columbia, and counties in both Virginia and Maryland received $82 million; *ibid.*, 14-16.

35. The proposed cuts were deeply criticized by law enforcement groups. In a press release, the President of the International Association of Police Chiefs, Joseph Estey stated that: "This administration talks about homeland security but then guts funding for the very programs that help secure our homeland. This budget cuts funding for critical law enforcement assistance programs by 90 percent, forcing many departments to continue using antiquated and inefficient communications equipment and others to lay off officers.

In smaller communities like mine, some chiefs won't be able to hire desperately needed officers. The administration is asking police agencies to take on even greater responsibilities with less and less funding. Discretionary funds for departments to use for equipment and technology have been virtually eliminated at the local level over the years and, under this budget, it has been eliminated at the federal level. It just doesn't add up;" International Association of Police Chiefs, "Police Chiefs Decry Deep Budget Cuts That Would Make Communities More Vulnerable," Press Release (7 February 2005).

36. Reese, *State and Local Homeland Security*, 6.

37. *Ibid.*, 6-7.

38. For state reactions in the aftermath of the first World Trade Center bombings, see Simon Reeve, *The New Jackals: Ramzi Yousef, Osama Bin Laden, and the Future of Terrorism* (Boston: Northeastern University Press, 1999); or Peter Caram, *The 1993 World Trade Center Bombing: Foresight and Warning* (London: Janus Publishing, 2002).

39. For instance, during Bush's early period in office, several commissions called for dramatic expansions in the nation's counterterrorism capabilities, most notably the Hart-Rudman Commission, see US Commission on National Security in the Twenty-first Century(Hart-Rudman Commission Phase III), *Roadmap for National Security: Imperative for Change* (15 February 2001). Meanwhile senior members of the Republican Party advocated a more robust counterterrorism policy; Raphael F. Perl, *National Commission on Terrorism Report: Background and Issues for Congress*, CRS Report RS 20598 (6 February 2001).

40. See, for instance, Randall J. Larsen and Ruth A. David, "Homeland Defense: Assumptions First, Strategy Second," *Strategic Review* 28/4 (Fall 2000).

41. Ashton Carter, John Deutch and Philip Zelikow, "Catastrophic Terrorism: Tackling the New Danger," *Foreign Affairs* 77/6 (November/December 1998), 82. See also, U.S., GAO, *Combating Terrorism: Issues to Be Resolved to Improve Counterterrorism Operations* (Washington, D.C.: GAO, May 1999), 12.

42. National Governors Association, *States' Homeland Security Practices*, Issue Brief (Washington, D.C.: NGA Center for Best Practices, 19 August 2002), 1.

43. Deil S. Wright, "Federalism and Intergovernmental Relations: Traumas, Tensions and Trends," *Spectrum: The Journal of State Government* (Summer 2003), 10.

44. National Governors Association, *Homeland Security in the States: Much Progress, More Work*, Issue Brief (Washington, D.C.: NGA Center for Best Practices, 24 January 2005), 3; online at http://www.nga.org/cda/files/0502homesec.pdf.

45. *Ibid.*, 1.

46. *Ibid.*, 3-4.

47. *Ibid.*, 2.

48. Most states derive an average of 40 percent of their revenues from personal income taxes and 33.3 percent from sales taxes; *ibid.*, 10-11.

49. Entitlements are those programs which provide a guaranteed level of benefits to individuals who meet the requirements for the initiative. Because the payment or benefit is guaranteed, government has no little control over the total outlays.

50. Wright, 11.

51. *Ibid.*, 11.

52. US, Department of Homeland Security, *National Response Plan* (Washington, D.C.: GPO, December 2004), 2.

53. US, Department of Homeland Security, *Select Homeland Security Accomplishments for 2005*, press release (20 December 2005).

54. National Governors Association, 1.

55. *Ibid.*

56. In Homeland Security Presidential Directive 3, from March 2002, Bush directed the

Homeland Security agency to develop an easily recognizable and identifiable alert system. In the directive, Bush noted that "the Nation requires a Homeland Security Advisory System to provide a comprehensive and effective means to disseminate information regarding the risk of terrorist acts to Federal, State, and local authorities and to the American people. Such a system would provide warnings in the form of a set of graduated "Threat Conditions" that would increase as the risk of the threat increases. At each Threat Condition, Federal departments and agencies would implement a corresponding set of "Protective Measures" to further reduce vulnerability or increase response capability during a period of heightened alert;" George W. Bush, Homeland Security Presidential Directive 3 (March 2002), online at http://www.whitehouse.gov/news/releases/2002/03/20020312-5.html. The system put in place relied on a color-coded system in which "Low = Green; Guarded = Blue; Elevated = Yellow; High = Orange; [and] Severe = Red;" *ibid.*

57. US, General Accounting Office, *Homeland Security: Communications Protocols and Risk Communication Principles Can Assist in Refining the Advisory System* (Washington, D.C.: GPO, June 2004), 25; online at http://www.gao.gov/new.items/d04682.pdf.

58. Ronald Marks, "Homeland Security's Biggest Problem: Too Much Information," *The Christian Science Monitor* (21 November 2005), online at http://www.csmonitor.com/2005/1121/p09s02-coop.html. Marks contends that the need for the federal agencies to take on a greater coordinating role is especially important in light of recent history in which there was a culture of not sharing information, what Marks describes as "compartmentalyzing information through security classification. Washington is still grappling with the mentality that information gathered must be classified 'secret' based on who gathered it not on what the information is about. Further, this 'compartmentalization' is usually handled differently by each federal agency that 'owns' the information"; *ibid.*

59. United States Conference of Mayors, "A National Action Plan for Safety and Security in America's Cities," (December 2001), online at http://www.usmayors.org/uscm/news/press_releases/documents/ActionPlan_121101.pdf.

60. *Ibid.*, 2-9.

61. For instance, the mayors' group wanted local officials included on federal task forces formed to oversee both broad areas of homeland security and local investigations (a practice not always utilized by the Justice Department). The mayors also called for the granting of security clearances to local police chiefs and other law enforcement officials in order to allow them to access sensitive intelligence; *ibid.*, 15-16.

62. *Ibid.*, 17-18.

63. United States Conference of Mayors, "One Year Later: A Status Report on the Federal-Local Partnership on Homeland Security" (9 September 2002).

64. *Ibid.*

65. In 2004, the Department of Homeland Security had to send a memo to state agencies "reminding" them that local emergency management bodies were eligible for chemical and biological preparedness grants. At the local level, there remains a high degree of uncertainty about federal or state assistance; Mimi Hall, "Report: EMS Lacks Terrorism Training, Equipment," *USA Today* (11 March 2005). Jay Bradshaw who directs Maine's Emergency Management System noted that there is "a lot of confusion about what resources are available;" quoted in *ibid.* One reason for the lack of resources is that emergency management systems "get overlooked" according to Robert Bass, the Director of Maryland's system; *ibid.*

66. *Ibid.*

67. *Ibid.*

68. *Ibid.*
69. *Ibid.*
70. In October 2001, in Homeland Security Presidential Directive 2, Bush ordered the creation of a federal task force to improve immigration policy and border control. Bush ordered that: "By November 1, 2001, the Attorney General shall create the Foreign Terrorist Tracking Task Force (Task Force), with assistance from the Secretary of State, the Director of Central Intelligence and other officers of the government, as appropriate. The Task Force shall ensure that, to the maximum extent permitted by law, Federal agencies coordinate programs to accomplish the following: 1) deny entry into the United States of aliens associated with, suspected of being engaged in, or supporting terrorist activity; and 2) locate, detain, prosecute, or deport any such aliens already present in the United States;" George W. Bush, Homeland Security Presidential Directive 2, "Combating Terrorism Through Immigration Policy" (29 October 2001); online at: http://www.fas.org/irp/offdocs/nspd/hspd-2.htm. The new group did not include state representation and was viewed as another example of the failure of the federal government to incorporate states into immigration policy.
71. US, Congress, Senate Committee on Appropriations, 107th Congress, 2nd session, *VA/HUD Firefighting Testimony: Harold Schaitberger*, press release (6 February 2002), online at http://appropriations.senate.gov/releases/record.cfm?id=180447.
72. US, Congress, House Science Committee, *Testimony Before the House Science Committee on Meeting the Needs of the Fire Service*, 107th Congress, 2nd session, hearing (2 October 2002), online at http://www.house.gov/science/hearings/full02/oct02/monihan.htm.
73. *Ibid.*
74. US, Congress, Senate Governmental Affairs Committee, *Investing in Homeland Security: Streamlining and Enhancing Homeland Security Grant Programs,* 108th Congress, 1st session, hearing on 1 May 2003 (Washington, D.C.: GPO 2003); cited in Reese, *State and Local Homeland Security*, 3.
75. See "Representative Abercrombie Requests First Responders Grants Restored to Police, Firefighters," *US Federal News* (28 February 2005; and "Representative Tierney Spearheads Efforts for First Responder Funding in Fiscal 2006 Budget," *US Federal News* (12 January 2005); both cited in *ibid.*
76. US, Congress, House Committee on Government Reform, Subcommittee on National Security, Emerging Threats, and International Relations, *Homeland Security: Keeping First Responders First*, 107th Congress, 2nd session, hearing on 30 July 2002 (Washington, D.C.: GPO, 2003), 31; cited in *ibid.*
77. US, Congress, House Science Committee, *Testimony Before the House Science Committee on Meeting the Needs of the Fire Service.*
78. National Governors Association, *Homeland Security in the States*, 4.
79. *Ibid.*, 5.
80. Reese, *State and Local Homeland Security*, 4.
81. US, Congress, *VA/HUD Firefighting Testimony.*
82. John Mintz and Mike Allen, "Homeland Security, a Politicized Issue," *The Washington Post* (27 June 2004), A6.
83. Stephen Dinan, "Terror-War Stance Hurting Democrats," *The Washington Times* (30 May 2003), online at http://www.washingtontimes.com/national/20030530-124908-6112r.htm.
84. Paul Glastris, "How Democrats Could Have Won," *The Washington Monthly* (December 2002), online at http://www.washingtonmonthly.com/features/2001/0212.glastris.html.
85. *Ibid.*
86. US House Committee on Homeland Security Democratic Staff, *Leaving the Nation at*

Risk: 33 Unfulfilled Promises From the Department of Homeland Security (December 2005), online at http://hsc-democrats.house.gov/NR/rdonlyres/1C607310-3228-4CCC-B13A-04A808A4C19B/0/HomelandSecurityDemocratsRevealUnfulfilledPromises.pdf.

87. Quoted in Lara Jakes Jordan, "Democrats Cite Gaps in DHS Record," *Associated Press* (28 December 2005).

88. US House Committee on Homeland Security Democratic Staff.

89. National Governors Association, *Homeland Security in the States: Much Progress, More Work.*

Chapter 6

Homeland Security in a Comparative Perspective

Introduction

The four states in this chapter range greatly in how they deal with homeland security and represent a broad spectrum of examples. France, the United Kingdom, Israel, and Russia have each dealt with the threat of terrorism, both in their present and in their past, to varying levels. The process of dealing with that threat, more than anything, has influenced the structures that have developed over the years and the culture in which the various agencies involved operate. For example, in Israel, its geographic location and the constant threat of terrorist activity, have led to a highly proactive structure geared almost totally toward counter terrorism and counter insurgency. In Russia, the Chechen conflict and the legacy of the Soviet Union have pushed the system toward a heavy, top down approach focused on internal security. Both France and the United Kingdom have developed broader systems of homeland security, each having dealt with terrorism from the perspective of a well developed state.

In each case, the states have strong central governments with a great deal of authority granted to the executive branch. In the cases of Israel, France and the United Kingdom, parliamentary style governments with entrenched links between the cabinet and the legislature assure a great deal of political participation. In the case of Russia, an almost authoritarian presidential federation exists. All four states face increased threats from terrorist attacks and all four states have responded to the increased level of threat in different ways.

The four states use a combination of general and special laws to prosecute and define terrorist activities within their respective countries. In the case of France, the general laws are supplemented with special laws detailing increased punishments and authority for prosecution as well as broader powers for investigations and detentions. Special courts and officers that deal only with the terrorist threat have developed a niche understanding of the problem. The United Kingdom has completely overhauled the legislative framework in which they work and has taken a broad based perspective dealing with preparation and increased powers of investigation, detention and surveillance. Israel's laws are holdovers from the founding of the state and represent the stark realities of a nation at war. Israel relies greatly on precedent to fill the gaps within its legislative framework. Russian laws have worked to increasingly blur the distinction between terrorism and other criminal activities granting the state increased authority over civil liberties. In all four cases, the governments have enacted legislation and policies that go well beyond what is acceptable in the United States in terms of infringing upon the privacy of citizens.[1]

All four countries rely heavily on the executive department for oversight of the various activities involved. Each ministry is expected to review processes and procedures as part of its day to day operations. The United Kingdom provides the greatest depth of oversight with a layered system of committees within the central government. Each has senior level executive committees that perform this function as well as permanent and ad-hoc legislative committees. In addition, Israel's State Comptroller's Office has oversight and review functions. For Israel, France and the United Kingdom, the judicial branch serves an important function in overseeing the legality of operations of the various functions of government. In the case of Russia, independent oversight remains an issue in need of review. Each state also recognizes the need to coordinate homeland security operations across departments. As such, each has developed committees and organizations designed to plan and implement broad policies across ministries and agencies. Even so, in each case one department can be recognized as the principal agency involved in homeland security – for example, the Home Office in the United Kingdom or France's Ministry of the Interior.

In all four cases, intelligence is viewed as of vital importance to the homeland security apparatus. The most tightly knit coordination amongst the intelligence agencies rests with the intelligence services of Israel. The Mossad, Shin Bet, and Aman coordinate counter intelligence collections and operations to a very high degree. The United Kingdom and France each have unique agencies that have experienced a great deal of success without the same degree of operational freedom as Israel's services. The Russian intelligence apparatus has a great deal of authority to suppress personal freedoms in its efforts to carry out its mandate.

In each case the military plays a role in dealing with homeland security. In the case of the United Kingdom, the role is largely a support role or deals mainly with specialty units specific to the services, including search and rescue or chemical, biological, and radiological teams. In Israel, the military is intimately linked with the civil services through the Home Front Command and has primary policing power in the occupied territories. For France, the Ministry of Defense is responsible, nominally, for the Gendarmerie Nationale, the main policing force for rural regions. In each case, the police also have a number of highly trained counter terrorism units that operate as Special Forces.

The bulk of this chapter involves short case studies of the four systems with an eye for the specific character of the institutions, laws and policies involved. Each state is different and demands a slight variation in how it is presented. Further confounding the issue, specific policies dealing with such concern as counter terrorism are often closely guarded national secrets or, at the very least, difficult to find. This is in stark contrast to the United States in which the policies and procedures of homeland security are often open and freely debated across news services on a day to day basis. One observation that can be made at this point is the broad nature of the US homeland security undertaking. In contrast, with the exception of the United Kingdom, the states in this study all seem to focus on the threat from terrorism with other disasters almost as an afterthought.

France

France is largely considered to have one of the best counter-terrorism infrastructures in Europe, mainly due to a contemporary history rife with terrorist episodes. While France escaped much of the violence that occurred in the 1970s, it took heed of the mounting European danger that was occurring at the time in countries like West Germany and Spain with movements such as the Weather Underground or the Red Brigades.[2] By 1980, however, the French had been subjected to a series of increasingly violent domestic terrorist encounters. The French experience with terrorism has led to the establishment of effective tools to combat the phenomenon from a legal and an operational perspective.

Legal Framework

The French legal system, in chapters I and II of title II of the Penal Code and the Code of Criminal Procedure, defines terrorism as "an act by an individual or group that uses intimidation or terror to disrupt public order."[3] Essentially, the same laws are used regardless of terrorist intent; however, the difference is made in sentencing guidelines. Illegal actions that are found to have been committed with political motives in mind have increased maximum penalties, as opposed to other similar acts of criminal intent. The French system also includes preparation for such attacks and terrorist recruitment within this special category of law warranting increased penalties. This has streamlined the process by integrating emerging terrorist threats within well established French law. From this perspective, the French expend a great deal of effort toward preparation and prevention.

Established in 1978, in the administration of Valéry Giscard d'Estaing, the anti-terrorist plan *Vigipirate* allows the French government to step up internal security during periods of elevated threat. While the exact protocol is classified, it sets provisions for a series of preplanned actions to occur upon the order of the government without specific legislative approval.[4]

There are two broad categories of *Vigipirate* that permit an escalation of government's infringement upon French society. *Vigipirate Simple* demands enhanced controls over safety measures and surveillance efforts.[5] It also places an emphasis on maintaining open lines of communication. *Vigipirate Renforcé* calls for the deployment of military and special police units to augment security in high traffic areas and additional surveillance efforts at key installations.[6] *Plan Vigipirate* was updated in 1995, 2000 and 2003 and now includes a system of classification similar to the US Department of Homeland Security Threat Advisory. With four levels of increasing alert (yellow, orange, red, and scarlet), *Vigipirate* has grown over the years to encompass the new dimensions of international terrorism. *Vigipirate* has been deployed since the 1991 Gulf War with marked escalation during periods of increased terrorist activities.

Coordination

While no one agency within the French government is directly responsible for all counter terrorist related activities, the French Interministerial Liaison Committee Against Terrorism serves as the principal policy organizing mechanism for the government.[7] Included within this committee are the Prime Minister and the Ministers of the Interior, Defense, and Foreign Affairs. The principal function of the committee is to coordinate activities with relevant ministries towards combating terrorism and to supervise the Anti-Terrorism Coordination Unit.[8] Formed in 1984, the Anti-Terrorism Coordination Unit works at the operational level to coordinate the various activities within the Ministries of Defense and Interior.[9] With three main missions – intelligence gathering, prevention, and repression – the Anti-Terrorism Coordination Unit oversees the counter terrorist activities of agencies including the police, border security, intelligence and domestic military response.[10] While this discussion is in no way complete, the Ministries of the Interior and Defense comprise the bulk of France's counter terrorism operations.

Practices

The Ministry of the Interior contains a number of primary counter terrorist outfits within its overview, including the Director General of the National Police, who takes lead in the aforementioned Anti-Terrorist Coordination Unit. In addition, the Ministry contains the Directorate of Territorial Security (DST), the Central Directorate of General Information (DCRG), and Central Directorate Judicial Police (DCPJ). The DST was formed in 1944 as the principal internal intelligence agency within France tasked with internal security from external threats.[11] DST has three primary missions: 1) counter terrorism, 2) counter espionage, and 3) protection of economic and scientific infrastructure.[12] The 1,500 member DST gathers information through an extensive system of informers, through community outreach programs, by a number of monitoring activities of immigrants and other suspects, and through external government and non-governmental sources.[13] The DCRG is the main political intelligence gathering apparatus of the government protecting internal security from internal threats.[14] With some 4,000 members, it is divided into four broad sub-directorates: 1) Sub-Directorate of Research; 2) Sub-Directorate of Analysis; 3) Sub-Directorate of Races and Backlashes; 4) Sub-Directorate of Resources and Methods.[15] The 7,400 members of the DCPJ investigate and apprehend individuals involved in complex criminal operations of an economic, financial, criminal, technical or scientific nature, including terrorist activities. In addition, the Ministry of the Interior includes approximately 150,000 National Police who are responsible for security mainly in large towns and cities.

The Ministry of Defense is responsible for security in rural France, including towns of less than 10,000 inhabitants. The two organizations that have particular counter terrorist tasking within the ministry are the General Directorate for External Security (DGSE) and the Gendarmerie Nationale. The DGSE is the French foreign intelligence service and is largely tasked at counter proliferation operations and counter terrorism.[16] Gendarmerie forces are the primary entity responsible for enforcing law and public security in some 95 percent of France. As a paramilitary organization, it has grown increasingly important to the internal security of France, expanding from 78,000 members in 1980 to around 104,000 in 2005; as compared to a decrease in the regular armed forces from 494,730 in 1980 to 294,430 in 2000.[17] Specific to the Gendarmerie, the Mobile Gendarmerie acts as a rapid response force for internal emergencies. In addition, regular military forces can be called into troubled areas where needed.

France has also expanded the judicial arm of its overall terrorism plan largely with the Act of 9 September 1986. The 1986 legislation created a number of institutional changes modeled after the US National Security Council – namely the formation of interagency coordination groups within the ministry of the interior and the ministry of justice. More particular to the French system in contrast with the American system was the formation of a centralized judicial process for dealing with terrorist activities.[18] Once a terrorist act has been committed, specialized magistrates with both prosecutorial and judicial powers are charged with investigating. These nominally non-political investigators have become experts in understanding the judicial difficulties in dealing with terrorism in a democratic society in addition to creating a professional cadre of experts with an in depth understanding of the phenomena.

The French have a well established track record for countering terrorism within their space. Since the events of September 11 2001, they have worked to strengthen the institutions that were in place previously. Most notably, the November 2001 Law on Everyday Security reinforced already aggressive counterterrorist law to include the ability to monitor email and internet use, less stringent surveillance guidelines, and the hampering of terrorist financing. In addition, the French have long standing ties with and within many Middle Eastern nations of concern that may help them curb Islamic terrorism at home and abroad.

French Homeland Security in a Comparative Perspective

The French have the longest history with terrorists of Middle Eastern descent on the European continent. Including two waves in 1986 and another in 1995, their experience is much broader than the experience of the United States in dealing with terrorists internally. Thus, over the years they have developed an effective system of police work, infiltration and diplomacy that the United States is just beginning to appreciate. Likewise, the development of French law to encompass greater powers for the government, and particularly the police force, are very popular in some circles of US government even as the decrease in civil liberties that these enforcement laws generate is viewed with a great deal of trepidation. "French strategy relies heavily on preemptive arrests, ethnic profiling, and an efficient domestic intelligence-gathering network."[19] Because of the unique history and culture of the United States, these same strategies would be very difficult to implement. For example, the French allow the detention of suspects for up to three years while an investigation is in process – a practice that is on trial in American courts namely with the case of Jose Padilla.[20]

With the obvious similarities between the Homeland Security Advisory System and France's *Vigipirate* in mind, the ways the United States and France are structured are different in a few key ways. The most obvious is the decentralized structure of police forces within the United States as compared to the French National Police and Gendarmerie Nationale. France bypasses many of the problems associated with having a large number of independent local and regional forces by having a centralized command structure. This would seem to forestall many of the coordination issues the Department of Homeland Security is facing today. Another important difference mentioned earlier rests with the specialized courts and police powers granted to special magistrates that investigate and have prosecution powers centrally located in Paris. Finally, but not all encompassing, France relies on its criminal legislation with increased sentencing guidelines for terrorism instead of the American attempt to reinvent the wheel as demonstrated in the Patriot Act and other legislation.[21]

United Kingdom

The United Kingdom has a history rife with experiences dealing with terrorism and other threats to the homeland; however, much of its efforts have been directed toward the Irish Republican Army and Northern Ireland. With the notable exception of the explosion of a bomb aboard Pan Am Flight 103 over Lockerbie in 1988, the United Kingdom had not needed to deal with international terrorism up until the recent London bombings in July 2005. With that said, the United Kingdom has been aware of the growing threat of international terrorism for some years as various groups have used Britain as a staging ground for fund raising and planning operations abroad with relative impunity. With the 9/11 attacks in the United States, the United Kingdom, as America's closest partner, has begun a plan to update and upgrade its ability to deter terrorist attacks and deal with the aftermath of major catastrophic events. One example of its preparations is the installation of large number of monitoring systems throughout the nation.

Legal Framework

The principal legal document defining terrorism rests with the Terrorism Act of 2000. It serves to update the legal framework within the UK in recognition of the increasing danger of terrorism. Before the introduction of this act, UK antiterrorism law was a patchwork of jurisprudence emplaced to deal with the threat of terrorism over the years. The Terrorism Act of 2000 updates the laws and serves as the foundation for future legislation.

Through the Terrorism Act of 2000, effective as of March 2001, terrorism is defined as an action that involves serious violence against an individual, damage to property, endangers life, creates a risk to the health or safety of the public, or disrupts electronic systems and is designed to influence the government or intimidate the public for the purpose of advancing a political, religious or ideological cause.[22] Particularly, the Act empowered the Home Secretary to outlaw terrorist groups within the United Kingdom and made it illegal to incite, recruit, or train for terrorist purposes. In addition, it authorized the government to detain suspects for up to seven days with a magistrate's approval. The Anti-Terrorism, Crime and Security Act of 2001 and the Prevention of Terrorism Act of 2005 serve to enhance the Terrorism Act of 2000 by strengthening measures such as tougher financial restriction on terrorist funding and greater search and seizure power to law enforcement.[23] The Prevention of Terrorism Act of 2005 also authorizes the use of "control orders" that can be imposed upon suspected terrorists that prevent or limit their access to potential targets or resources.[24]

The principal legislation dealing with emergency preparation and response is the Civil Contingencies Act of 2004. The Act is divided into two substantive parts outlining local arrangements for civil protection and emergency powers in the face of more serious events.[25]

Coordination

Overall responsibility for coordination of the homeland security rests with the Cabinet Office. However, the Home Office primarily protects the domestic population and infrastructure from terrorist threats, and manages the British terrorism programs, as well as authority over the nation's law enforcement, domestic intelligence gathering enterprises, and emergency management.[26] Under the guidance of the Home Secretary, the Home Office chairs a number of cabinet level coordination committees on domestic preparedness.

The Ministerial Civil Contingencies Committee (CCC) job is "[t]o consider, in an emergency, plans for assuring the supplies and services essential to the life of the community and to supervise their prompt and effective implementation where required."[27] In the immediate aftermath of a crisis, CCC is responsible for overseeing the lead department's response.[28] Members of the CCC include the Home Secretary (chair), Head of the Economic and Domestic Secretariat of the Cabinet Office (deputy chair), The Prime Minister's Chief Press Secretary, and representatives from the various departments of government.[29]

In addition, the Home Secretary chairs the Ministerial Group on Protective and Preventive Security (DOP (IT)(T)) and the Ministerial Group on Resilience (DOP (IT)(R)). DOP (IT)(T) terms of reference are "to keep under review the Government's policy on preventive and precautionary security measures to counter the threat of terrorism in the United Kingdom and to British interests overseas; and to report to the Sub-Committee on International Terrorism as appropriate."[30] It meets every two to three months and consists of, in addition to the Home Secretary, the various Secretaries of State as well as the President of the Association of Chief Police Officers and the heads of the Intelligence Agencies as required. DOP (IT) (R) develops policy on managing the consequences of major events and includes three sub-committees: the UK Resilience Committee, the London Resilience Committee, and the Chemical, Biological, Radiological and Nuclear (CBRN) Committee.[31]

The Civil Contingencies Secretariat (CCS), as part of the Cabinet office, serves as the central organization guiding and coordinating activity within and across governmental departments dealing with domestic preparedness for emergencies. Established in 2001, it provides expertise across departments and various committees in order to better prepare the government for domestic emergencies. As part of this task, it fulfills a number of duties such as: coordinating risk assessment activities of potential challenges, coordinating the development of capabilities designed to face such risks, implementing topical legislation, providing training and expertise in the field of emergency management, and coordinating consequence management.[32]

In addition to these elements, a number of other coordination entities exist within the government to assure interagency cooperation and a firm grasp on command and control of any event.

Practices

The United Kingdom has not gone the route of the United States by having a national level system similar to the American threat advisory system. Instead, the United Kingdom increases or decreases security based on where and what the threat is. For any given event, the Chief of Police for the area has primary responsibility for an emergency at the local level. At the point in which the emergency is deemed in need of a central governmental response, the United Kingdom utilizes a system by which a Lead Government Department (LGD) takes over all control. In each case, usually predetermined based on the nature of the event, the LGD is expected to have maintained a state of readiness for any event under its umbrella. In a case in which it is not predetermined or clear who the LGD is, the CCS makes the determination.

The LGD has three broad levels of engagement based on the severity of the event.[33] A Level 1 emergency is handled by the LGD Minister using his own facilities. A Level 2 event is coordinated through the Cabinet Office Briefing Rooms in order to better facilitate assistance from other departments. A Level 3 event is lead by the Prime Minister or a nominated Secretary of State and is expected to involve all aspects of government.

In terms of terrorist prevention, the United Kingdom has a number of organizations preventing and investigating terrorism. Most notably, MI5, an organization similar to the FBI, with the exception of having no police powers, protects the homeland from threats both domestic and abroad.[34] With approximately 1,900 members and a budget between £200 million and £300 million, MI5 has expanded its role substantially since the 9/11 attacks.[35] Some 67 percent of MI5's resources are directed toward International or Irish counter terrorism. Within MI5, three branches have an expressed role in counter terrorism.[36] The Joint Terrorism Analysis Center (JTAC) acts as an information and assessment clearing house for the UK government in terms of domestic and international threats to the UK, and includes representatives from all of the United Kingdom's various intelligence agencies. The International Counter terrorism, Counter Proliferation, and Counter Espionage branch and the Irish and Domestic Counter terrorism branch deal with investigations and deterrence. MI5 is under the guidance of the Home Office.

MI6, in contrast to MI5, is directly responsible for collecting intelligence overseas and the Government Communications Headquarters (GCHQ), akin to the US National Security Agency, is responsible for signals intelligence and information assurance.[37] Both agencies are under the control of the Foreign Secretary. All three agencies, as well as the UK Military's Defense Intelligence Staff, coordinate their activities, mainly through the JTAC, for counter terrorism issues. The three services combined have an annual budget of £1,355 million as of 2005/2006 but the numbers are expected to increase modestly over the next several years. All three derive legislative and oversight functions through the Security Act of 1989 amended in 1996, the Intelligence Service Act of 1994 and the Regulation of Investigatory Powers Act of 2000.[38]

The security services, through JTAC and specifically MI5, work closely with the United Kingdom's police forces in terms of counter terrorism and serious criminal activity. The police forces have primary responsibility for investigating terrorist activity as part of their central role in all criminal investigations. In particular, the Metropolitan Police have a number of specific branches dedicated to counter terrorism including SO12 and SO13, the Special Branch and the Anti-Terrorist Branch, respectively. The 43 separate organizations that amount to the police forces of the United Kingdom coordinate under the auspices of the Association of Chief Police Officers, which also houses the Terrorism and Allied Matters Committee in setting policy and procedure. The United Kingdom stations dedicated Counter Terrorism Security Advisors in every police force, as well as having dedicated units in every force geared toward counter terrorism and coordination with MI5.[39] At present, the United Kingdom boasts of a record level of police officers, more than 141,000 as of July 2005, with some £31 billion set aside for public order and safety of which about a third is dedicated to policing.[40]

In addition, the military plays a role in the United Kingdom's efforts, namely in terms of specialized equipment and expertise generally called upon when needed, in consultation with the Home Office and the Ministry of Defense. Military assistance comes in three broad forms as outlined in *Operations in the UK: The Defence Contribution to Resilience.*[41] Military Assistance to Civil Authorities (MACA) is guided by principles designed to minimize the operations of the military within the country and to maintain its dependence and subservience to civil authorities. MACA is broken down into Military Assistance to Government Departments (MAGD), Military Aid to the Civil Power (MACP), and Military Aid to the Civil Community (MACC). MAGD is reserved for duties involving the maintenance of supplies and services. MACP entails assistance dealing with the maintenance of law and order, for example drug interdiction and counter terrorism. MACC is unarmed assistance dealing with such issues as search and rescue and natural disasters.

Legal authority for the use of armed forces is derived from the Civil Contingencies Act of 2004 and the Emergency Powers Act of 1964. Each service has personalized regulations that are being replaced by a common Tri-Service agreement in 2006.[42]

United Kingdom Homeland Security in a Comparative Perspective

The United Kingdom and the United States have both taken a very broad perspective on Homeland Security as not just a mechanism for counter terrorism, but as a total package. Both arrangements highlight the partnership between local, regional and the central government in protecting the nation internally. With a broad based focus on preparation and mitigation, both UK Resilience and the Department of Homeland Security share a culture of technological measures, with less of an emphasis on preparing the population for increased responsibility and purpose.[43] This is in contrast to the example presented in Israel which places a great deal of emphasis on the vigilance and preparation of the citizenry. In contrast to the United States, perhaps because of the lengthy history with Irish terrorism, the United Kingdom places more emphasis on intelligence than the United States, going as far as assuring that each regional police area has dedicated intelligence and counter terrorism aspects. In addition, the best practices offered by the United Kingdom's Association of Chief Police Officers have no real equivalent within the United States, although efforts in that direction are being made.

In addition, the United Kingdom has taken a stance of increased levels of surveillance through the integration of closed circuit television systems (CCTV) and increased powers to the police to conduct wiretap, internet and preemptive interrogations.[44] While the size of the United States makes the installation of CCTV impractical on a wide scale, many of the same police powers have been adopted within the United States, as both those states have drastically overhauled legislation dealing with counter terrorism and homeland security in general.

Israel

Of the four states discussed in this short review, Israel has arguably encountered the greatest degree of terrorist activity. Since its founding in 1948, Israel has been subjected to numerous attacks by both state and non-state actors. Its geographical location and ongoing troubles with various Palestinian terrorist organizations have necessitated a very proactive strategy that has been built upon a strong intelligence service and a tightly integrated police and military infrastructure. Israel's history has lead to a number of steps that would otherwise be unacceptable in a democracy and are highly contentious within Israel and international society. The targeting for assassination of various individuals deemed threatening and the construction of a security fence designed to separate Israel from Palestinian territories can serve as examples of such actions.

Because of Israel's long experience with extremism, Israel is on the cutting edge of development when it comes to security technology, doctrine and policy. As such, many governments, including the United States, have looked at the Israeli example when formulating their own doctrines. However, it has been argued that terrorism cannot be simply answered within the security sphere. It may take a multi pronged effort that Israel has been somewhat hesitant to utilize for political reasons.[45]

Legal Framework

The principal framework for Israeli anti-terrorism law rests with two acts that are almost as old as the state itself. The Defense and Emergency Act (1945) is a remnant from the British era and has been updated a number of times.[46] Generally, this Act is used to enforce rules against unlawful associations, imposing curfews, regulation of the media, and policing powers in the occupied territories. The 1948 Prevention of Terrorism Ordinance, updated in 1980, 1986, and 1993, contains judicial, administrative and criminal wording designed to limit and deter terrorist related activities within Israel. It has been noted that neither of these basic frameworks actually defines terrorism; however, the Prevention of Terrorism Ordinance defines terrorist organizations as "a body of persons resorting in its activities to acts of violence calculated to cause death or injury to a person or to threats of such acts of violence."[47]

Coordination

The Bureau of Counter Terrorism in the Office of the Prime Minster, formed in 1996, serves as the principal policy coordination body within Israel. The body answers directly to the Prime Minister and consists of representatives from the various agencies involved.[48] In addition, the Department for Counter Terrorism and Non Proliferation within the Ministry of Foreign Affairs' Division for Strategic Affairs, formed in 2001 partially in response to the 9/11 attacks, handles domestic and international issues that concern the increasing threat of terrorism.[49] The National Security Council, formed in 1999, provides security oversight as well as serves as a coordination body dealing with broader security questions.[50] In addition, the National Security Council deals with formulating long term planning and strategy.[51] Within the Knesset, the Foreign Affairs and Defense Committee provides legislative oversight over the various security services.

Practices

Israeli counter terrorism trends along three distinct tracts: offensive, defensive and punitive measures.[52] Offensive measures are used by the Israel Defense Force and the various other security agencies to both deter and hamper terrorist activity through preemptive action. Various examples of this type of action include the selective targeting of terrorist leaders or various sweeps within suspect areas through the use of air, sea and ground forces. Defensive measures include various barriers and checkpoints designed to limit access to potential targets. The security fence designed to separate Israel from Palestinian controlled areas, currently being built, is the best example of a defensive move and is credited by Israel for substantially decreasing the number of terrorist incidents – a decrease of some 45 percent between 2003 and 2004 in the number of people killed through terrorist activities.[53] Punitive measures differ in occupied territories and in Israel proper. Within the borders of Israel, the rule of law is generally limited to imprisonment. Within the occupied territories, punitive action can range from arrest to exile and has often involved the destruction of housing.[54]

It is worth noting that Israel places strong reliance on intelligence gathering as a means of prevention. The intelligence apparatus of Israel is considered one of the best. Through a vigilant population and traditional means of collecting information, Israel has proved highly successful in infiltrating and foiling terrorist activities.[55] However, the intelligence services of Israel have also been known to utilize techniques that are questionable from a humanitarian perspective. The three main intelligence organizations – Shin Bet, Mossad, and Aman – coordinate closely across multiple levels.

Shin Bet, or officially Israel Security Agency, is the lead agency for internal security within Israel, the West Bank and the Gaza Strip.[56] Shin Bet is divided into three operational departments plus five support departments. The Arab Affairs Department devotes its time to antiterrorism and political subversion, and maintains files on known terrorists. The Non-Arab Affairs Department concerns itself with counter intelligence work of other countries. The Protective Security Department protects the national airline, various government and strategic buildings, as well as the lives of various senior officials. It is believed that Shin Bet consists of some 5,000 employees.

Israel's foreign intelligence service, Mossad, is also internationally known and respected for its effectiveness.[57] The principal goals of Mossad, officially known as the Institute for Intelligence and Special Operations, involve intelligence collection, counter terrorism and special operations. Mossad employs approximately 1,200 agents divided into eight departments, including Collections, Political Action and Liason, Special Operations, LAP (Psychological warfare and propaganda), Research, and Technology.

Both Shin Bet and Mossad are responsible to the Prime Minister; however, the military has its own agency, Aman, separate from the Army, Navy, or Air Force; it consists of approximately 7,000 personnel.[58] Aman produces national intelligence estimates, daily intelligence briefs, country studies, as well as houses a number of special operations teams with specialized counter terrorism and intelligence gathering missions.

Both the military and the Israel police force play roles during an emergency. In Israel proper, the national police have primary authority over any incident, whereas in the occupied territories the military retains control. The National Police of Israel consist of some 30,000 officers with a supplementary volunteer corps of approximately 70,000. The combat components of the police force are the Border Police (Magav) that undergo infantry training and act as a mobile gendarmerie. Within Magav are a number of special operations units dedicated to counter intelligence and counter terrorism operations. The Israel National Police are under the Ministry of Public Security.

The Israel Defense Force (IDF), under the Ministry of Defense, has been created to secure the occupied territories, as well as "to defend the existence, territorial integrity and sovereignty of the state of Israel" and "to protect the inhabitants of Israel and to combat all forms of terrorism which threaten the daily life."[59] Israel has a compulsory military service requirement for both men and women. Upon completion of a three year commitment, reserve service is mandatory until the age of 54, with women subject to recall until the age of 34. Within the IDF, the Home Front Command is the principal military organization designed to assist the civilian population during times of emergencies. Formed in 1992, the command is responsible for protecting the civilian population during attacks or natural disasters and houses a number of search and rescue, and other specialized units.

Israel Homeland Security in a Comparative Perspective

While many have compared the terrorism faced by Israel with the new threats facing the United States, the comparison lacks depth when one accounts for the daily struggle over the entire history of the Jewish State to the relatively recent attack on the United States. This has been the motivating factor in many of the policies that Israel has in place now. Over the years, Israeli citizens have accepted decreased civil liberties in exchange for the increased security offered by more draconian methods of dealing with terrorism. This has forced Israel to defend its policies on the international front for accused violations of human rights and democratic traditions. The lessons from the Israeli system are important as much for their similarities as they are for their differences from the US model.

One lesson that the United States has been attempting to integrate in its system, unfortunately with little progress, is the high levels of cooperation that are demonstrated throughout the Israeli security services. The tightly integrated intelligence services are in stark contrast to the rivalry and suspicion that seems to plague the CIA and the FBI. The high level of commitment of the majority of the population through reserve duty or in terms of observation and reporting is also not seen within the United States. The hand on approach of the military permeates the occupied territories as well as Israel at large. Of course, the protections granted to US citizens prohibit the same level of general information sharing and military intrusiveness within civil society. Indeed, perhaps the largest difference between the two states lays in the level of independence the executive branch and the individual agencies have in acting against threats. Many of Israel's policies are based on laws written at the beginning of its statehood and are in need of updating. The emergency powers that have become institutions in the occupied territories are often viewed as less than democratic. While many of the policies that are being implemented within the United States have been in place for years in Israel, it is important that Washington recognizes the sacrifices to civil liberties that are being made in order to increase a security that is based on a highly different threat.

Russia

Nothing in Russia officially happens without the approval of the powerful presidential office, including the organization and operation of the homeland security infrastructure. According to the Russian Constitution, the President is not only a main architect of domestic politics, but is also in charge of foreign and security policies. Homeland defense plays as important of a role in Russia's politics today as it did in communist times when the system, lacking legitimacy from its people, protected itself through strong security. Given the acts of terrorism by Chechen rebels in such prominent cities as Moscow, Volgodonsk, and Buyanaksk, the Russian internal security apparatus had to change its focus and its role has since become increasingly intrusive. Since the infamous events of 9/11, and particularly the politically disgraceful Moscow theater hostage fiasco of the fall of 2002, the Chechen issue has dominated homeland security, now viewed as a terrorist threat, rather than a problem of a separatist and rebellious region. Despite the change in terminology, the government's policy and public's perception have not altered. However, as much as a strong homeland security structure in Russia is needed, the current Russian security system appears to be "adrift and leaderless, without any clear guidelines, and in serious trouble,"[60] effects of which are evident in the increasingly brutal and frequent nature of terrorist attacks on Russian soil.

The security environment in Russia changed as the Cold War ended. From relatively rare and unrelated incidents, in the 1990s terrorist activity in Russia proper took the form of a "systemic and large-scale threat to the state and society in general."[61] This shift was caused by deteriorating economic and political morale of the governing elites and the society at large. Viktor Petrishchev, a member of the Russian Duma, cites the following as the factors contributing to the spread of terrorist activity in Russia: a decline in economic conditions; ethnic tensions in the former republics; rising unemployment and declining standard of living; a high level of corruption among the governing elites; the rise of organized and street crime; and the rise of political and religious extremism.[62]

Political Framework

The Russian Federation, in its national security strategies, outlines its most essential internal and external threats, and provides a general outline of the future security policy. Although this document is not binding, it is essential for understanding the Russian security policy. It reflects not only the priorities based on extensive negotiations among the governing elites and the general economic, social and political climate in the country, but also provides a clear indication for the direction of the future security policy.

On 17 December 1997, President Boris Yeltsin signed the National Security Concept of the Russian Federation, providing a blueprint for Russia's domestic and international security.[63] This decree, surprisingly liberal in nature, outlined threats facing Russian national interests in the post-Cold War environment, placing them in Russia's interior rather than in the international setting.[64] It called for economic and social reforms as solutions to the growing problems. In 2000, President Vladimir Putin issued a decree changing and adapting the national security strategy.[65] The new security concept took into account developments in Kosovo and Chechnya, as well as the growing scope of NATO, expanding the external threat to Russian national security.[66] In contrast to the 1997 document, the new concept emphasized terrorism, rising crime and societal dissonance, and called for strengthened governmental authority and amplified intrusion into the social and political lives of its citizens.[67]

Legal Framework

The Criminal Code of the Russian Federation, established in 1996, and the 1998 Federal Law on Combating Terrorism serve as the basis for the Russian antiterrorism legal framework. The Criminal Code defines terrorist actions, sets forth appropriate punishments, outlines the responsibilities of the law enforcement and intelligence agencies, along with formulating their goals, structures, and operational means for uncovering, suppressing and preventing terrorism.

Chapter 24, Article 205 of the Criminal Code defines terrorism as "the perpetration of an explosion, arson, or any other action endangering the lives of people, causing sizable property damage, or entailing other socially dangerous consequences, if these actions have been committed for the purpose of violating public security, frightening the population, or exerting influence on decision-making by governmental bodies."[68] With such a broad definition, there is not much legal differentiation between criminal and terrorist activity.[69] Such an approach affords the State maximum authority over its citizens, consistent with the current direction of Russian politics.

Homeland Security Infrastructure

The Security Council[70] of the Russian Federation in the Federal Law of 25 July, 1998, with the latest revision in August 2004, determines the lawful and organizational bases of combating terrorism in the Russian Federation, the chain of command for the responsible agencies beyond the outlines of the Constitution of the Russian Federation, the Criminal Code and the Federal Law.[71] It also defines in much greater detail what terrorism, a terrorist, a terrorist action, group, organization are, giving the concept of terrorism a broad scope in an attempt to "break away from the recent trend of narrowing the definition of counter terrorism to a mere response to terrorist acts."[72] Furthermore, it provides a detailed blueprint for the legislative and executive structure. Directly responsible for internal security in the Russian Federation are the Federal Security Service of the Russian Federation; the Ministry of Internal Affairs; Federal Foreign Intelligence Service; the Federal Service for the Protection of the Russian

Federation; and the Ministry of Defense. The President can liquidate, reorganize or rename the powers of each agency. He also determines the scope of cooperation among the agencies, as well as between regional and federal levels, effectively remaining in the position of the final authority.

The Federal Security Service[73] and its territorial organs develop the security structure, uncovering and preventing security breaches, and act to diffuse and suppress terrorist threats. They work in cooperation with the border police in controlling the inflow of illegal traffic of people, weapons, explosives, toxic and radioactive materials, and other objects used for terrorist activities into the country. Along with the Ministry of Internal Affairs, they directly control counter-terrorist operations, usually headed by the regional leaders in case of regional threats. In an event of a national threat, the leadership position is determined by the nature of the threat and appointed by the federal anti-terrorist commission composed of the representatives of all the federal organs involved or the President of the Russian Federation.[74]

The Ministry of Internal Affairs, in addition, serves as an internal intelligence and development agency, whereas the Federal Foreign Intelligence Service, along with other organs of external reconnaissance, provides safety outside of Russia's borders. The Federal Service for the Protection of the Russian Federation safeguards "the security of facilities subject to state protection and defending protected facilities;"[75] and the Ministry of Defense provides protection of the weapons of mass destruction arsenals, rockets and small arms, ammunition and explosives, military targets, and participates in providing security to Russian water and air space.

In terms of infringing upon personal freedoms of citizens where security concerns are involved, the Russian government prefers to err on the side of security. In a stark contrast to French or British policies, the Russian legislature allows for drastic limitation of personal freedoms and violation of personal rights in order to maintain national security. The territorial and operational scope of an anti-terrorist operation is determined by the appointed leader. If necessary, the commanding leader may at his discretion limit or prohibit means of transportation within and outside of the outlined locality, remove citizens out of the territory in question, perform security checks, detain citizens, enter and search their property, use their property if necessary to carry out the operation.[76]

Russian Homeland Security in a Comparative Perspective

Despite the obvious differences in the political and social cultures of the Russian Federation and the United States, the antiterrorist policies of the two states display some similarities. They both restrict mass media coverage of incidents related to terrorist actions;[77] use military for large scale operations and the undercover tactics to infiltrate terrorist networks; protect the personnel involved in national security activities; assign higher priority to terrorism prevention; promote little or no deal-making with terrorist organizations; and follow a single chain of command during operations.[78] However, the similarities end there. The legal frameworks, financial resources, as well as the scope of governmental authority and infringement on personal freedoms and rights, vary drastically between American and Russian domestic security infrastructure.

The Russian case is unlike any of the other discussed here. While the United Kingdom has struggled with similar separatist forces, the high level of civil controls over the government are in stark contrast to what exists within Russia. Recently comparisons have been made with the United States in terms of a radical Islamist threat; however, the configuration of this threat is drastically different. Russia's failing struggle with terrorism reflects the dire state of its military infrastructure and morale, economic and social needs, and political restriction comparable to the old Soviet system – all of which are specific to Russia, rather than reflecting any commonalities. In that respect, Russia is a classic case of what not to do when assuring homeland security within a democracy. Notwithstanding the comparable experiences of terrorist attacks on American and Russian soil, Presidents Putin and Bush do not perceive terrorism in the same way.[79] While the United States is experiencing "new security normalcy," Russian "public's view of the terrorist threat remains largely unchanged ... Russians see the state as under attack not from the outside, but from the inside, as a result of its military, political, and economic weakness."[80] In contrast to the United States, Russia through its policies, instigates a good deal of home grown terrorism.[81] In this sense, the Russian Federation creates its own homeland security threat.[82]

Conclusion

The United States seems to be on the more moderate side of the homeland security fence as compared to the states presented here. While several laws recently legislated into the US legal framework have been questionable as to their damage to civil liberties, the massive surveillance and internal intelligence gathering that takes place within these four states would assuredly face serious challenges politically and judicially. In common with these four nations, the military can be called into use domestically; however, severe limitations as to what roles they can play bring the US more in line with the policies of the United Kingdom. Also similar to the United Kingdom, the United States has focused on a broad based system of homeland security that relies on the traditions first developed in the natural disasters of the past and incorporates the dangers that terrorism also presents. Similar to France's *Vigipirate* system, the threat warning system of the United States is designed to provide clear indication of the threat that is facing the nation. However, the intrusion upon civil society and the unclear powers of France's special judicial police units would contradict the spirit of America's ideas on freedom and limitations on government. Likewise, the gross intrusions of the Israeli military and intelligence services upon Israeli society would never be tolerated within the United States. However, the security fence being built in Israel is comparable to that being built along the US-Mexico border. Of course, the immigrant workers coming into the United States are different than the threat faced by Israel. Russia would appear to offer few comparative points, only lessons. The lack of checks on the central government and an internal security apparatus with very little controls placed on it[83] would spell disaster for what passes for rights in the United States. It should be noted however, that with the exception of the 11 September 2001 attacks, the United States has not experienced the same degree of terrorist activity as the four states presented here. Perhaps, under similar circumstances, the reduction of civil liberties would be tolerated to a greater level as would the focus away from other disasters and more toward terrorism.[84]

Notes

1. Gus Hosein, "Threatening the Open Society: Comparing Anti-terror Policeis and Strategies in the U.S. and Europe," *Privacy International*, 13 December 2005.
2. Samuel T. Francis, "Terrorist Renaissance: France, 1980-1983," *World Affairs*, 146/1 (Summer 1983), 54-58.
3. "Combating Terrorism: How Five Foreign Countries Are Organized to Combat Terrorism," *GAO/NSIAD-00-85* (April 2000).
4. Paul Gallis, "France: Factors Shaping Foreign Policy, and Issues in U.S.-French Relations," *CRS Report for Congress* RL32464, 4 February 2005.
5. "France's Experiences with-and Methods Combating-Terrorism," as viewed 26 Nov 2005 on the Embassy of France in the United States website.
6. *Ibid.*
7. "Combating Terrorism: How Five Foreign Countries Are Organized to Combat Terrorism"; Peter Chalk and William Rosenau, "Confronting the Enemy Within: Security Intelligence, the Police, and Counter terrorism in Four Democracies," *Rand Corporation* MG-100, 2004.
8. Erik van de Linde, Kevin O'Brien, Gustav Lindstrom, Stephan de Spiegeleire, Mikko Vayrynen and Han de Vries, "Quick Scan of post 9/11 national counter-terrorism policymaking and implementation in selected European countries," *RandEurope* MR-1590, May 2002.
9. Report submitted by France to the Counter-Terrorism Committee pursuant to paragraph 6 of Security Council resolution 1373 (2001) of 28 September 2001.
10. Shaun Gregory, "France and the War on Terrorism," *Terrorism and Political Violence* 15/1 (2003), 124-147.
11. "Combating Terrorism: How Five Foreign Countries Are Organized to Combat Terrorism."
12. Chalk and Rosenau, 2004.
13. *Ibid.*
14. "Combating Terrorism: How Five Foreign Countries Are Organized to Combat Terrorism."
15. "RG-General Information," available at http://www.fas.org/irp/world/france/interieur/rg/index.html
16. Stéphane Marchand, 'Enquête sur les trois grands services de renseignement français', *Le Figaro,* 8 April 1995; Jeremy Shapiro and Bénédicte Suzan, 'The French Experience of Counter-Terrorism', *Survival*, 45/1(2003), 67-98.
17. Derek Lutterbeck, "Blurring the Line: The Convergence of Internal and External Security in Western Europe," *European Security*, 14:2 (June 2005), 231-253.
18. Jeremy Shapiro and Bénédicte Suzan.

19. Craig Whitlock, "French Push Limits in Fight On Terrorism," *The Washington Post*, 2 November 2004.
20. "Profile: Jose Padilla," *BBCNews,* 22 November 2005; Jerry Markon, "U.S. Can Confine Citizens Without Charges, Court Rules," *The Washington Post,* 10 September 2005; harging Padilla: Mootness and Chief Justice Rehnquist," *Jurist,* 23 November 2005; *Rumsfeld v. Padilla* No. 03-1027, 28 June 2004.
21. Rebecca Cox, "Counterterrorism legislation: A Question of Reaction?" *RUSI/ Jane's Homeland Security and Resilience Monitor,* 30 December 2005.
22. Terrorism Act 2000, available at http://www.opsi.gov.uk/acts/acts2000/00011--b.htm#1
23. Anti Terrorism, Crime and Security Act 2001, available at http://www.opsi.gov.uk/acts/acts2001/20010024.htm.
24. Prevention of Terrorism Act 2005, available at http://www.opsi.gov.uk/ acts/ acts2005/20050002.htm.
25. "Civil Contingencies Act 2004: A Short Guide," available at http://www.ukresilience.info/ ccact/3octshortguide.pdf.
26. "Combating Terrorism: How Five Foreign Countries Are Organized to Combat Terrorism."
27. Ministerial Committee in Civil Contingencies, available at http://www.cabinetoffice.gov.uk/ secretariats/committees/ccc.asp.
28. "Memorandum submitted by the Home Office," *Select Committee on Home Affairs Written Evidence*, The United Kingdom Parliament, 26 February 2004.
29. "Civil Contingencies Committee," *Written Answers to Questions (17 November 1997)*, The United Kingdom Parliament.
30. "Campaign Against Terrorism," *Written Answers to Questions (27 November 2001)*, The United Kingdom Parliament.
31. "Memorandum submitted by the Home Office," *Select Committee on Home Affairs Written Evidence*, The United Kingdom Parliament, 26 February 2004.
32. "Civil Contingencies Secretariat," http://www.cabinetoffice.gov.uk/secretariats/ civil_contingencies/index.asp. The UK uses the term *Resilience* to define the aspect of coordination, preparation and response to various national emergencies.
33. "The Lead Government Department and its role- Guidance and Best Practices," *Civil Contingencies Secretariat*, available at http://www.ukresilience.info/publications/lgds.pdf.
34. Tod Masse, "Domestic Intelligence in the United Kingdom: Applicability of the MI-5 Model to the United States," Report for Congress *CRS* RL31920, 19 May 2003.
35. "MI5," *Federation of American Scientists*, available at http://www.fas.org/irp/ world/uk/mi5/budget.htm; Richard Norton-Taylor and Riazat Butt, "Queen is target for al-Qaida Security Sources Confirm," *The Guardian*, 14 November 2005.
36. "About MI5," available at http://www.mi5.gov.uk.
37. "National Intelligence Machinery," *Cabinet Office* available at http://www.cabinetoffice. gov.uk/publications/reports/intelligence/nationalintelligence machinery.pdf.
38. Available from the Office of Public Sector Information at http://www.opsi.gov.uk.
39. Paul Howard, ed. "Hard Won Lessons: How Police Fight Terrorism in the United Kingdom," *Safe Cities Project*, Manhattan Institute, December 2004.
40. "Budget 2005 Summary," *HM Treasury* available at http://budget2005.treasury.gov.uk/ page_09.html; "National Policing Plan 2005-08: Safer, Stronger Communities," *Home Office*, November 2004.
41. "Operations in the UK: The Defence Contribution to Resilience," Interim Joint Doctrine Publication 02, *Joint Doctrine & Concepts Centre* available at http://www.ukresilience.info/ publications/index.shtm.
42. *Ibid.*

43. "Security, Terrorism and the UK," *Chatham House* ISP/NSC Briefing Paper 05/01, July 2005.
44. Steve Conner, "Surveillance UK: Why This Revolution is Only the Start," *The Independent,* 22 December 2005; Martin Gill and Angela Spriggs, "Assessing the Impact of CCTV," *Home Office Research Study 292*, Home Office Research, Development and Statistics Directorate, February 2005.
45. Bruno S. Frey, *Dealing with Terrorism: Stick or Carrot?* (Cheltenham: Edward Elgar, 2005).
46. "Combating Terrorism: How Five Foreign Countries Are Organized to Combat Terrorism"; "Defence (Emergency) Regulations," *The Palestine Gazette*, No. 1442. Published by the British Government, Palestine (Sept. 27, 1945); David Kretzmer, *The Occupation of Justice: The Supreme Court of Israel and the Occupied Territories* (SUNY Press, Albany, NY: 2002).
47. "Prevention of Terrorism Ordinance No.33 of 5708-1948," 23 September 1948, available at http://www.mfa.gov.il/MFA/MFAArchive.
48. Israeli Report to the UN Committee on Counter terrorism, 27 December 2001.
49. *Ibid.*
50. "Combating Terrorism: How Five Foreign Countries Are Organized to Combat Terrorism."
51. *Ibid.*; Israeli Government Press Office, 3 September 1999.
52. "Background – The Components of Counter-Terrorism," *The Institute for Counter-Terrorism*, available at http://www.ict.org.il/; Jerry D. Smith, "The Effectiveness of Israel's Counter-Terrorism Strategy," *Naval Post Graduate School*, Thesis, March 2005.
53. Abigail Cutler, "Security Fences," *The Atlantic Monthly* 295:2, 40 (March 2005).
54. Jerry D. Smith, "The Effectiveness of Israel's Counter-Terrorism Strategy"; According to Amnesty International, Israel outlawed the death penalty with the exception of special circumstances in 1954 and has not executed an individual since 1962.
55. Jonathan B. Tucker, "Strategies for Countering Terrorism: Lessons from the Israeli Experience," *Journal of Homeland Security*, March 2003.
56. "Israel Security Agency," *Global Security.org*; "Inside Israel's Secret Organizations," *Jane's Intelligence Review*; October 1996.
57. "The Institute for Intelligence and Special Operations," *Global Security.org;* "Inside Israel's Secret Organizations," *Jane's Intelligence Review* October 1996.
58. "Aman Military Intelligence," *Global Security.org*; "Inside Israel's Secret Organizations," *Jane's Intelligence Review* October 1996.
59. Israel Defense Forces: The Official Website.
60. Roman Kupchinsky, "Russia: the loosing battle against terrorism and insurgency," Radio Free Europe/Radio Liberty, 18 September 2004, available at www.terrorisme.net.
61. Viktor Petrishchev, "Russian Legislation and the Fight Against Terrorism," in: *High-Impact Terrorism: Proceedings of a Russian American Workshop* (The National Academies Press: 2002) p. 25.
62. *Ibid.*, 27.
63. Alexander A. Sergounin, "Russia: A long Way to the National Security Doctrine," March 1998, Columbia Interantional Affairs Online, available at www.ciaonet.org/wps/sea03/#17.
64. Celeste A. Wallander, "The Russian National Security Concept: A Liberal –Statist Synthesis," July 1998, PONARS Policy Memo 30, Harvard University, Center for Strategic and International Studies, available at www.csis.org/media/csis/pubs/pm_0030.pdf.
65. See Concept of national Security of the Russian Federation (Endorsed by the Decree of the President of the Russian Federation No. 1300 of December 17, 1997 in the wording of the

Decree of the President of the Russian Federation No. 24 of January 10, 2000), available at www.nyu.edu/globalbeat/nuclear/Gazeta012400.html.

66. Celeste A Wallander, "Russian National Security Policy in 2000," January 2000, PONARS Policy Memo 102, Harvard University, Center for Strategic and International Studies, available at www.csis.org/media/csis/pubs/pm_0102.pdf.

67. *Ibid.*, 4.

68. Text and translation provided by the Anti-Corruption Gateway for Europe and Eurasia, available at www.nobribes.org.

69. Mikhail Kireev, "Russian Legislation and the Struggle Against Terrorism," in: *High-Impact Terrorism: Proceedings of a Russian American Workshop*, p. 19.

70. This body coordinates the security policy between the Russian President, who chairs it, and the federal bodies. For more information regarding the security and intelligence agencies of the Russian Federation please see Soviet/Russian Intelligence Agencies provided by Federation of American Scholars, available at www.fas.org/irp/world/russia/index.html.

71. Федеральный закон от 25 июля 1998 г. № 130-ФЗ "О борьбе с терроризмом," Trans.: Russian Federation Federal Law No. 130-FZ "On combating terrorism," available at www.scrf.gov.ru.

72. Petrishchev, 32.

73. For in-depth information on the history, structure and operation of FSB, please consult Структура органов Федеральной Службы безопасности РФ (утверждена Указом Президента Российской Федерации от 11 августа 2003 г. N 960), Trans: Structure of the Organs of Federal Security Service of the Russian Federation (legislated by the decree of the President of the Russian Federation on 11 August 2003); available at www.fsb.ru/structure/ukaz/. Also please see ИСТОРИЧЕСКАЯ СПРАВКА ОБ ОРГАНАХ ГОСУДАРСТВЕННОЙ БЕЗОПАСНОСТИ, Trans: Historical Information on the Organs of National Security, available at www.fsb.ru/history/organi.html.

74. Федеральный закон от 25 июля 1998 г. № 130-ФЗ.

75. Russian Federation Federal Law No. 130-FZ, Signed by Russian Federation President B. Yeltsin, 25 July 1998, Russian Intelligence-Related Legal Documents provided by Federation of American Scientists, available at www.fas.org/irp/world/russia/docs/law_980725.htm; This document is a translation of its equivalent in Russian provided by the Security Council of the Russian Federation.

76. Федеральный закон от 25 июля 2002 г. № 114-ФЗ "О противодействии экстремистской деятельности," Trans: Federal Law of 25 July, 2002, No. 114-FZ "On the Opposition to Extremist Activity," available at www.scrf.gov.ru.

77. For a broader scope of information on this subject please see The Brookings Institution/Harvard Forum on "The Role of the Press in the Anti-Terrorism Campaing; Assessing the Media and the Government." *A Quarterly Review,* January 9th, 2002, available at http://www.brookings.edu/GS/Projects/Press/Press.htm. Especially Michael Getler, the ombudsman for *The Washington Post*, who said: "A large question is, we don't know what we don't know. We really don't know. This is a very, very closely held war in terms of information and secrecy. There are obviously some reasons that make that legitimate. My concern, just as an observer, and it's not provable, but my concern as an observer is that it goes well beyond that. I think what we're seeing now is a situation where the public really, the United States has been attacked, the public wants the enemy defeated as they should be, and they really are not concerned about press concerns or access concerns or secrecy concerns."

78. Petrishchev, 35.

79. For an in-depth discussion of the nature of terrorist threat facing Russia and the

governmental policies regarding it, please see Dmitri Trenin, "Russia and anti-terrorism," Carnegie Endowment for International Peace: Carnegie Moscow Center, March 22, 2005, available at www.carnegie.ru/en/pubs/media/72290.htm.

80. Fiona Hill, "Putin and Bush in Common Cause? Russia's View of the Terrorist Threat After September 11," The Brookings Institution Global Politics, *The Brookings Review*, 20:3 (Summer 2002); 33-35, available at www.brookings.edu/press/review/summer2002/hill.htm.

81. See also Igor Torbakov, "War on Terrorism in the Caucasus: Russia Breeds Jihadists," *Chechnya Weekly*, 6:42 (November 10, 2005), The Jamestown Foundation, available at www.jamestown.org/publications_details.php?volume_id=409&issue_id=3522&article_id=2370458.

82. See also Fiona Hill, "Central Asia: Terrorism, Religious Extremism, and Regional Stability," Testimony before the House Committee on International Relations Subcommittee on the Middle East and Central Asia, July 23, 2003, available at www.brookings.edu/views/testimony/hill/20030723.pdf.

83. On March 6, 2005, the Council of Europe issued a public report in which it criticizes Russia for incompliance with the CoE guidelines and standards regarding laws on federal security services. The Russian Federation has been a member of the Council of Europe for the past eight years and, upon accession, committed to revising the law on federal security within a year. In particular, the report states: "The current Law on Organs of the Federal Service126 of 3 April 1995 gave the President direction of the activities of the security service, which has the status of a federal executive organ and outlined the FSB's mission in detail. The FSB regained a number of the functions that had been eliminated in earlier post-KGB reorganizations … To date, the 1995 law has been neither repealed nor substantially modified: it still provides that, apart from the normal activities of a secret service127, the FSB also performs law enforcement duties that are traditionally in most member states, if not all, entrusted to specialised departments of the police or the public prosecutor's office. Indeed, the main problem with the FSB is not that it is still authorised to run a number of pre-trial detention centres but that it retains to date a number of specific investigation powers seriously affecting individuals' rights which it should not have … Although we have no compelling reason to doubt that the thousands of agents working today for the FSB act only in the national interest and in conformity with the law, fully respect fundamental freedoms and are not being used as a means of oppression or undue pressure, as was the case with the KGB, the present set-up of the FSB is clearly contravening European standards and, in particular, the Assembly's Recommendation 1402 (1999) on the control of internal security services in Council of Europe member states. We do not believe, contrary to what was stated by our interlocutors, that the necessity to fight terrorism and organised crime justifies the sweeping powers still afforded to the FSB … We therefore urge the Russian authorities to honour this outstanding commitment without further delay and to revise the 1995 law on the federal security services in line with Council of Europe standards." Issued by Parliamentary Assembly of the Council of Europe, "Hounouring of obligations and commitments by the Russian Federation," June 3, 2005, available at http://assembly.coe.int/Documents/WorkingDocs/Doc05/ EDOC10568.pdf.

84. Of note, the recent fiasco during the aftermath of Hurricane Katrina has created a push to remove the Federal Emergency Management Organization away from the Department of Homeland Security. See the concluding chapter for a more detailed overview of the issues surrounding the aftermath of Hurricane Katrina.

Conclusion

The Present and Future Threats

Introduction

In the aftermath of the September 11 2001 attacks, homeland security was focused almost exclusively on the prevention of, and response to, terrorism. There was a dramatic increase in funding for federal, state and local efforts to prevent terrorism and to prepare response plans for major terrorist attacks. With the creation of the Department of Homeland Security, federal counterterrorism efforts became much better coordinated and integrated across all levels of government. Two major issues stand out in US homeland security policy. The first is the ongoing effort to identify the most significant contemporary and future threats. Threat recognition will guide the allocation of resources and the overall parameters of policy for the near-term future. Among the main areas of concern are: critical infrastructure, cybersecurity, and the potential for catastrophic attacks involving the use of nuclear, chemical or biological weapons. The second major issue bedeviling current policy efforts concerns assessment. A Congressional Research Service report notes that: "How one perceives and measures progress is central to formulating and implementing anti-terror strategy. Perception has a major impact, as well, on how nations prioritize and allocate resources. On the flip side, the parameters used to measure progress can set the framework for the measurement of failure."[1] The lack of a significant attack within the United States since the September 11 strikes has created a perception of success. However, questions remain about the contemporary priorities of homeland security policy and the use of resources. The development of a national system to assess policies and programs is critical to the success of those policies.

The creation of the Department of Homeland Security brought together all of the federal agencies tasked to respond to major disasters. Between 2001 and 2006, the greatest threats to stability and economic prosperity in the United States have come from non-human sources, specifically natural disasters. A succession of hurricanes hit the state of Florida in 2004, causing billions of dollars in damage and leading to the displacement of thousands of people. The following year, Hurricane Katrina devastated the Gulf Coast region. More than one million people were displaced by the storm. The recovery costs rivaled the expenditures necessitated by the September 11 attacks. In the immediate aftermath of the storm, Congress appropriated $10.5 billion for the recovery effort in fiscal year 2005.[2] Congress subsequently allocated an additional $29 billion for fiscal year 2006. The timeframe for economic recovery for the region was three to five years. In light of criticism of the Federal Emergency Management Agency (FEMA), within the Department of Homeland Security, its director, Michael Brown, was forced to resign. The impact of the hurricane has led to a reevaluation of the functions and missions of the Homeland Security Department and its agencies. Increasingly, homeland security within the United States will necessitate the ability to balance the hard security threats presented by terrorism and the soft security threats posed by natural disasters or other catastrophic events.

Terrorism and Weapons of Mass Destruction

The cornerstone of the Bush administration's homeland security policy is codified in the July 2002 *National Strategy for Homeland Security* (NSHS). Among the various goals identified in the plan, the administration argues that the priorities of homeland security are twofold: first, to protect the "physical well-being of the American people"; second, to "safeguard our way of life."[3] The administration contends that protecting the American way of life includes five major components: 1) democracy; 2) liberties; 3) security; 4) economics; and 5) culture.[4]

These elements, which comprise the core of the United States, are vulnerable to terrorist attacks. The NSHS notes that:

> Terrorism is not so much a system of belief, like fascism or communism, as it is a strategy and a tactic – a means of attack. In this war on terrorism, we must defend ourselves against a wide range of means and methods of attack. Our enemies are working to obtain chemical, biological, radiological, and nuclear weapons for the stated purpose of killing vast numbers of Americans. Terrorists continue to employ conventional means of attack, such as bombs and guns. At the same time, they are gaining expertise in less traditional means, such as cyber attacks. Lastly, as we saw on September 11, out terrorist enemies are constantly seeking new tactics or unexpected ways to carry out their attacks and magnify their effects.[5]

The NSHS divides potential terrorist threats into four broad risk categories. First, the United States is susceptible to attack by nuclear, biological or chemical weapons. This category of attack has the highest risk quotient and could cause the greatest number of casualties. Throughout the 1990s, a range of terrorist attacks and plots across the world showcased the desire and willingness of terrorist groups to utilize weapons of mass destruction to attack civilian populations. For instance, in 1994, members of the Aum Shinrikyo cult attacked a neighborhood in Matsumoto where they dispersed Sarin gas (a chemical, nerve agent) through an aerosol system from a refrigerator truck. The attack killed seven and made 500 people sick. Aum Shinrikyo then attacked the Tokyo Subway with Sarin in 1995. The cult placed five packages of Sarin at different locations in the subway system. The attack killed twelve and injured 3,800. Fortunately, the subway system's ventilation system dispersed the agent in such a fashion that the casualties were actually much lower. The subsequent investigation of the cult discovered that the cult had chemical and biological weapons as early as 1990 and that the cult had endeavored to launch a biological attack in June 1993 by releasing botulin toxin.[6] In addition, in 1994, the cult attempted to bring samples of the ebola virus from Africa in an effort to weaponize the virus for use in a future terrorist strike.[7]

In 2001, there were a series of anthrax attacks in the United States.[8] Lethal doses of anthrax were delivered through the US postal system. The disease proved fatal in 45 percent of the cases (five out of 11 people infected).[9] The perpetrator, or perpetrators, of the attacks have yet to be identified or apprehended.[10] The FBI estimated that the clean-up costs and investigation cost more than $1 billion.[11] The Aum Shinrikyo and anthrax examples demonstrate the relative ease with which groups can obtain chemical or biological weapons. The precursors for the weapons often have legitimate dual-use purposes. In addition, there is a large international community of researchers, military officers and scholars who have intimate knowledge of the weapons. As the NSHS notes, "biological weapons are especially dangerous because we may not know immediately that we have been attacked, allowing an infectious agent time to spread. Moreover, biological agents can serve as a means of attack against humans as well as livestock and crops, inflicting casualties as well as economic damage."[12]

The potential for a nuclear strike includes the use of a nuclear weapon or a radiological strike. While nuclear weapons have enormous destructive potential, the difficulties in acquiring and transporting the weapons are significant. Nonetheless, a variety of terrorist groups have sought to acquire the weapons. An ad hoc group assembled by the Washington think tank, the Nuclear Control Institute, noted that there are a range of hurdles that groups would have to overcome to acquire a nuclear, although the possibility exists:

> Assuming the existence of a subnational group equipped for the activist role of acquiring the necessary fissile material and the technical role of making effective use of it, the question arises as to the time they might need to get ready. The period would depend on a number of factors, such as the form and nature of the material acquired and the form in which the terrorists proposed to use it; the most important factor would be the extent of the preparation and practice that the group had carried out before the actual acquisition of the material. To minimize the time interval between acquisition and readiness, the whole team would be required to prepare for a considerable number of weeks (or, more probably, months) prior to acquisition. With respect to uranium, most of the necessary preparation and practice could be worked through using natural uranium as a stand-in.[13]

The time required to develop a nuclear would vary, but could be considerably short:

> The time intervals might range from a modest number of hours, on the supposition that enriched uranium oxide powder could be used as is, to a number of days in the event that uranium oxide powder or highly enriched (unirradiated) uranium reactor fuel elements were to be converted to uranium metal. The time could be much longer if the specifications of the device had to be revised after the material was in hand. For plutonium, the time intervals

would be longer because of the greatly increased hazards involved (and the absolute need of foreseeing, preparing for, and observing all the necessary precautions). In addition, although uranium could be used as a stand-in for plutonium in practice efforts, there would be no opportunity to try out some of the processes required for handling plutonium until a sufficient supply was available.[14]

The second form of nuclear strike would be through the use of a Radiological Dispersal Device (RDD) or "dirty bomb." An RDD could be a conventional explosive devise, combined with radioactive materials, or it could simply be radioactive material placed in an area that would contaminate people or drinking water or food supplies. The most likely source of material for an RDD is nuclear waste or radioactive devices used in medical treatments. The impact of an RDD would vary depending on a range of factors. Most experts agree that the costs and number of casualties of an RDD attack would be potentially lower than other weapons of mass destruction, and that the main risk is the long-term potential for cancer (with deaths from cancer ranging from one-in-one hundred to one-in-one hundred thousand, depending on proximity to the attack).[15] The US Nuclear Regulatory Agency has noted that:

> The extent of local contamination would depend on a number of factors, including the size of the explosive, the amount and type of radioactive material used, and weather conditions. Prompt detectability of the kind of radioactive material employed would greatly assist local authorities in advising the community on protective measures, such as quickly leaving the immediate area, or going inside until being further advised. Subsequent decontamination of the affected area could involve considerable time and expense.[16]

The potential for the use of an RDD was reinforced by the case of Jose Padilla, an American citizen and former gang member, who was arrested in May 2002 on suspicion of ties to Al Qaeda and plans to conduct an RDD attack within the United States.[17]

Conventional Attacks

The most likely potential attack on the United States remains a conventional strike using explosive devices or personal weapons. The low cost and relative ease in planning and launching a conventional strike make this tactic especially attractive to terrorist groups. Bombs, or other improvised explosive devices (IEDs), can be delivered in a variety of means. In the past terrorists, including domestic terrorists such as the Unibomber or the Oklahoma City Bombers, have utilized a range of methods, including letter bombs, car bombs, and suicide/homicide bombs, to conduct attacks against government and civilian targets around the world. Suicide/homicide bombers have proven to be especially effective in conducting strikes around the world. The British intelligence agency, MI5, notes that "Suicide bombers fall broadly into one of two categories: either, as with the 11 September terrorists, they hijack a plane or use any other kind of vehicle and turn it into a bomb; or they conceal explosive on their persons and detonate it wherever it will cause most damage."[18] Suicide/homicide attacks often provide the most damage for the least cost for terrorist groups (these strikes also involve far less planning). Writing in the *Atlantic Monthly*, Bruce Hoffman provides an overview of the attractiveness of suicide/homicide attacks:

> Such are the weapons of war in Israel today: nuts and bolts, screws and ball bearings, any metal shards or odd bits of broken machinery that can be packed together with homemade explosive and then strapped to the body of a terrorist dispatched to any place where people gather – bus, train, restaurant, café, supermarket, shopping mall, street corner, promenade. These attacks probably cost no more than $150 to mount, and they need no escape plan – often the most difficult aspect of a terrorist operation. And they are reliably deadly. According to data from the Rand Corporation's chronology of international terrorism incidents, suicide attacks on average kill four times as many people as other terrorist acts. Perhaps it is not surprising, then, that this means of terror has become increasingly popular. The tactic first emerged in Lebanon, in 1983; a decade later it came to Israel, and it has been a regular security problem ever since. Fully two thirds of all such incidents in Israel have occurred in the past two and a half years – that is, since the start of the second intifada, in September 2000. Indeed, suicide bombers are responsible for almost half of the approximately 750 deaths in terrorist attacks since then.[19]

While the casualties and economic damage of these strikes is often limited, their psychological impact can be considerable. Hoffman notes that the potential impact of suicide/homicide attacks on the United States could change forever the social and economic environment. One result may be the transformation of American society so that it more resembles states such as Israel that have developed a substantial domestic security infrastructure. Hoffman specifically writes that:

> In the United States in the 20 months since 9/11 we, too, have had to become accustomed to an array of new, often previously inconceivable security measures – in airports and other transportation hubs, hotels and office buildings, sports stadiums and concert halls. Although some are more noticeable and perhaps more inconvenient than others, the fact remains that they have redefined our own sense of normality. They are accepted because we feel more vulnerable than before. With every new threat to international security we become more willing to live with stringent precautions and reflexive, almost unconscious wariness. With every new threat, that is, our everyday life becomes more like Israel's.[20]

One significant implication for future suicide/homicide bombings is the need for greater private/government cooperation in site security. Israel, a nation of 5.3 million, has at least 20,000 private security contractors.[21] When suicide/homicide bombers strike the United States, there will a immediate demand for more, and both better trained and better armed, private security guards in public spaces, including shopping malls and sports venues.

Cyber Attacks

The potential damage from cyber attacks is enormous, although the vulnerabilities are mainly economic and quality of life, as opposed to direct casualties (although some cyber attacks could damage medical and emergency response capabilities). In general, there has been a steady increase in the number of cyber threats world wide. Dorothy E. Denning summarizes the increase in incidents in a report for the Social Science Research Council:

> The Computer Emergency Response Team Coordination Center (CERT/CC), for example, reported 2,134 incidents in 1997. This number rose to 21,756 in 2000 and to almost 35,000 during the first three quarters of 2001 alone. Considering that many, perhaps most, incidents are never reported to CERT/CC or indeed to any third party, the numbers become even more significant. Further, each incident that is reported corresponds to an attack that can involve thousands of victims. The Code Red worm, which infected about a million servers in July and August [2001] and caused $2.6 billion in damages, was a single incident.[22]

The NSHS presented the Bush administration's view of cyber terrorism as a major new threat to the United States. Among the administration's main concerns are the potential for cyber terrorism to harm "critical infrastructures such as our energy, financial, and securities networks."[23] Because of its potential impact on the private sector, cyber terrorism is another area which calls for greater cooperation and coordination between government and the private sector. In this regard, progress has been made (although considerable work remains to be done). One example of effective partnership is the United States Computer Emergency Readiness Team (US-CERT). It was created in 2003 as "partnership between the Department of Homeland Security and the public and private sectors ... to protect the nation's Internet infrastructure, US-CERT coordinates defense against and responses to cyber attacks across the nation."[24] The organization is the operational side of the National Cyber Security Division of the Department of Homeland Security, and it works with some 250 organizations around the world to coordinate cyber security (one of US-CERT's major partners is Carnegie Mellon's own Computer Emergency Readiness Team or CERT which was established in 1988). US-CERT works with its partners to identify threats and vulnerabilities and to respond to cyber attacks, including the full spectrum of viruses and worms. By incorporating the expertise and resources of the private sector into the broader effort to prevent cyber attacks and cyber terrorism, the government is able to greatly enhance its capabilities and assets. Further expansion of this type of cooperative initiative will be critical to protect against cyber terrorism.

Concurrently, the government must ensure that resources are allocated according to the most significant threat quotients. While the risks of cyber terrorism are great, various entities and scholars have warned about overemphasizing the potential threats of cyber attacks at the expense of other counterterrorism initiatives. For instance, the United States Institute of Peace (USIP) noted that:

> Psychological, political, and economic forces have combined to promote the fear
> of cyberterrorism. From a psychological perspective, two of the greatest fears of
> modern time are combined in the term "cyberterrorism." The fear of random,
> violent victimization blends well with the distrust and outright fear of computer
> technology.[25]

The US government spends approximately $4.5 billion per year on defense against cyber terrorism. Symantec, one of the world's largest virus protection firms, reported that "software holes" which lead to vulnerabilities in programs and systems had increased by 80 percent in 2002 as more and more new programs and software became available to the market.[26] Although there have yet to be instances of large-scale cyber terrorism, there have been episodes which point to the potential harm that could be caused by such attacks (including examples where terrorists are involved in the design and implementation of software which would therefore make systems highly vulnerable to attack).[27]

Terrorism and Innovative Attacks

The terrorist strikes of 2001 demonstrated that groups such as Al Qaeda could develop and implement innovative and unconventional attacks. As noted, terrorism is a form of asymmetrical warfare in which the terrorists seek to exploit any weaknesses they identify within the target nation. The NSHS identifies "new or unexpected tactics" as a special category of attack and describes the category in the following manner:

> Our terrorist enemies are constantly seeking new tactics or unexpected ways to
> carry out attacks. They are continuously trying to find new areas of
> vulnerability and apply lessons learned from past operations in order to achieve
> surprise and maximize the destructive effect of their next attack. Our society
> presents an almost infinite array of potential targets, allowing for an enormously
> wide range of potential attack methods.[28]

The attack on the USS *Cole* in September 2000 and the September 11 attacks are demonstrative of ability of terrorists to utilize unexpected tactics.[29] Writing for the Rand Corporation, Brian Jackson uses the example of the Irish Republican Army to demonstrate the adaptability of terrorist groups. Jackson writes that "the Irish Republican Army gradually evolved their explosive designs to incorporate first crude timers, then radio control, and finally triggers using radar detectors or remote photographic flash units in response to British efforts to jam or defeat their bomb detonation."[30] Jackson also describes the ability of groups such as Al Qaeda, the Revolutionary Armed Forces of Columbia (FARC), and Egyptian Islamic Jihad, to adapt tactics and strategy and undertake new methods of attack and targets.[31]

Adaptive terrorist groups pose special challenges for counterterrorism policy. It is difficult to develop strategies to ameliorate threats when those risks cannot be easily identified. One response of the Bush administration has been an increasing emphasis on response capabilities. To prepare for the potentially unknown, the Bush administration has endeavored to better coordinate across the range of federal, state and local law enforcement and first responders. The Defense Threat Reduction Agency, the Center for Disease Control and the Commerce Department's National Institute of Standards and Technology are working together to improve the testing ability of various bodies to detect chemical or biological attacks through quick and highly accurate medical testing.[32] Nonetheless, as discussed in Chapter 5, in order to implement more effective response abilities, the federal government will need to expand its coordination and cooperation with the state and local levels of government. (in addition to bolstering capabilities through more efficient resources allocation for homeland security initiatives).

The Bush administration has also asserted that its global war on terror provides the best means to keep terrorist groups off-balance and reactive, instead of proactive. For instance, in response to suggestions that the United States withdraw form Iraq, National Security Advisor Stephen Hadley declared "advocates of withdrawal fail to explain how abandoning Iraq to the terrorists and Ba'athists would make American more secure. We [the Bush administration] contend it would only encourage further attacks on the America."[33] In February 2003, the Bush administration released *The National Strategy for Combating Terrorism* (NSCT), an effort to further integrate the foreign and domestic implications of the *National Security Strategy*. The NSCT emphasizes the asymmetric nature of terrorism and governmental responses to the threat. Just as terrorism attempts to exploit the weaknesses of the government-in-power, the NSCT asserts that the United States will use its geo-strategic and economic advantages to defeat terrorist groups.[34] Through proactive and aggressive policies which integrate national- and homeland security strategies, the Bush administration hopes to utilize asymmetric warfare to its advantage and utilize its strengths to keep terrorist groups on the defensive.

Assessing Homeland Security

One of the greatest challenges emerges in the effort to assess the effectiveness of homeland security policy is the question of measurement: how can one tell if homeland security policies are working? At one level, the lack of a significant attack can be seen as a sign of accomplishment. However, the lack of a major attack or incident could just as easily be tied to the failure, or unwillingness, of terrorist groups to launch attacks (following the aforementioned argument, for instance, the lack of attack could be the result of Al Qaeda and other groups concentrating their energy and resources in Iraq). This would mean that the United States could still possess critical vulnerabilities to attack, risks which would not be exposed until the next attack. Nevertheless, the ultimate test by which homeland security policies are judged is whether or not attacks have occurred.

Attitude is also important in assessment. Since one of the goals of terrorist activity is to disrupt normal patterns of behavior and economic activity, "perception" is a major component in assessing policy. For instance, a study done by Carnegie Mellon highlighted the impact that emotions and perceptions have on policy implementation. Jennifer Lerner, who helped oversee the survey, noted that feelings "clearly influence everything from future support for military action to decisions to travel."[35] The Carnegie Mellon study specifically developed four main conclusions:

- Americans who experience anger are more optimistic about the future, less likely to take precautionary actions, and are more likely to favor aggressive policy responses than those who experience fear.
- Individuals see themselves as less vulnerable than the "average American," while still perceiving strikingly high personal risk in the wake of September 11.
- Men experience more anger about terrorism than women, leading them to be more optimistic than women are.
- Media portrayals of the terrorist attacks strongly influence emotional responses, producing anger in some instances and fear in others.[36]

Nevertheless, surveys generally indicate public support for the Bush administration's management of homeland security. For instance, a January 2006 Fox News poll showed that 46 percent of Americans believe that the absence of terrorist attacks since 2001 are the result of administration policies, while 22 percent believe that terrorist groups have simply not planned any new attacks (20 percent assert that the lack of incidents is attributable to both).[37] Tracking numbers within the poll show that homeland security has become less of a concern for Americans as time has gone by so that in August 2004, 8 percent of those surveyed rated homeland security as the number one priority for the country (20 percent rated Iraq as the main issue); while in January 2006, only 3 percent of people polled ranked homeland security as number one, while 27 percent stated that Iraq was the most important issue facing the United States.[38] Concurrently, rankings over terrorism have also declined from 9 percent in August 2004 to 5 percent in January 2006.[39] Other polls mirror the Fox survey. For instance, a CBS poll conduct between January 5–8, 2006, found terrorism was rated as the main issue confronting the United States by 5 percent of Americans (Iraq was 19 percent); while an NBC/Wall Street Journal poll from December 2005 found 12 percent of Americans thought terrorism was the nation's main issue (Iraq was 22 percent).[40]

Any measurement of homeland security must incorporate means which assess the effectiveness of government information efforts. One criticism of the Department of Homeland Security has been the agency's use of a color-coded alert system and the practice of using news conferences to announce changes to the alert level. A news report in the *Washington Post* reports that the current system "is unloved even by its creators."[41] Instead, the Department is examining a range of methods to communicate threats and dangers which mirror the systems used by other government agencies, including the State Department and its travel advisory system.[42] Importantly, the Homeland Security Department will use surveys and polls to assess any new system. The *Washington Post* notes that "the department may launch a years-long public education campaign, including television documentaries and participation in made-for-TV movies ... The idea would be to help Americans understand the difference between various types of terrorist attacks, and explain the typically fragmentary nature of the government's intelligence about where and how they may be carried out."[43]

Raphael Perl points out that an integrated system of measurement is important, one which integrates "incidents, attitudes and trends."[44] An escalation of attacks, or potential attacks, may indicate growing stress on a nation's homeland security system. For instance, during the 1990s, there was a succession of terrorist strikes within the United States (accompanied by an even more significant rise in the number of attacks on US interests around the globe).[45] This trend culminated in 2001 with the attacks on New York and Washington. Perl goes on to identify several trends that could help determine the success or failure of homeland security: "1) the number of governments that do not embrace appeasement policies, 2) the number of defectors from the terrorist ranks, 3) the terrorists' levels of Internet activity; 4) the amount of media coverage they [the terrorist groups] receive, and 5) the number of supports and recruits they gain."[46] In a Rand study, Bruce Hoffman warns that trends in the volume of terrorism should be carefully examined since there has been a worldwide decrease in the number of terrorist strikes in the 1990s (from 481 in 1991 to 250 in 1996), but there was an increase in the number of fatalities caused by the attacks.[47]

Of significant interest to policymakers, scholars and the general public in the United States are patterns whereby civil liberties are eroded in exchange for increased domestic security. As a Congressional Research Service report, "Terrorism and National Security: Issues and Trends," notes, "a growing issue bedeviling policymakers is how to minimize the economic and civil liberties costs of an enhanced security environment."[48]

Other trends may measure the increasing effectiveness of domestic security, especially if those patterns reveal increases in resources or capabilities for homeland preparedness. Since the 9/11 terrorist attacks, there has been a dramatic increase in spending on homeland security. According to figures compiled by the Congressional Budget Office (CBO), in 2001, the federal government spent approximately $20.7 billion on homeland security. That figure rose to $33 billion in 2002, $42.5 billion in 2003, before declining slightly to $41.4 billion in 2004. For 2005, the CBO estimates that homeland security spending would increase by about 14 percent over 2004, for a total of $47.3 billion.[49] This is in addition to funds spent overseas in order to protect the domestic United States.[50] Related to the increase in funding is a corresponding rise in capabilities and resources. The creation of the Department of Homeland Security initiated a period of mission revision and reorientation as various agencies in the federal, state and local levels of government all adopted new, or in some cases expanded existing, missions devoted to domestic security and preparedness.

In response, the administration and a variety of governmental and academic bodies have sought to develop a comprehensive method to judge homeland security policy. In addition, under federal law, all agencies are required to develop tools to measure effectiveness. Perl writes that: "the Government Performance and Results Acts (GPRA) requires agencies to set goals and objectives for their performance, and to measure progress against these goals and objectives ... anti-terror efforts are not exempt from these requirements."[51] A definitive assessment remains elusive, however, instead, as noted in Chapter Four, homeland security is increasing becoming politicized within the United States as both the Democratic and Republican parties seek to use the issue to gain political advantage. Hence, the United States continues to lack an effective and utilitarian rubric to assess homeland security.

Disaster Response and Homeland Security

Linking homeland security and emergency management is a logical step in formulating and implementing effective policies. The Federal Emergency Management Agency (FEMA) was moved within the newly created Department of Homeland Security and tasked to enhance its response capabilities for terrorist incidents or other hard security threats. Yet, the agency also remains the main federal body to oversee the response and recovery efforts following natural disasters. During 2004, FEMA spent a record (at that time) $4.27 billion to assist Florida and other states impacted by a series of hurricanes (in all there were 27 major disaster areas in 15 states and Puerto Rico).[52] The Agency also provided a range of other assistance, including aid for people displaced by fires in the western areas of the country and those harmed by flooding in the East and Midwest. While FEMA was generally given positive reviews for its management of the Florida recovery effort, the Agency was roundly criticized for waste and overspending. For example, an investigation by the Orlando *Sun-Sentinel* found widespread waste and fraud. The newspaper reported that:

> FEMA paid $31 million in Miami-Dade County for Hurricane Frances, even though the Labor Day weekend storm made landfall 100 miles to the north. Subsequent reports detailed how FEMA inspectors receive little training; that the agency paid for funerals for deaths unrelated to the storm; and that some criminals were hired to inspect damage. The reports resulted in recommendations by a US Senate committee and the inspector general of the Department of Homeland Security for widespread changes in the way the agency administers its program.[53]

In addition to financial oversight problems, a host of other issues emerged in the aftermath of Hurricane Katrina in 2005, which dramatically illustrated flaws in FEMA and the federal government's ability to manage major disasters.

Hurricane Katrina

After crossing Florida as a Category One storm, Katrina moved in the Gulf of Mexico, where it became the first Category Five storm of the 2005 hurricane season. It also developed into the sixth strongest-storm in the Atlantic basin in the modern era of record keeping on hurricanes. On 29 August 2005, the storm struck the lower islands of Louisiana and then moved ashore into coastal Mississippi. Katrina was the worst natural disaster in American history and it devastated the city of New Orleans and the Mississippi Gulf Coast. In Mississippi alone, damage estimates exceed $125 billion with more than 65,000 homes destroyed and some 44 million cubic yards of debris created.[54] Throughout the Gulf region, Katrina killed 1,386 people, although there remain a large number of missing persons. The storm also displaced some 1.2 million people and left 2.3 million homes without power. In both economic, infrastructure and personal terms, Katrina's losses were comparable to those that would result from a catastrophic terrorist strike or even a direct attack on the United States by a foreign power.

In the face of the devastation caused by the storm, a massive relief effort was undertaken. Traditionally, the control and oversight of relief efforts have been the domain of state and local government. However, the federal government has increasingly taken on a larger role in disaster relief. FEMA is charged with coordinating disaster response as part of the Department of Homeland Security's Emergency Management and Preparedness Directorate.[55] Following the storm, Bush declared some 90,000 square miles disaster areas (the declaration cleared the way for federal assistance and for FEMA to take over relief and recovery efforts). During the relief effort for Katrina, a range of problems emerged in FEMA's preparations and operations. FEMA chief Brown eventually resigned over the agency's management of the Katrina response.[56] Brown's lack of leadership and focus had led the initial stages of the recovery effort to become plagued by critical lack of haste and organization.

In the immediate aftermath of the storm in Louisiana, a disconnect quickly emerged between FEMA's public pronouncements and the reality on the ground. FEMA Director Brown issued glowing reports and declared at one point that "considering the dire circumstances that we have in New Orleans, virtually a city that has been destroyed, things are going relatively well." Homeland Security head Michael Chertoff stated that "Now, of course, a critical element of what we're doing is the process of evacuation and securing New Orleans and other areas that are afflicted. And here the Department of Defense has performed magnificently, as has the National Guard, in bringing enormous resources and capabilities to bear in the areas that are suffering."[57] However, the Mayor of New Orleans, Ray Nagin, countered that FEMA and the federal government and FEMA "don't have a clue what's going on down here."[58] Even Bush admitted that "Katrina exposed serious problems in our response capability at all levels of government and to the extent the federal government didn't fully do its job right, I take responsibility."[59]

For example, New Orleans was not in Katrina's path, but the levee system protecting the city was overwhelmed by the combination of wind, storm surge and increased strain. There were a few areas of the city that were flooded by rain and in some cases, the storm surge topped the levees, but the major flooding occurred after several sections of the levee system collapsed.[60] The flooding displaced almost all of the city's population and put 80 percent of New Orleans under water. Shelters were established at the New Orleans Superdome and the Convention Center; however, these sites, and the city in general, were wracked by violence, looting and break-downs in aid distribution. In an understated summary, the *Guardian* reported that: "Unrest broke out in the Superdome, where more than 20,000 people have been awaiting evacuation. Conditions have been deteriorating after part of the roof was blown off and the toilets blocked. Fights broke out and rubbish caught fire. In a scuffle, a police officer was shot in the leg."[61]

Ultimately, federal, state and local officials were cited for lapses and errors in the response to Katrina. FEMA officials were criticized for being too heavy-handed and unresponsive to the specific needs of individual communities. Many aspects of the federal response were also disorganized and slow. Meanwhile, the governor of Louisiana, Kathleen Blanco, and various state officials made a number of mistakes. CNN described Blanco as "engaging in a bureaucratic turf war that delayed the National Guard response as New Orleans spiraled into anarchy."[62] For instance, the federal government sought to take control of the evacuation of New Orleans after the storm (so that a unified command and control structure could be implemented). Blanco resisted for fear that federal officials would blame problems on state and local officials.[63] In addition, Nagin was criticized for his poor handling of the evacuation, and his confrontational approach toward both state and federal officials.[64]

In Mississippi, the governmental response was better and demonstrated the benefits of closer federal-state coordination. A key difference seems to have been the personality and tactics of Mississippi Governor Haley Barbour. Unlike Blanco, a Democrat, the Republican Barbour had close ties to the Bush administration and used those connections to the state's advantage. In addition, the Barbour administration was far more willing to work with the various federal agencies to coordinate planning and response. Finally, Barbour demonstrated a style that resonated well with the public and gave the impression that he was a strong leader. Daniel C. Vock offers this summary of Barbour's management of the crisis:

> Barbour, former Republican National Committee chairman, conveyed a take-charge demeanor in leading Mississippi's relief effort. He quickly convened a special legislative session and appointed a high-octane recovery commission headed by former Netscape chief executive Jim Barksdale.
>
> Barbour persuaded the Legislature to let the shipwrecked Gulf riverboat casinos move 800 feet inland and secured a $25 million package of interest-free $25,000 loans for small businesses.[65]

Barbour also managed to forge a bipartisan consensus in the recovery effort that was lacking in Louisiana.[66] Vock goes on to assert:

> Still, Barbour seemed to strike the right notes as he rallied the state's 2.8 million citizens to the recovery.
>
> "Frankly, in 20 years, we'll be glad Haley Barbour was governor when he was," said Marty Wiseman, director of the Stennis Institute of Government at Mississippi State University. Wiseman, a Democrat, said Barbour artfully balanced working with the White House and his friends in Washington, D.C., and giving voice to the frustrations of ordinary Mississippians.[67]

Mississippi also benefited from having two senators as part of the majority in Congress (while Louisiana's delegation was split with one Republican and one Democrat). That Mississippi Senator Thad Cochran was the chairman of the Senate appropriations Committee further aided the state, as Mississippi ultimately received about five-times as much per capita as Louisiana in federal assistance.

Conclusions

The federal response to Hurricane Katrina reinforces the fact that homeland security remains an evolving concept in the United States. Before the storm, most officials and the general public viewed terrorism or the war in Iraq as the greatest threat to the United States. Katrina demonstrated that natural disasters can inflict catastrophic damage and loss of life even in advance societies with well-developed emergency management systems. One of the key lessons of Katrina is the continuing importance of non-security threats to the economic and societal stability of the United States. Thus, homeland security policy in the country will need to do a better job of balancing preparedness and response capabilities to deal with both human and natural threats.

The different experiences of Louisiana and Mississippi demonstrate the potential positive and negative attributes of the contemporary homeland security system. As was the case following the September 11 attacks, in the aftermath of Katrina, a range of reforms and changes in the Department of Homeland Security are being undertaken in order to address the problems highlighted by the storm. After Brown resigned as FEMA director, he was replaced by acting Director R. David Paulison, a 30-year veteran of fire and emergency response work in Florida, including work during the recovery effort from Hurricane Andrew. Once in office, Paulison worked to streamline the FEMA assistance process for those affected by Katrina (and future disasters) and to enhance planning and response capabilities. Coast Admiral Thad Allen was tasked to oversee the recovery efforts in the Gulf Coast. Allen's appointment brought a strong leader to the federal effort.[68] In addition, in November, Bush appointed Donald E. Powell, the Chairman of the Federal Deposit Insurance Corporation (FDIC), as the Coordinator of Federal Support and charged him as "the Administration's primary point of contact with State and local governments, the private sector, and community leaders on long-term recovery and rebuilding plans. As Federal Coordinator, he [Powell] will work with Congress and Federal departments and agencies to provide effective, integrated, and fiscally responsible support for Gulf Coast recovery."[69] Nonetheless, considerable progress needs to be made to ensure that the mistakes of the Katrina response are not repeated.

Homeland Security Challenges

The United States continues to face a range of challenges in homeland security. There are a variety of threats that remain to domestic security. Following the September 11 attacks, the main thrust of US homeland security policy was counterterrorism. The

Department of Homeland Security became the lead agency in the national anti-terror effort which was supported by dramatic increases in funding and resources. In the post-September 11 era, the Department continues to focus on protecting critical infrastructure and developing strategies to prevent or respond to cyber attacks or strikes by weapons of mass destruction, including nuclear, biological or chemical incidents. The hurricanes of 2004 and 2005 reinforced the necessity of the disaster response functions inherent within homeland security. The need for closer federal-state-local coordination to prepare for, and to respond to, natural disasters remains a high priority for the Department of Homeland Security as it attempts to digest the lessons from Katrina. Overriding the disparate, but interrelated, components of homeland security policy is the need to develop comprehensive methods of assessment. The response to the September 11 attacks and Hurricane Katrina highlighted problems in the contemporary system. In order for the United States to be more proactive, the creation of utilitarian assessment rubrics will be the key to future policy success.

Notes

1. Raphael Perl, "Combating Terrorism: The Challenge of Measuring Effectiveness," Congressional Research Service Report RL 33160 (23 November 2005), Summary.
2. Of this amount, $10 billion was designated for use by the Federal Emergency Management Agency (FEMA) of the Department of Homeland Security, and the remaining $500 million was allocated for the Department of Defense; Jennifer E. Lake and Ralph M. Chite, "Emergency Supplemental Appropriations for Hurricane Katrina Relief," Congressional Research Service Report RS 22239 (7 September 2005), 1; online at http://www.fas.org/sgp/crs/misc/RS22239.pdf.
3. US, Office of Homeland Security, *National Strategy for Homeland Security* (July 2002), 7; online at http://www.whitehouse.gov/homeland/book/nat_strat_hls.pdf.
4. *Ibid.*
5. *Ibid.*, 9.
6. Kyle B. Olson, "Aum Shinrikyo: The Once and Future Threat?" *Emerging Infectious Diseases* 5/4 (July-August, 1999); online at http://www.cdc.gov/ncidod/EID/vol5no4/olson.htm.
7. *Ibid.*
8. See Marilyn W. Thompson, *The Killer Strain, Anthrax and a Government Exposed* (New York: HarperCollins, 2003) or Leonard A. Cole, *The Anthrax Letters, A Medical Detective Story* (Washington, D.C.: Joseph Henry Press, 2003).
9. See Michael Stebbins, "Anthrax Fact Sheet" (updated 4 October 2005); online at http://www.fas.org/main/content.jsp?formAction=297&contentId=481.
10. Writing in the *Washington Post*, Allan Lengel notes that: "Four years after the deadly 2001 anthrax attacks, one of the most exhaustive investigations in FBI history has yielded no arrests and is showing signs of growing cold as officials have sharply reduced the number of agents on the case. FBI agents and postal inspectors have pursued leads on four continents, conducted more than 8,000 interviews and carried out dozens of searches of houses, laboratories and other locations. They traveled to Afghanistan twice in the past 16 months to follow up on tips that proved fruitless, said law enforcement sources, who spoke

on the condition of anonymity because of the sensitive nature of the issue;" Allan Lengel, "Little Progress in FBI Probe of Anthrax Attacks," *The Washington Post* (16 September 2005), A1.

11. *Ibid.*
12. US, Office of Homeland Security, *National Strategy for Homeland Security*, 9.
13. Carson Mark, Theodore Taylor, Eugene Eyster, William Maraman, and Jacob Wechsler, "Can Terrorists Build a Nuclear Weapons: Paper Prepared for the International Task Force on the Prevention of Nuclear Terrorism," (1987); online at http://www.nci.org/nuketerror.htm.
14. *Ibid.*
15. US, Congress, Senate Committee on Foreign Relations, "Testimony of Dr. Henry Kelly, President, American Federation of Scientists," 107th Congress, 2nd session (6 March 2002); online at http://www.nci.org/nuketerror.htm.
16. US, Nuclear Regulatory Commission, "Fact Sheet on Dirty Bombs," (updated 25 February 2004); online at http://www.nrc.gov/reading-rm/doc-collections/fact-sheets/dirty-bombs.html.
17. See Amanda Ripley, "The Case of the Dirty Bomber," *Time* (16 June 2002), online at http://www.time.com/time/nation/article/0,8599,262917,00.html; or Dan Eggen and Susan Schmidt, "'Dirty Bomb' Plot Uncovered, US Says," *The Washington Post* (11 June 2002), A1.
18. UK, MI5, "Security Advice: Suicide Bombs," online at http://www.mi5.gov.uk/output/Page51.html.
19. Bruce Hoffman, "The Logic of Suicide Terrorism," *The Atlantic Monthly* (June 2003); online at http://www.theatlantic.com/doc/200306/hoffman.
20. *Ibid.*
21. "Suicide Bombing: Events Related to Suicide Bombing," *Harpers Magazine*; online at http://www.harpers.org/SuicideBombing.html.
22. Dorothy E. Denning, "Is Cyber Terrorism Next?" *After September 11: New War?* Social Science Research Council (1 November 2001); online at http://www.ssrc.org/sept11/essays/denning.htm.
23. US, Office of Homeland Security, *National Strategy for Homeland Security*, 9.
24. US, Computer Emergency Readiness Team, "About US," online at http://www.us-cert.gov/aboutus.html.
25. Gabriel Weiman, "Cyberterrorism: How Real is the Threat?" United States Institute of Peace, Special Report 119 (December 2004); online at http://www.usip.org/pubs/specialreports/sr119.html.
26. *Ibid.*
27. The most dramatic instance of this sort of occurred with the aforementioned Japanese cult, Aum Shinrikyo. The USIP report notes that: "In March 2000, Japan's Metropolitan Police Department reported that a software system they had procured to track 150 police vehicles, including unmarked cars, had been developed by the Aum Shinryko cult, the same group that gassed the Tokyo subway in 1995, killing 12 people and injuring 6,000 more. At the time of the discovery, the cult had received classified tracking data on 115 vehicles. Further, the cult had developed software for at least 80 Japanese firms and 10 government agencies. They had worked as subcontractors to other firms, making it almost impossible for the organizations to know who was developing the software. As subcontractors, the cult could have installed Trojan horses to launch or facilitate cyber terrorist attacks at a later date; *ibid.*
28. US, Office of Homeland Security, *National Strategy for Homeland Security*, 9.

29. There is a body of literature which asserts that terrorist groups are actually not very innovative. Instead, some scholars argue that terrorists can be very staid. Brian Jackson observes that a range of authors declare terrorist groups to be "generally operationally conservative and usually use a limited set of tactics. For example, over time, groups have shown a strong preference for staging bombings and firearms attacks;" Brian Jackson, "Organizational Learning and Terrorist Groups," Working Paper: RAND Corporation, WR 133 NIJ (February 2004); online at http://www.rand.org/pubs/working_papers/2004/RAND_WR133.pdf.

30. Jackson cites Bruce Hoffman, *Inside Terrorism* (New York: Columbia University Press, 1998), 180-182; in *ibid.*

31. *Ibid.*

32. For instance, see US, National Institute of Standards and Technology (NIST), "Technologies for Public Safety and Security: Activities at the National Institute of Standards and Technology," NIST Fact Sheet (23 March 2004); online at http://www.nist.gov/public_affairs/factsheet/homeland.htm. The NIST is also in the midst of a five-year plan (due to be completed) to establish 42 standards for "protective equipment, detection and decontamination technologies;" *ibid.*

33. Stephen Hadley, "Victory in Iraq," Address at the Center for Strategic and International Studies (CSIS), (20 December 2005); online at http://www.csis.org/media/csis/events/051220_hadley_transcript.pdf.

34. US, White House, *The National Strategy for Combating Terrorism* (February 2003); online at http://www.fas.org/irp/threat/ctstrategy.pdf.

35. Teresa Sokol Thomas, "Study Reveals Impact of Fear, Anger on Perception of Americans," Press Release (10 May 2002); online at http://www.cmu.edu/cmnews/020510/020510_terrorism.html.

36. *Ibid.*

37. Fox News, "Fox News Opinion/Dynamics Poll" (12 January 2006); online at http://www.foxnews.com/projects/pdf/poll_011206.pdf.

38. *Ibid.*

39. *Ibid.*

40. These and other polls are available at Pollingreport.com, "Problems and Priorities," online at http://www.pollingreport.com/prioriti.htm.

41. John Mintz, "DHS Considers Alternatives to Color-coded System," *The Washington Post* (10 May 2005), A6.

42. Among the changes being considered are the replacement of the color-coded system with a numeric system with as many as six different levels. The Department is also likely to employ the same tactics as the State Department which announces lower level threats via its website or other public information systems; ibid.

43. *Ibid.*

44. Perl, "Combating Terrorism."

45. See, for instance, Center for Arms Control and Non-Proliferation (CACNP), "Significant Terrorist Attacks Against the United States and its Citizens, 1946-2001," online at http://www.armscontrolcenter.org/terrorism/101/timeline.html.

46. Perl, "Combating Terrorism," 1.

47. Bruce Hoffman, "Chapter Two: Terrorism Trends and Prospects," in Ian O. Lesser, Bruce Hoffman, John Arquilla, David Ronfeldt, Michele Zanini, and Brian Michael Jenkins, eds., *Countering the New Terrorism* (Santa Monica: Rand Corporation, 1999), 1-17; online at http://www.rand.org/pubs/monograph_reports/MR989/index.html. Hoffman also describes the rise in religious-based terrorism. In 1968, none of the eleven major terrorist groups could be classified as religious (they were nationalist formations), but by 1992, a

quarter of the major groups (11 out of 48) were religiously-based and by 1995, almost half of all terrorist organizations were religious in nature (26 of 56); Hoffman, 16-17.

48. Raphael Perl, "Terrorism and National Security: Issues and Trends," Congressional Research Service Report IB 10119 (21 December 2004), 1; online at http://www.fas.org/irp/crs/IB10119.pdf.

49. US, Congressional Budget Office (CBO), "Federal Funding for Homeland Security," CBO Economic and Budget Issue Brief (30 April 2004); online at http://www.cbo.gov/showdoc.cfm?index=5414&sequence=0.

50. The CBO notes that: "Another definition of homeland security could identify a different set of activities and funding amounts. For example, the executive branch's definition focuses only on activities aimed at preventing or responding to terrorist attacks within U.S. borders and not on those devoted to combating terrorism overseas. Overseas activities, such as security at U.S. embassies and military facilities and some intelligence activities, are accounted for separately; OMB [Office of Management and Budget] estimates that 2004 funding for those purposes totals about $12 billion. Of that amount, DoD [Department of Defense] and other national security agencies receive over $8 billion, and the Department of State, about $1.8 billion; ibid. The CBO report also points out that "... none of DoD's security and counterterrorism operations in response to the September 11 attacks – operations such as Noble Eagle, which includes combat air patrols over the United States and increased security at military facilities. Over $2 billion was appropriated for Noble Eagle for 2004"; *ibid.*

51. Perl, "Combating Terrorism," 1.

52. FEMA also reported that there were 15,560 federal emergency response workers involved in the recovery effort following storms which impacted some 1.6 million people. The agency distributed "163 million pounds of ice, 10.8 million gallons of water, 14 million meals-ready-to-eat and 151,000 rolls of plastic roofing material were delivered to help meet immediate emergency needs;" US, Federal Emergency Management Agency, "FEMA Reports Record Aid for 2004 Hurricane Season Response," *FEMA News* (29 November 2004); online at http://www.fema.gov/news/newsrelease.fema?id=15508.

53. "FEMA: A Legacy of Waste," *The Sun-Sentinel* (18 September 2005); online at http://www.sun-sentinel.com/news/local/southflorida/sfla-emareport,0,7651043.story gallery?coll=sfla-home-headlines.

54. "Mississippi's Invisible Coast," *The Sun Herald* (14 December 2005); online at http://www.sunherald.com/mld/sunherald/13402585.htm.

55. FEMA was created in 1979 by President Jimmy Carter through Executive Order 12148. In the order, Carter declared that "The Director of the Federal Emergency Management Agency shall establish Federal policies for, and coordinate, all civil defense and civil emergency planning, management, mitigation, and assistance functions of Executive agencies;" James Carter, Executive Order 12148 Federal Emergency Management (20 July 1979); online at http://www.archives.gov/federal-register/codification/executive-order/12148.html. FEMA thus became the lead federal agency in disaster response efforts and was moved into the Department of Homeland Security in 2003.

56. See "FEMA Chief Brown Resigns," *Fox News* (13 September 2005); online at http://www.foxnews.com/story/0,2933,169169,00.html; or "FEMA Director Brown Resigns," *CNN* (12 September 2005); online at http://www.cnn.com/2005/POLITICS/09/12/brown.resigns/. Brown had actually planned to resign before Katrina struck, but his performance during the crisis; Spenser Hsu, "Brown had Resignation Plans Before Katrina Hit," *The Washington Post* (26 October 2005), A9.

57. Brown and Chertoff quoted in "The Big Disconnect on New Orleans," *CNN* (2 September 2005); online at http://www.cnn.com/2005/US/09/02/katrina.response/.

58. Quoted in *ibid.*
59. George Bush quoted in "People Making Decisions Hesitated," *CNN* (13 September 2005); online at http://www.cnn.com/2005/US/09/13/katrina.response/.
60. The major flooding came from four significant breaks. A 450-feet break in the 17th Street Canal levee occurred when flood waters topped the levee and caused a collapse. The Industrial Seaway Canal had two breaks (one 100-feet and the second 500-feet), and the London Street Canal also had a 500-feet breach; Nicole T. Carter, "New Orleans Levees and Floodwalls: Hurricane Damage Protection," Congressional Research Service Report RS 22239 (6 September 2005); online at http://www.fas.org/sgp/crs/misc/RS22238.pdf.
61. Julian Borger, "Mayor Issues SOS as Chaos Tightens its Grip," *The Guardian* (2 September 2005); online at http://www.guardian.co.uk/katrina/story/0,16441,1561314,00.html.
62. "People Making Decisions Hesitated."
63. In addition, Blanco did reach a "multi-state mutual aid compact" until the Wednesday after the storm (this would allow neighboring states to lend National Guard forces and other assets to the recovery effort; Manuel Roig-Franzia and Spencer Hsu, "Many Evacuated, But Thousands Still Waiting," *The Washington Post* (4 September 2005), A4. Writing in *Stateline.Org* Daniel C. Vock asserted that "Blanco, a Democrat who spent two decades as a state legislator, public service commissioner and lieutenant governor, appeared hesitant in the first days of the disaster. She vented about federal incompetence but had trouble marshaling the resources to rescue the thousands stranded in attics, on rooftops and at the Superdome and Convention Center;" Daniel C. Vock, "Katrina Alters Vista for Barbour, Blanco," *Stateline.Org* (2 January 2006). Vock does note that after initial missteps, Blanco was able to secure a range of political victories, including wide-ranging legislation from a special session of the legislature.
64. Nagin dramatically altered his tactics in the aftermath of the storm and after initially "denouncing" the Bush administration, he made switched strategies and began working with the administration, although he still bypassed state officials. The *Wall Street Journal* reported that "When the state's congressional delegation introduced a $250 billion Katrina-relief bill, Mr. Nagin ignored it. Instead, he went to the White House on Oct. 17 to lay out his own recovery strategy. That meeting yielded a $45.5 million tax-stimulus plan to encourage displaced residents and businesses to return, and a request for $412 million to repair city facilities;" Corey Dade, "Nagin Works Both Sides of the Aisle for Aid," *The Wall Street Journal* (10 January 2006); A4.
65. Vock.
66. For instance, during the contentious debate over casino gambling in the state legislature, Barbour work with his oft-times nemesis, House Speaker and Democratic leader Billy McCoy. After the passage of legislation to allow onshore casinos, Barbour roundly praised McCoy and his efforts in the Mississippi House. Barbour declared that "The speaker has shown true courage and leadership and statesmanship ... He understands that the public has elected these legislators to face up to these tough decisions as leaders;" Geoff Pender, Melissa Scallan, and Tom Wilemon, "Hose OKS Onshore Casinos," *The Sun Herald* (1 October 2005); online at http://www.sunherald.com/mld/sunherald/12791433.htm. McCoy's role in the legislation was all the more significant in light of his personal opposition to gambling and the unpopularity of casinos in Rienzi, his northern Mississippi district.
67. Vock.
68. The choice of Allen was widely praised because of his vast experience and credentials; see "Allen Brings Rescue Savvy to Job," *CBS News* (9 September 2005); online at

http://www.cbsnews.com/stories/2005/09/09/katrina/main832548.shtml.   Democratic Louisiana Senator Mary Landrieu stated in a press release that "Vice Admiral Allen brings serious credentials to the table and the people of Louisiana are supportive of all the work he and the Coast Guard have done over the past two weeks to help save lives and bring hope to our state;" Mary Landrieu, "Senator Landrieu Statement on Appointment of Vice Admiral Allen," Press Release, Washington, D.C. (9 September 2005); online at http://landrieu.senate.gov/~landrieu/releases/05/2005909D48.html.

69. US, White House, "Fact Sheet: Coordinating Federal Support for Gulf Coast Rebuilding," Press Release (1 November 2005); online at http://www.whitehouse.gov/news/releases/2005/11/20051101-6.html.

Bibliography

Documents and Official Sources

Allen, Charles. "Written Statement of Charles Allen Chief Intelligence Officer of Department of Homeland Security House Committee on Homeland Security Subcommittee on Intelligence, Information Sharing and Terrorism Risk Assessment and House Permanent Select Committee on Intelligence Subcommittee on Terrorism/HUMINT, Analysis and Counterintelligence," 19 October 2005.

Anti Terrorism, Crime and Security Act 2001, available at: http://www.opsi.gov.uk/acts/acts2001/20010024.htm.

Bea, Keith. "Urban Search and Rescue Task Forces: Facts and Issues." CRS Report RS21073, 10 January 2005.

Best, Richard, Jr., Alfred Cumming, and Todd Masse. "Director of National Intelligence: Statutory Authorities." CRS Report RS22112, 11 April 2005.

"Budget 2005 Summary," *HM Treasury* available at: http://budget2005.treasury.gov.uk/ page_09.html.

Bush, George W. Addresses and Speeches (various).

Структура органов Федеральной Службы безопасности РФ (утверждена Указом Президента Российской Федерации от 11 августа 2003 г. N 960), Trans: "Structure of the Organs of Federal Security Service of the Russian Federation" (legislated by the decree of the President of the Russian Federation on 11 August 2003); available at www.fsb.ru/structure/ukaz/.

"Campaign Against Terrorism." *Written Answers to Questions (27 November 2001).* The United Kingdom Parliament.

"Civil Contingencies Act 2004: A Short Guide," available at: http://www.ukresilience.info/ccact/3octshortguide.pdf.

"Civil Contingencies Committee." *Written Answers to Questions (17 November 1997).* The United Kingdom Parliament.

"Combating Terrorism: How Five Foreign Countries Are Organized to Combat Terrorism." *GAO/NSIAD-00-85* (April 2000).

"Department of Homeland Security Reorganization: The 2SR Initiative." *CRS Report RL33042*, 19 August 2005.

Department of Homeland Security. Press releases and reports. Various.

"Domestic Nuclear Detection Office." Available athttp://www.dhs.gov/dhspublic/interapp/editorial/_editorial_0766.xml; "Domestic Nuclear Detection Office," Statement by the Honorable Fred C. Ikle before the Committee on Homeland Security Subcommittee on the Prevention of Nuclear and Biological Attack House of Representatives, 19 April 2005.

Doyle, Charles, and Jennifer Elsea. "Terrorism: Some Legal Restrictions on Military Assistance to Domestic Authorities Following a Terrorist Attack." *CRS Report*

RS21012, 27 May 2005.

Gallis, Paul. "France: Factors Shaping Foreign Policy, and Issues in U.S.-French Relations." *CRS Report for Congress* RL32464, 4 February 2005.

ИСТОРИЧЕСКАЯ СПРАВКА ОБ ОРГАНАХ ГОСУДАРСТВЕННОЙ БЕЗОПАСНОСТИ, Trans: "Historical Information on the Organs of National Security," available at www.fsb.ru/history/organi.html.

Hadley, Stephen. "Victory in Iraq." Address at the Center for Strategic and International Studies (CSIS), (20 December 2005); online at http://www.csis.org/media/csis/events/051220_hadley_transcript.pdf.

Hill, Fiona Hill. "Central Asia: Terrorism, Religious Extremism, and Regional Stability." Testimony before the House Committee on International Relations Subcommittee on the Middle East and Central Asia, July 23, 2003, available at www.brookings.edu/views/testimony/hill/20030723.pdf.

"Intelligence and Information Analysis within the Department of Homeland Security." Prepared Statement of Richard Ben-Veniste, Member of the 9/11 Commission. *US House of Representatives,* 19 October 2005.

Kean, Thomas H., Lee H. Hamilton, Richard Ben-Veniste, Fred F. Fielding, Jamie S. Gorelick, Slade Gorton, Bob Kerrey, John F. Lehman, Timothy J. Roemer and James R. Thompson, *The 9/11 Commission Report: Final Report of the National Commission on Terrorist Attacks on the United States.* New York: W.W. Norton & Company, 2004.

Landrieu, Mary. "Senator Landrieu Statement on Appointment of Vice Admiral Allen," Press Release, Washington, D.C. (9 September 2005); online at http://landrieu.senate.gov/~landrieu/releases/05/2005909D48.html.

Masse, Todd. "The 9/11 Commission and a National Counterterrorism Center: Issues and Options for Congress." CRS Report RL32558, 3 September 2004.

_____. "Domestic Intelligence in the United Kingdom: Applicability of the MI-5 Model to the United States." Report for Congress *CRS* RL31920, 19 May 2003.

"Memorandum submitted by the Home Office." *Select Committee on Home Affairs Written Evidence.* The United Kingdom Parliament, 26 February 2004.

"Mitigating Catastrophic Events Through Effective Medical Response." Testimony of Roy L. Alson, Ph.D., MD, FACEP Before the House Committee on Homeland Security Subcommitte on Prevention of Nuclear and Biological Attack.

National Governors Association. *Homeland Security in the States: Much Progress, More Work*, Issue Brief. Washington, D.C.: NGA Center for Best Practices, 24 January 2005, online at http://www.nga.org/cda/files/0502homesec.pdf.

National Governors Association. *States' Homeland Security Practices*, Issue Brief. Washington, D.C.: NGA Center for Best Practices, 19 August 2002.

"National Policing Plan 2005-08: Safer, Stronger Communities," *Home Office*, November 2004.

Nunez-Neto, Blas. "Border Security: Key Agencies and Their Missions." *CRS Report RS21899*, 9 May 2005.

Office of the Mayor, New York City. "Direction and Control of Emergencies in the City of New York." New York: Office of the Mayor, July 2001.

Федеральный закон от 25 июля 2002 г. № 114-ФЗ "О противодействии экстремистской деятельности," Trans: "Federal Law of 25 July, 2002," No. 114-FZ "On the Opposition to Extremist Activity," available at www.scrf.gov.ru.

"Operations in the UK: The Defence Contribution to Resilience." Interim Joint Doctrine Publication 02, *Joint Doctrine & Concepts Centre* available at http://www.ukresilience.info/publications/index.shtm.

O'Prey, Kevin. "Homeland Security: Framing the Problem." Speech, Massachusetts Institute of Technology (21 February 2001).

O'Rourke, Ronald. "Homeland Security: Coast Guard Operations-Background and Issues for Congress." CRS Report RS21125.

Perl, Raphael. "Terrorism and National Security: Issues and Trends." *CRS Issue Brief IB1011*, 21 December 2004.

_____. "Combating Terrorism: The Challenge of Measuring Effectiveness." Congressional Research Service Report RL 33160. Washington, D.C.: Library of Congress, 23 November 2005.

_____. "Terrorism and National Security: Issues and Trends." Congressional Research Service Report IB 10119 (21 December 2004), 1; online at http://www.fas.org/irp/crs/IB10119.pdf.

_____. "National Commission on Terrorism Report: Background and Issues for Congress." Congressional Research Service Report RS 20598 (6 February 2001).

Prevention of Terrorism Act 2005, available at http://www.opsi.gov.uk/acts/acts2005/20050002.htm.

"Prevention of Terrorism Ordinance No.33 of 5708-1948," 23 September 1948, available at http://www.mfa.gov.il/MFA/MFAArchive.

Reese, Shawn. "State and Local Homeland Security: Unresolved Issues for the 109th Congress." Congressional Research Service Report RL 32941. Washington, D.C.: Library of Congress, 9 June 2005.

_____. "Fiscal Year 2005 Homeland Security Grant Program: State Allocations and Issues for Congressional Oversight." Congressional Research Service Report *RL 32696*. Washington, D.C.: Library of Congress, 16 February 2005.

Relyea, Harold C. "Homeland Security: Department Organization and Management-Implementation Phase." *CRS Report RL31751*, 3 January 2005.

_____. "Homeland Security: The Presidential Coordination Office." *CRSReport RL31148*, 30 March 2004.

Russian Federation Federal Law No. 130-FZ, Signed by Russian Federation President B. Yeltsin, 25 July 1998, Russian Intelligence-Related Legal Documents provided by Federation of American Scientists, available at www.fas.org/irp/world/russia/docs/law_980725.htm.

Shepherd, Scott, and Steve Bowman. "Homeland Security: Establishment and Implementation of the United States Northern Command." *CRS Report RS21322*, 10 February 2005.

Stephan, Robert B. "Statement of Assistant Secretary for Infrastructure Protection Robert B. Stephan U.S. Department of Homeland Security Before the Economic Security, Infrastructure Protection, and Cyber Security Subcommittee of the House

Homeland   Security   Committee,"   20   October   2005,
http://homeland.house.gov/files/TestimonyStephan.pdf.

Terrorism Act 2000, available at http://www.opsi.gov.uk/acts/acts2000/00011--
b.htm#1.

"The Lead Government Department and its role- Guidance and Best Practices." *Civil
Contingencies   Secretariat,*   available   at   http://www.ukresilience.info/
publications/lgds.pdf.

UK. MI5. "Security Advice: Suicide Bombs," online at http://www.mi5.gov.uk/
output/Page51.html.

United Nations. Office on Drugs and Crime. "Terrorism: Definitions." Online at
http://www.unodc.org/unodc/terrorism_definitions.html.

United States (US) Commission on National Security in the 21st Century (Hart-
Rudman Commission Phase III). *Roadmap for National Security: Imperative for
Change* (15 February 2001).

US Commission on National Security for the Twenty-First Century (Hart-Rudman
Commission Phase I), New World Coming: *American Security in the Twenty-First
Century* (15 September 1999).

US Conference of Mayors. "One Year Later: A Status Report on the Federal-Local
Partnership on Homeland Security" (9 September 2002).

US Conference of Mayors. "A National Action Plan for Safety and Security in
America's Cities." (December 2001), online at http://www.usmayors.org/
uscm/news/press_releases/documents/ActionPlan_121101.pdf.

US. Congress. House Committee on Government Reform, Subcommittee on National
Security, Emerging Threats, and International Relations. *Homeland Security:
Keeping First Responders First,* 107th Congress, 2nd session, hearing on 30 July
2002. Washington, D.C.: GPO, 2003.

US. Congress. House Science Committee. *Testimony Before the House Science
Committee on Meeting the Needs of the Fire Service,* 107th Congress, 2nd session,
hearing (2 October 2002), online at http://www.house.gov/science/hearings/
full02/oct02/monihan.htm.

US. Congress. Senate Committee on Appropriations, 107th Congress, 2nd session.
VA/HUD Firefighting Testimony: Harold Schaitberger, press release (6 February
2002), online at http://appropriations.senate.gov/releases/record.cfm?id=180447.

US, Congress. Senate Committee on Foreign Relations. "Testimony of Dr. Henry
Kelly, President, American Federation of Scientists," 107th Congress, 2nd session (6
March 2002); online at http://www.nci.org/nuketerror.htm.

US. Congress. Senate Governmental Affairs Committee. *Investing in Homeland
Security: Streamlining and Enhancing Homeland Security Grant Programs,* 108th
Congress, 1st session, hearing on 1 May 2003. Washington, D.C.: GPO 2003.

US. Department of Defense. *Army Modernization Plan 2002.* Washington, D.C.:
DOD, 2002.

US.   Department of Homeland Security, *Emergencies and Disasters: First
Responders*,   online   at   http://www.dhs.gov/dhspublic/interapp/editorial/
editorial_0197.xml.

US. Department of Homeland Security. *Select Homeland Security Accomplishments for 2005*, press release (20 December 2005).

US. Department of Homeland Security. *National Response Plan*. Washington, D.C.: GPO, December 2004.

US. Department of Homeland Security. "Fact Sheet: Department of Homeland Security Funding for States and Cities." Press Release (21 May 2003), online at http://www.dhs.gov/dhspublic/display?content=755.

US. General Accounting Office (GAO). *Homeland Security: Communications Protocols and Risk Communication Principles Can Assist in Refining the Advisory System*. Washington, D.C.: GPO, June 2004, online at http://www.gao.gov/new.items/d04682.pdf.

US. General Accounting Office. *Unfunded Mandates: Analysis of Reform Act Coverage*. Washington, D.C.: GPO, May 2004, online at http://www.gao.gov/new.items/d04637.pdf.

US. GAO. *Combating Terrorism: Issues to Be Resolved to Improve Counterterrorism Operations*. Washington, D.C.: GAO, May 1999.

US. House. Committee on Homeland Security Democratic Staff. *Leaving the Nation at Risk: 33 Unfulfilled Promises From the Department of Homeland Security* (December 2005), online at http://hsc-democrats.house.gov/NR/rdonlyres/1C607310-3228-4CCC-B13A-04A808A4C19B/0/HomelandSecurityDemocrats RevealUnfulfilledPromises.pdf.

US. House Committee on International Relations [now Foreign Affairs], Subcommittee on International Security and Scientific Affairs, *Background Information on the Use of U.S. Armed Forces in Foreign Countries, 1975 Revision*. Committee Print, 94th Congress,1st Session, 1995, prepared by the Foreign Affairs Division, Congressional Research Service, Library of Congress.

US. Nuclear Regulatory Commission. "Fact Sheet on Dirty Bombs," (updated 25 February 2004); online at http://www.nrc.gov/reading-rm/doc-collections/fact-sheets/dirty-bombs.html.

US. Office of Homeland Security. *National Strategy for Homeland Security* (July 2002).

US. US Code, Title 50, Section 1801, Chapter 36, Subchapter 1. Online at http://www.law.cornell.edu/uscode/.

US. White House. *National Security Strategy of the United States*. Washington, D.C.: GPO, September 2002.

US. White House. *National Strategy for Homeland Security*. Washington, D.C.: GPO, 2002.

US. White House. *A National Security Strategy for a Global Age*. Washington, D.C.: GPO, December 2000.

US. White House. *A National Security Strategy for a New Century*. Washington, D.C.: GPO, 1999.

US. White House. *Analysis for the Department of Homeland Security Act of 2002: Title 1*. Washington, D.C.: White House, Office of the Press Secretary, 2002.

US. White House. Office of Management and Budget. *Annual Report to Congress on Combating Terrorism*, July 2001.

US. White House. *Securing the Homeland, Strengthening the Nation.* Washington, D.C.: White House, 2002, online at http://www.whitehouse.gov/ homeland/homeland_security_book.html.

US. White House. *The National Strategy for Combating Terrorism* (February 2003); online at http://www.fas.org/irp/threat/ctstrategy.pdf.

Newspapers, News Sources and Serials

Associated Press.
CNN.com.
Fox News Channel.
Le Figaro.
National Review.
Newsweek: US Edition.
Radio Free Europe/Radio Liberty.
RUSI/ Jane's Homeland Security and Resilience Monitor.
The Christian Science Monitor.
The Columbus Dispatch.
The Guardian.
The Independent.
The Sun-Sentinel.
The Sun Herald.
The Wall Street Journal.
The Washington Post.
The Washington Times.
The Weekly Standard.
Time.
USA Today.
US Federal News.
US Medicine.

Books

Albright, Madeleine, with Bill Woodward. *Madame Secretary: A Memoir.* New York: Miramax Books, 2003.

Arnold-Baker, Charles. *The Companion to British History.* New York, Routledge, 2001.

Baker, James A., with Thomas M. DeFrank. *The Politics of Diplomacy: Revolution, War and Peace, 1989-1992.* New York: G.P. Putnam's Sons, 1995.

Baldwin, David, ed. *Neorealism and Neoliberalism: The Contemporary Debate.* New York: Columbia University Press, 1993.

Beck, Ulrich. *World Risk Society.* Cambridge: Polity, 1999.

Benjamin, Daniel, and Steven Simon. *The Age of Sacred Terror.* New York: Random House, 2002.

Bergen, Peter L. *Holy War, Inc.: Inside the Secret World of Osama bin Laden.* New York: The Free Press, 2001.

Black, Jeremy. *War: Past, Present & Future.* New York: St. Martin's Press, 2000.

Blight, James G., Bruce J. Allyn and David A. Welch, *Cuba on the Brink: Castro, the Missile Crisis and Soviet the Collapse.* New York: Pantheon, 1992.

Boot, Max. *The Savage Wars of Peace: Small Wars and the Rise of American Power.* New York: Basic Books, 2002.

Brandt, Irving. *The Bill of Rights: Its Origin and Meaning.* Indianapolis: Bobbs-Merrill, 1965.

Brown, Michael, ed. *Theories of War and Peace.* Cambridge: Massachusetts Institute of Technology, 1998.

Brown, Michael E., Owen R. Coté, Jr., Sean M. Lynn-Jones, and Steven E. Miller, eds. *Offense, Defense and War, An International Security Reader.* Cambridge: MIT Press, 2004.

Brzezinski, Zbigniew. *Out of Control: Global Turmoil on the Eve of the Twenty-first Century.* New York: Touchstone Books, 1993.

Buzan, Barry, Ole Weaver and J. de Wilde. *Security: A New Framework for Analysis.* Boulder: Lynne Rienner, 1998.

Caram, Peter. *The 1993 World Trade Center Bombing: Foresight and Warning.* London: Janus Publishing, 2002.

Carr, E.H. *The Twenty Years Crisis, 1919-1939: An Introduction to the Study of International Relations.* London: Macmillan, 1939.

Chace, James, and Caleb Carr. *America Invulnerable: The Quest for Absolute Security from 1812 to State Wars.* New York: Summit Books, 1988.

Childs, John Brown, ed. *Hurricane Katrina: Response and Responsibilities.* Santa Cruz, CA: New Pacific Press, 2005.

Clinton, Bill. *My Life.* New York: Alfred A. Knopf, 2004.

Cole, Leonard A. *The Anthrax Letters, A Medical Detective Story.* Washington, D.C.: Joseph Henry Press, 2003.

Daadler, Ivo, ed. *Assessing the Department of Homeland Security.* Washington, D.C.: Brookings Institution, 2002.

Daniels, Ronald J., Donald F. Kettl and Howard Kunreuther, eds. *On Risk and Disaster: Lessons from Hurricane Katrina.* Philadelphia, PA: University of Pennsylvania Press, 2006.

Deger, Saadet, and Somnath Sen. *Military Expenditures: The Political Economy of International Security.* Oxford: Oxford University Press, 1990.

Denning, Dorothy E. "Is Cyber Terrorism Next?" *After September 11: New War?* Social Science Research Council (1 November 2001); online at http://www.ssrc.org/sept11/essays/denning.htm.

Dietze, Gottfried. *The Federalist: A Classic on Federalism and Free Government.* Baltimore: The Johns Hopkins Press, 1960.

Duric, Mira. *The Strategic Defense Initiative: US Policy and the Soviet Union.* Aldershot: Ashgate, 2003.

Epstein, David F. *The Political Theory of the Federalist.* Chicago: University of Chicago Press, 1984.

Ferguson, Niall. *Colossus: The Price of America's Empire.* New York: The Penguin Press, 2004.

Flynn, Stephen. *America the Vulnerable: How Our Government is Failing to Protect Us from Terrorism.* New York: HarperCollins Publishers, 2004.

Freeman, Joseph, and Joseph Nearing. *Dollar Diplomacy: A Study in American Imperialism.* New York: Monthly Review Press, 1928.

Frey, Bruno S. *Dealing with Terrorism: Stick or Carrot?* Cheltenham: Edward Elgar, 2005.

Fukuyama, Francis. *The End of History and the Last Man.* New York: Avon, 1993.

Gaddis, John Lewis. *Surprise, Security and the American Experience.* Cambridge, MA: Harvard University Press, 2004.

_____. *We Now Know: Rethinking Cold War History.* New York: Oxford University Press, 1997.

_____. *Strategies of Containment: A Critical Appraisal of Postwar American National Security Policy.* Oxford: Oxford University Press, 1982.

Gurr, Ted Robert, and Barbara Harff. *Ethnic Conflict in World Politics.* Boulder: Westview Press, 1994.

Haar, Roberta N. *Nation States as Schizophrenics: Germany and Japan as Post-Cold War Actors.* Westport: Praeger, 2001.

Hanson, Victor Davis. *Ripples of Battle: How Wars of the Past Still Determine How We Fight, How We Live and How We Think.* New York: Doubleday, 2003.

_____. *An Autumn of War: What America Learned from September 11 and the War on Terrorism.* New York: Anchor Books, 2002.

Hastedt, Glenn, and Kay Knickrehm, eds. *Toward the Twenty-First Century: A Reader in World Politics.* New York: Prentice Hall, 1994.

Hayes, Stephen F. *The Connection: How Al Qaeda's Collaboration with Saddam Hussein has Endangered America.* New York: HarperCollins *Publishers*, 2004.

Haynes, John Earl, and Harvey Klehr. *Venona: Decoding Soviet Espionage in America.* New Haven: Yale University Press, 2002.

High-Impact Terrorism: Proceedings of a Russian American Workshop. The National Academies Press: 2002.

Hobbes, Thomas. *Leviathan.* Richard E. Flathman and David Johnson, eds. Norton Critical Edition. New York: W.W. Norton, 1997.

Hoff, Joan, and Richard K. Vedder, eds. *The European Union: From Jean Monnet to the Euro.* Athens: Ohio University Press, 2000.

Hoffman, Bruce. *Inside Terrorism.* New York: Columbia University Press, 1998.

Howard, Paul, ed. "Hard Won Lessons: How Police Fight Terrorism in the United Kingdom." *Safe Cities Project*, Manhattan Institute, December 2004.

Howard, Russell D., and Reid Sawyer, eds. *Terrorism and Counterterrorism: Understanding the New Security Environment.* Guilford, Connecticut: The McGraw-Hill Companies, 2002.

Hulnick, Arthur S. *Keeping Us Safe: Secret Intelligence and Homeland Security.* Westport, CT: Praeger, 2004.

Huntington, Samuel P. *The Clash of Civilizations and the Remaking of World Order.* New York: Simon & Schuster, 1996.

Ikenberry, G. John, ed. *American Foreign Policy: Theoretical Essays.* 5th ed. New York: Pearson Longman, 2005.

Jackson, Brian. "Organizational Learning and Terrorist Groups." Working Paper: RAND Corporation, WR 133 NIJ (February 2004); online at http://www.rand.org/pubs/working_papers/2004/RAND_WR133.pdf.

Jervis, Robert. *Perception and Misperception in International Politics.* Princeton: Princeton University Press, 1976.

Johnson, Paul. *A History of the American People.* New York: HarperCollins Publishers, 1998.

Kaplan, Robert D. *Imperial Grunts: The American Military on the Ground.* New York: Random House, 2005.

Katzenstein, Peter J., ed., *The Culture of National Security: Norms and Identity in World Politics.* New York: Columbia University Press, 1996.

Kegley, Jr., Charles W. *Controversies in International Relations: Realism and the Neoliberal Challenge.* New York: St. Martin's, 1995.

Keohane, Robert O. *After Hegemony: Cooperation and Discord in the World Political Economy.* Princeton: Princeton University Press, 1984.

_____., ed. *Neorealism and its Critics.* New York: Columbia University Press, 1987.

Kennedy, Robert F. *Thirteen Days: A Memoir of the Cuban Missile Crisis.* New York: W.W. Norton & Company, 1969.

Kissinger, Henry A. *Diplomacy.* New York: Simon & Shuster, 1994.

Kratochwil, Friedrich. *Rules, Norms and Decisions.* Cambridge: Cambridge University Press, 1989.

Kretzmer, David. *The Occupation of Justice: The Supreme Court of Israel and the Occupied Territories.* Albany, NY: SUNY Press, 2002.

Lagon, Mark P. *The Reagan Doctrine: The Sources of American Conduct in the Cold War's Last Chapter.* Westport, CT: Praeger, 1994.

Lansford, Tom. *All for One: Terrorism, NATO and the United States.* Aldershot, UK: Ashgate Publishing Limited, 2002.

Lansford, Tom, and Robert J. Pauly, Jr. *Strategic Preemption: US Foreign Policy and the Second Iraq War.* Aldershot, UK: Ashgate Publishing Limited, 2004.

Laqueur, Walter. *Europe in Our Time: A History, 1945-1992.* New York: Penguin, 1992.

Lesser, Ian O., Bruce Hoffman, John Arquilla, David Ronfeldt, Michele Zanini, and Brian Michael Jenkins, eds. *Countering the New Terrorism.* Santa Monica: Rand Corporation, 1999.

Linklater, Andrew. *Beyond Realism and Marxism: Critical Theory and International Relations*. New York: St. Martin's, 1989.

Mandelbaum, Michael. *The Nuclear Question: The United States & Nuclear Weapons, 1946-1976*. Cambridge: Cambridge University Press, 1979.

Mead, Walter Russell. *Power, Terror, Peace, and War: America's Grand Strategy in a World at Risk*. New York: Alfred A. Knopf, 2004.

_____. Walter. *Special Providence: American Foreign Policy and How it Changed the World*. New York: Routledge, 2002.

Metz, Steven, and Douglas V. Johnson, II. *Asymmetry and US Military Strategy: Definition, Background, and Strategic* Concepts. Carlisle Barracks: Army War College, 2001.

Miniter, Richard. *Losing Bin Laden: How Bill Clinton's Failures Unleashed Global Terror*. Washington, D.C.: Regnery Publishing, Inc., 2003.

Morgenthau, Hans J. *Politics Among Nations*. New York: Knopf, 1948.

Morris, Dick. *Off With Their Heads: Traitors, Crooks & Obstructionists in American Politics, Media & Business*. New York: ReganBooks, 2003.

Morris, Richard B., ed. *Encyclopedia of American History*. Sixth edition. New York: Harper & Row, 1982.

Mylroie, Laurie. *Study of Revenge: The First World Trade Center Attack and Saddam Hussein's War against America*. Washington, D.C.: The AEI Press, 2001.

Nathan, James A., ed. *The Cuban Missile Crisis Revisited*. New York: St. Martin's Press, 1992.

New York Times. *Portraits: 9/11/01: The Collected "Portraits of Grief."* New York: Times Books, 2002.

Nyatepe-Coo, Akorlie A., and Dorothy Zeisler-Vralsted, eds. *Understanding Terrorism: Threats in an Uncertain World*. Upper Saddle, NJ: Pearson, 2004.

Paul, T.V. *Asymmetric Conflicts: War Initiation by Weaker Powers*. Cambridge: Cambridge University Press, 1994.

Rapp, Theodore. *War in the Modern World*. Revised edition. New York: Macmillan Books, 1962.

Reeve, Simon. *The New Jackals: Ramzi Yousef, Osama Bin Laden, and the Future of Terrorism*. Boston: Northeastern University Press, 1999.

Roskin, Michael G. *National Interest: From Abstraction to Strategy*. Carlisle, Pa.: US Army Strategic Studies Institute, 1994.

Ruggie, John. *Constructing the World Polity: Essays on International Institutionalization*. New York: Routledge, 1998.

Sarkesian, Sam C., John Allen Williams and Stephen J. Cimbala. *U.S. National Security: Policymakers, Processes, and Politics*. Third edition. Boulder: Lynne Rienner, 2002.

Schweikart, Larry, and Michael Allen. *A Patriot's History of the United States: From Columbus's Great Discovery to the War on Terror*. New York: Sentinel, 2005.

Serfaty, Simon. *Stay the Course: European Unity and Atlantic Solidarity*. Westport, Conn.: Praeger, 1997.

Sjdjanski, Dusan. *The Federal Future of Europe: From the European Community to the European Union*. Ann Arbor: University of Michigan Press, 2000.

Smith, David G. *The Convention and the Constitution: The Political Ideas of the Founding Fathers*. Lanham, MD: University Press of America, 1987.

Stern, Paul C., Robert Axelrod, Robert Jervis and Roy Radner, eds. *Perspectives on Deterrence*. London: Oxford University Press, 1989.

Taylor, Paul Graham. *The European Union in the 1990s*. New York: Oxford University Press, 1996.

Tickner, J. Ann. *Gender in International Relations*. New York: Columbia University Press, 1992.

Thompson, Marilyn W. *The Killer Strain, Anthrax and a Government Exposed*. New York: HarperCollins, 2003.

Tuchman, Barbara. *The Guns of August*. New York: Random House, 1962.

Quester, George. *Offense and Defense in the International System*. New York: John Wiley & Sons, 1977.

Van Evera, Stephen. *Causes of War: Power and the Roots of Conflict*. Ithaca: Cornell University Press, 1999.

Viotti, Paul Viotti, and Mark Kauppi, eds. *International Relations Theory: Realism, Pluralism, Globalism*. New York: Macmillan, 1993.

Wallace, William. *The Transformation of Western Europe*. New York: Council on Foreign Relations Press, 1990.

Wallerstein, Immanuel. *Geopolitics and Geoculture: Essays on the Changing World System*. Cambridge: Cambridge University Press, 1991.

_____. *The Modern World System: Capitalist Agriculture and the Origins of the European World Economy in the Sixteenth Century*. New York: Academic Press, 1974.

Waltz, Kenneth N. *Man, the State and War: A Theoretical Analysis*. New York: Columbia University Press, 1959.

_____. *The Theory of International Politics*. Reading, MA: Addison Wesley, 1979.

We Will Prevail: President George W. Bush on War Terrorism and Freedom. New York: Continuum, 2003.

Weiman, Gabriel. "Cyberterrorism: How Real is the Threat?" United States Institute of Peace, Special Report 119 (December 2004); online at http://www.usip.org/pubs/specialreports/sr119.html.

Woodward, Bob. *Bush at War*. New York: Simon & Schuster, 2002.

Journal Articles, Reports and Essays

Acharya, Amitav. *Constructing a Security Community in Southeast Asia: ASEAN and the Problem of a Regional Order*. London: Routledge, 2001.

Adler, Emanuel. "Seizing the Middle Ground: Constructivism in World Politics." *European Journal of International Affairs* 3 (September 1997).

Arreguin-Toft, Ivan. "How the Weak Win Wars: A Theory of Asymmetrical Conflict." *International Security*, 26/1 (Summer 2001).

Bilgin, Pinar. "Individual and Societal Dimensions of Security." *International Studies Review*, 5 (2003).

Brinkerhoff, John R. "The Posse Comitatus Act and Homeland Security." *Journal of Homeland Security* (February 2002).

Brookings Institution/Harvard Forum on "The Role of the Press in the Anti-Terrorism Campaing; Assessing the Media and the Government." *A Quarterly Review*, January 9th, 2002, available at http://www.brookings.edu/GS/Projects/Press/Press.htm.

Buzan, Barry, and Ole Weaver. "Slippery? Contradictory? Sociologically Untenable?:The Copenhagen School Replies." *Review of International Studies*, 23/2 (1997).

Carafano, James Jay. "The Truth About FEMA: Analysis and Proposal." The Heritage Foundation, Backgrounder #1901, 7 December 2005.

Carafano, James Jay, Richard Weitz, and Alan Kochens. "Department of Homeland Security Needs Under Secretary for Policy." *The Heritage Foundation*, Backgrounder #1788, 17 August 2004.

Carson, Mark, Theodore Taylor, Eugene Eyster, William Maraman, and Jacob Wechsler. "Can Terrorists Build a Nuclear Weapons: Paper Prepared for the International Task Force on the Prevention of Nuclear Terrorism," (1987); online at http://www.nci.org/nukterror.htm.

Carter, Ashton, John Deutch and Philip Zelikow. "Catastrophic Terrorism: Tackling the New Danger." *Foreign Affairs* 77/6 (November/December 1998).

Caruson, Kiki, and Susan A. MacManus. "Homeland Security Preparedness: Federal and State Mandates and Local Government." *Spectrum: The Journal of State Government* (Spring 2005).

Chalk, Peter, and William Rosenau. "Confronting the Enemy Within: Security Intelligence, the Police, and Counter terrorism in Four Democracies." *Rand Corporation* MG-100, 2004.

Checkel, Jeffrey T. "The Constructivist Turn in International Relations Theory," *World Politics*, 50/2 (January 1998).

"Combating Terrorism: How Five Foreign Countries Are Organized to Combat Terrorism." *Rand Corporation* MG-100, 2004.

Cox, Rebecca. "Counterterrorism legislation: A Question of Reaction?" *RUSI/Jane's Homeland Security and Resilience Monitor*, 30 December 2005.

Cutler, Abigail. "Security Fences." *The Atlantic Monthly* 295: 2, 40 (March 2005).

"DoD Roles and Missions in Homeland Security: Volume II-A: Supporting Reports." Defense Science Board 2003 Summer Study, May 2004.

Farrell, Theo. "Constructivist Security Studies: Portrait of a Research Program." *International Studies Review*, 4/1 (Spring 2002).

Florini, Ann. "The Evolution of International Norms." *International Studies Quarterly*, 40/3 (September 1996).

Francis, Samuel T. "Terrorist Renaissance: France, 1980-1983." *World Affairs*, 146/1 (Summer 1983).

Gaddis, John Lewis. "A Grand Strategy of Transformation." *Foreign Policy*, 133 (November/December 2002).

_____. "International Relations Theory and the End of the Cold War." *International Security*, 17/3 (Winter 1992-93).

Gill, Martin and Angela Spriggs, "Assessing the Impact of CCTV," *Home Office Research Study 292*, Home Office Research, Development and Statistics Directorate, February 2005.

Glastris, Paul. "How Democrats Could Have Won." *The Washington Monthly* (December 2002), online at http://www.washingtonmonthly.com/features/2001/0212.glastris.html.

Golinski, Jan. *Making Natural Knowledge*. Cambridge: Cambridge University Press, 1998.

Gregory, Shaun. "France and the War on Terrorism." *Terrorism and Political Violence* 15/1 (2003).

Haass, Richard N. "The Squandered Presidency: Demanding More From the Commander-in-Chief." *Foreign Affairs*, 79/3 (May/June 2000).

Hammond, Thomas H., and Brandon Prins. "Domestic Veto Institutions, International Negotiations, and the Status Quo: A Spatial Model of Two-Level Games with Complete Information." *Political Institutions and Public Choice Working Paper 98-05*. East Lansing: Michigan State University, Institute for Public Policy and Social Research, 1998.

Hill, Fiona. "Putin and Bush in Common Cause? Russia's View of the Terrorist Threat After September 11," The Brookings Institution Global Politics, *The Brookings Review*, 20:3 (Summer 2002); 33-35, available at www.brookings.edu/press/review/summer2002/hill.htm.

Hoffman, Bruce. "The Logic of Suicide Terrorism." *The Atlantic Monthly* (June 2003).

Hopf, Ted. "The Promise of Constructivism in International Relations Theory." *International Security*, 23/1 (Summer 1998).

Hosein, Gus. "Threatening the Open Society: Comparing Anti-terror Policeis and Strategies in the U.S. and Europe." *Privacy International*, 13 December 2005.

Iida, Keisuke. "Involuntary Defection in Two-Level Games." *Public Choice*, 89/2 (1996).

_____. "When and How do Domestic Constraints Matter? Two-Level Games with Uncertainty." *Journal of Conflict Resolution*, 34/3 (September 1993).

International Association of Police Chiefs. "Police Chiefs Decry Deep Budget Cuts That Would Make Communities More Vulnerable." Press Release (7 February 2005).

Jervis, Robert. "Realism in the Study of World Politics." *International Organization*, 52/4 (Autumn 1998).

_____. "From Balance to Concert: A Study of International Security Cooperation, *World Politics*, 38/1 (October 1985).

Kaplan, Robert D. "The Coming Anarchy." Atlantic Monthly 281 (Summer 1994).

Kennedy, Harold. "U.S. Northern Command Actively Enlisting Partners." *National Defense* (June 2004).

Kireev, Mikhail. "Russian Legislation and the Struggle Against Terrorism," *High-Impact Terrorism: Proceedings of a Russian American Workshop*, p. 19.

Kupchinsky, Roman. "Russia: the loosing battle against terrorism and insurgency," Radio Free Europe/Radio Liberty, 18 September 2004, available at www.terrorisme.net.

Lake, David A. "Leadership, Hegemony, and the International Economy: Naked Emperor or Tattered Monarch with Potential." *International Studies Quarterly*, 37/4 (December 1993).

Larsen, Randall J., and Ruth A. David. "Homeland Defense: Assumptions First, Strategy Second." *Strategic Review* 28/4 (Fall 2000).

Larson, Eric V., and John E. Peters. *Preparing the U.S. Army for Homeland Security: Concepts, Issues, and Options.* Rand Corporation, report MR-1251-A, 2001.

Lewis, Bernard. "Freedom and Justice in the Modern Middle East." *Foreign Affairs*, 84/3 (May/June2005).

Lutterbeck, Derek. "Blurring the Dividing Line: The Convergence of Internal and External Security in Western Europe," *European Security* 14:2 (June 2005), 231-253.

Mack, Andrew. "Human Security Report to Form Key Aspect of 2002 Policy Workshop." *Human Security Network News Bulletin,* 1/1 (December 2001).

Mahnken, Thomas G. "The Future of Strategic Studies." *The Journal of Strategic Studies*, 26/1 (March 2003).

Martin, Lisa L. "The Contributions of Rational Choice: A Defense of Pluralism," *International Security*, 24/2 (Fall 1999).

McGinnis, Michael D., and John T. Williams. "Policy Uncertainty in Two-Level Games: Examples of Correlated Equilibria." *International Studies Quarterly*, 37/1 (March 1993).

Mearsheimer, John J. "Back to the Future: Instability in Europe After the Cold War." *International Security* 15 (Summer 1990).

Milner, Helen V., and B. Peter Rosendorff. "Democratic Politics and International Trade Negotiations: Elections and Divided Government as Constraints on Trade Liberalization." *Journal of Conflict Resolution*, 41/1 (February 1997).

Mo, Jongryn. "The Logic of Two-Level Games with Endogenous Domestic Coalitions." *Journal of Conflict Resolution*, 38/3 (September 1994).

Nivola, Pietro S. "Reflections on Homeland Security and American Federalism." Brookings Institution Working Paper (13 May 2003), online at http://www.brookings.edu/views/papers/nivola/20020513.htm.

Nye, Joseph S., and Sean Lynn-Jones. "International Security Studies: A Report of a Conference on the State of the Discipline." *International Security*, 12/4 (Winter 1988).

Olson, Kyle B. "Aum Shinrikyo: The Once and Future Threat?" *Emerging Infectious Diseases* 5/4 (July-August, 1999); online at http://www.cdc.gov/ncidod/EID/vol5no4/olson.htm.

Pahre, Robert. "Endogenous Domestic Institutions in Two-Level Games: Parliamentary Oversight in Denmark and Elsewhere." *Journal of Conflict Resolution*, 41/1 (February 1997).

Peou, Sorpong. "Realism and Constructivism in Southeast Asian Security Studies Today: A Review Essay." *The Pacific Review*, 15/1 (2002).

Petrishchev, Viktor. "Russian Legislation and the Fight Against Terrorism," *High-Impact Terrorism: Proceedings of a Russian American Workshop* (The National Academies Press: 2002) p. 25.

Powell, Colin L. "A Strategy of Partnerships." *Foreign Affairs*, 83/1 (January/February 2004).

Prins, Gwyn. "The Four-Stroke Cycle in Security Studies." *International Affairs*, 74/4 (October 1998).

Putnam, Robert. "Diplomacy and Domestic Politics: The Logic of Two-Level Games." *International Organization*, 42/3 (Summer 1988).

Schliter-Lowe, Merrie. "USNORTHCOM and NORAD-Partners in Defending the Homeland." *Homeland Defense Journal* 2:11 (December 2004).

"Security, Terrorism and the UK." *Chatham House* ISP/NSC Briefing Paper 05/01, July 2005.

Sergounin, Alexander A. "Russia: A long Way to the National Security Doctrine." March 1998, Columbia International Affairs Online, available at www.ciaonet.org/wps/sea03/#17.

Shapiro, Jeremy, and Bénédicte Suzan. 'The French Experience of Counter Terrorism'. *Survival*, 45/1 (2003).

Smith, Jerry D. "The Effectiveness of Israel's Counter-Terrorism Strategy." *Naval Post Graduate School*, Thesis, March 2005.

Sostek, Anya. "Taking Action: New York's State of Mind: Out of the Twin Towers' Ashes, NY is building a World Class Terror-Fighting Machine." *Securing the Homeland: A Special Report From Governing Magazine and Congressional Quarterly*, online at http://www.manhattan-institute.org/html/_govmag-out_of_the_twin_towers.htm.

Stebbins, Michael. "Anthrax Fact Sheet" (updated 4 October 2005); online at http://www.fas.org/main/content.jsp?formAction=297&contentId=481.

Stubbs, Bruce. "Where to Place the U.S. Coast Guard for Success in the Department of Homeland Security." *The Heritage Foundation*, Backgrounder #1586, 11 September 2002.

"Suicide Bombing: Events Related to Suicide Bombing." *Harpers Magazine*; online at http://www.harpers.org/SuicideBombing.html.

Thomas, Teresa Sokol. "Study Reveals Impact of Fear, Anger on Perception of Americans," Press Release (10 May 2002); online at http://www.cmu.edu/cmnews/020510/020510_terrorism.html.

Tickner, J. Ann. "Feminist Responses to International Security Studies." *Peace Review*, 16/1 (March 2004).

Tomisek, Steven J. "Homeland Security: The New Role for Defense," *Strategic Forum*, 189 (February 2002).

Torbakov, Igor. "War on Terrorism in the Caucasus: Russia Breeds Jihadists," Chechnya Weekly, 6:42 (November 10, 2005), The Jamestown Foundation, at www.jamestown.org/publications_details.php?volume_id=409&issue_id=3522& article_id=2370458.

Trebilcock, Craig T. "The Myth of Posse Comitatus." *Journal of Homeland Security* (October 2000).

Trenin, Dmitri. "Russia and anti-terrorism," Carnegie Endowment for International Peace: Carnegie Moscow Center, March 22, 2005, available at www.carnegie.ru/ en/pubs/media/72290.htm.

Tucker, Jonathan B. "Strategies for Countering Terrorism: Lessons from the Israeli Experience." *Journal of Homeland Security*, March 2003.

Van de Linde, Erik, Kevin O'Brien, Gustav Lindstrom, Stephan de Spiegeleire, Mikko Vayrynen and Han de Vries. "Quick Scan of post 9/11 national counter-terrorism policymaking and implementation in selected European countries." *RandEurope* MR-1590, May 2002.

Wallander, Celeste A. "The Russian National Security Concept: A Liberal – Statist Synthesis." July 1998, PONARS Policy Memo 30, Harvard University, Center for Strategic and International Studies, at www.csis.org/media/csis/pubs/pm_0030.pdf.

Wallander, Celeste A. "Russian National Security Policy in 2000," January 2000, *PONARS Policy Memo 102*, Harvard University, Center for Strategic and International Studies, available at www.csis.org/media/csis/pubs/pm_0102.pdf.

Walt, Stephen M. "Rigor or Rigor Mortis: Rational Choice and Security Studies," *International Security*, 23/4 (Spring 1999).

_____. "The Renaissance of Security Studies." *International Studies Quarterly* 35/1 (1991).

Waltz, Kenneth N. "The Emerging Structure of International Politics." *International Security* 18 (Fall 1993).

Weber, Katja. "Hierarchy Amidst Anarchy: A Transaction Costs Approach to International Security Cooperation." *International Studies Quarterly*, 41/2 (June 1997).

Williams, Michael G. "Words, Images, Enemies: Securitization and International Politics." *International Studies Quarterly* 47 (2003).

_____. "Modernity, Identity and Security: A Comment on the Copenhagen Controversy." *Review of International Studies*, 24/3 (1998).

Wright, Deil S. "Federalism and Intergovernmental Relations: Traumas, Tensions and Trends." *Spectrum: The Journal of State Government* (Summer 2003).

Index